Daughters of the Union

Elizabeth and James Bowler
Minnesota Historical Society

DAUGHTERS
OF THE
UNION

Northern Women Fight the Civil War

NINA SILBER

HARVARD UNIVERSITY PRESS
Cambridge, Massachusetts
London, England
2005

Library of Congress Cataloging-in-Publication Data

Silber, Nina.
Daughters of the Union : northern women fight the Civil War /
Nina Silber.
p. cm.
Includes bibliographical references and index.
ISBN 0-674-01677-7
1. United States—History—Civil War, 1861–1865—Women.
2. United States—History—Civil War, 1861–1865—Social Aspects.
3. Women—Northeastern States—History—19th century.
4. Women—Northeastern States—Social conditions—19th century.
5. Women in politics—Northeastern States—Social conditions—
19th century.   6. Sex role—Northeastern States—History—
19th century.   I. Title.
E628.S55   2005
973.7′082′0974—dc22   2004059779

For Louis, Benjamin, and Franny

Contents

Daughters of the Union

Prologue: Summoned to War, Charged to Patriotism

🌿 🌿 🌿

Modern myth suggests that the truly embattled female participants in the Civil War were Southern white women like Scarlett
O'Hara—and the roots of that myth lie in the Civil War era itself.
From the outset there were the reports of Confederate women's
demonlike devotion to their cause: rumors that they used Union
soldiers' bones for jewelry or celebrated battlefield successes by
drinking wine from enemy skulls. As Northern soldiers moved
south, they reported that the women they encountered were
as vociferous as the men, if not more so, that they defied officers' orders and insulted federal troops, and that they were a
critical source of encouragement to their own fighting men and
willingly sacrificed male relatives, domestic comforts, even their
homes. Real, flesh-and-blood Confederate women, however, revealed considerable ambivalence about the conflict, especially as
the death toll mounted and no quick resolution seemed possible.
Nonetheless, in the North, the image of rebel women as intense
patriots was widely accepted as truth.[1]

By the Civil War's midpoint, some Northerners judged Southern women's patriotism worthy of emulation. Having endured
poverty, starvation, and innumerable deprivations, Confederate
women, they believed, remained unswerving in their devotion to
Confederate success and had made themselves crucial to the
South's continuing show of force. Northern women, they argued,

would do well to follow their example. "In the South, the ladies who are by far more bitter secessionists than the men, have long since discarded the use of silks and satins," the *New York Herald* proclaimed, thereby criticizing Northern women for not doing the same. "But for the courage and energy of the women of the South," another writer noted, "we believe the Rebellion would not have survived to this time. Had the women of the North with like zeal addressed themselves to the work of encouraging a loyal and devoted spirit among us," the Union struggle would have been more successful. By May 1863 such disparaging comparisons were frequent enough to prompt the political activist Elizabeth Cady Stanton to reflect on the "many complaints of the lack of enthusiasm among Northern women."[2]

In short, Northern women, less than two years after the war began, found their patriotism at the center of a public debate. With the Union army experiencing devastating losses on eastern battlefields and prolonged stalemates in western strongholds, some critics, both male and female, began to suggest that the Union cause was suffering not because of poor military leaders or low soldier morale, but because of women. The debate invited comparisons between the women of the two regions, and while some acknowledged that Southern women had not always acted with ladylike decorum, most praised their resolute adherence to the Confederate cause. Why, such critics wondered, could Northern women not be more like them?

One of the more prominent participants in this debate was Gail Hamilton. Born in Massachusetts in 1838 as Mary Abigail Dodge, Hamilton had been a schoolteacher and a governess before she turned to writing essays. By the war's outbreak, she had established herself as a frequent contributor to such influential periodicals as *The Congregationalist,* the New York *Independent,* and the *Atlantic Monthly.* Troubled by the North's lackluster patriotism, particularly in light of the stumbling Union war effort late in 1862, she launched her critique of Northern women that fall. In an essay entitled "Courage! A Tract for the Times," Hamilton chastised "able-bodied men and women, who have not, as yet, made a single sacrifice of personal comfort for the war; who have never, for one single moment, gone cold, or hungry, or thirsty for country's sake." Although she pointed to both "men and women," Hamilton made it clear in a subsequent essay whom she held most responsible. "The issue of this war depends quite as much upon American women as upon American men . . . It is to them I speak. It is they I wish to get ahold of." In Hamilton's view, Northern women had succumbed to the disease of insufferable domesticity, and were trying to support the war effort with their usual home-based tasks—praying, knitting, sewing—all fine contributions, but hardly enough. "Let us tear up our carpets to make blankets for the soldiers," she intoned, "as rebels have done, let us turn our houses and churches into hospitals; let us confine ourselves to two meals a day . . . before we begin to give the rein to our despondency."[3]

Although she offered no clear solutions, Hamilton had nonetheless recognized one of the central problems behind Northern women's responses to America's most devastating conflict: how could they show support for a war that would not, by and large, be fought on their own land and would not require the defense of their homes and domestic surroundings? In urging Northern women to follow a Southern model, Hamilton was resurrecting a traditional vision of female patriotism. She did not call on women to exchange hearth and home for battlefield discomforts; she did not urge them to become political activists. Instead she called on women to direct their domestic concerns in a patriotic direction: to give up meals, and carpets, and domestic contentment in the service of their country. This was a traditional vision of female patriotism rooted in long-standing notions of male and female roles in wartime. During the American Revolution, political leaders had argued that women's domesticity had to take on an increasingly political thrust to help advance the patriots' cause. By making homespun cloth, or by refusing to consume British tea, American women put their housekeeping at the service of politics. Some women counseled a more active display of patriotism—in helping wounded soldiers or aiding destitute war widows—but it was nonetheless a patriotism that sprang from a domestic focus. Women thus entered civic life through their family and domestic obligations.[4]

At the end of the American Revolution, republican theorists enshrined this model of female patriotism. Women, they argued, related to the polity not as individuals but through their familial, and especially marital, relationships. Legally, a married woman had no identity distinct from her husband's. And because marriage was assumed to be woman's natural state, this *feme covert* status symbolically extended to all women, whether married or not. When women did pursue civic and political activities, they did so through domestic endeavors. By educating their children in republican values, and rearing their sons to be wise republican citizens, American women brought the American family into the civic realm and gave their own responsibilities a patriotic focus. The ideology of "republican motherhood" encouraged women to demand greater access to education in the decades following the American Revolution. It compelled some women, especially in the North, to devote increasing attention to moral reform and church activity, particularly when aiding widows and orphans, who could benefit from their enlightened guidance. By the start of the War of 1812 American women were undertaking more organized patriotic activities than ever before, but the renewed war against the British continued to confine American women's politics to the domestic circle.[5]

In the years leading up to the Civil War, women chipped away at the model of Republican motherhood, exposing certain conflicts and contradictions implicit in the notion that women's patriotism had to be tied to the home. The rise of the second American party system during the 1830s and 1840s saw the mobilization of political participation at a mass level, assigning even women a part to play. Although not targeted as formal affiliates, women formed a significant base of party supporters. Especially in Whig circles, women cheered on candidates, attended political rallies, and listened to speakers. Democrats, too, had their female supporters, although the Whig Party, which drew its constituents from many of the reformers and benevolent crusaders, apparently did more to cultivate a feminine clientele. In doing so, the Whigs modified the language of republican motherhood, suggesting that women should not only be the repositories of public virtue but should also put their attributes of goodness and moral dignity at the service of partisan politics. In this context women, and their male supporters, attempted to create a new view of women's civic duty, one that drew on specific feminine characteristics while encouraging political affiliations.[6]

Yet the onset of the Civil War seemed to diminish their new political clout. By the 1860s the ideal of Confederate womanhood suggested that Southern women imbued the cause of Southern nationalism with a sense of purity and moral righteousness. They were expected to make the traditional kinds of domestic sacrifices, willingly giving up sons and husbands and brothers for the preservation of the new nation. While Confederates encouraged Southern women to be political, they defined politics for women less in terms of partisan identity and more as a force for unity. Southern women, just like men, continued to be divided in their sympathies regarding union or secession. But as the secessionist cause became more prominent, it also resurrected a notion of womanhood that further disconnected women from practical political issues and connected them to more exalted, patriotic concerns, with a renewed emphasis on domestic sacrifice.[7]

In the North, the Republican Party inherited the Whig tradition of promoting women's moral strength and political legitimacy. As it more emphatically embraced an antislavery perspective, the party garnered the support of numerous Northern women who had long sympathized with abolitionism. Republicans also infused their political vision with domestic imagery, especially in portraying the secessionist threat from the South and the need to uphold the sanctity of the Union home against the divisive, immoral, and home-wrecking influence of slavery. In 1858 Abraham Lincoln famously used the metaphor of the "house divided" to refer to the growing schism between free and slave states. Northern women, employing the language of home and family, viewed the sectional conflict as something that could strike at the very core of domestic life. Harriet Beecher Stowe, who in 1852 published the most popular novel yet produced on American soil, focused on the domestic reverberations of sectional politics. Slavery, as Stowe depicted it in *Uncle Tom's Cabin*, tore at households North and South, white as well as black. Moreover women's good domestic sense, represented in the book by kindly, antislavery women who resided in both sections of the country, could be a potent force for change.[8]

Less well known women drew on the domestic metaphor to make sense of the unfolding crisis. "The whole United States," wrote young Caroline Richards of upstate New York in her diary in April 1861, "has been like one great household for many years." In November 1860, when South Carolinians were calling for secession, Elizabeth Cabot, a wealthy Bostonian, remarked "that a baby might as well say it would separate from its Mother since the South would simply starve and go naked without the North." After South Carolina had made good on its threat, Cabot envisioned a different type of domestic breakdown. "It seems to me," she wrote in December 1860, "very much like a family quarrel which may be unavoidable but must always be profoundly painful and distressing, at any rate to the *ladies* of the family." During the secession crisis, Republican women like Cabot believed that in opposing the South's threats, and especially its defense of slavery, they were defending American homes and families. Caroline Dunstan, who was living in New York during the "secession winter" of 1860–61, believed that women must devote themselves to defying Southern secession and keeping the nation whole. In December Dunstan went to church and prayed "for our United States, that they may be kept in peace & unity." But once that unity was no more and the traitorous South had made its departure, how would Northern women demonstrate their patriotism? And how would they reconcile the demands of patriotism with their domestic concerns?[9]

Such questions, however, did not trouble most Northern women that winter. They watched the unfolding developments with increasing interest, but more as attentive observers than embroiled participants. Elizabeth Cabot, for one, anticipated financial repercussions if secession came but felt certain she could meet the challenge. "I shan't dare to complain," she wrote to her sister-in-law soon after Lincoln's election, ". . . but shall peaceably try to make $2000 take the place of $6000 which would be the practical working of it on our incomes." Elizabeth

Cooper looked forward to peace and stability in light of Lincoln's victory, not diminished income. "Lincoln is this day to take his seat as President of the United States," the young Pennsylvania Quaker wrote on March 4, 1861. "We are hoping for better times, hope we will not be disappointed this time, after so much labor." As many recognized, Lincoln's focus would now be on the South, but few would have tried to predict the outcome of Lincoln's sectional negotiations. "Abraham Lincoln," wrote Annie Dudley of New Hampshire, "is inaugurated President of the United States, and everyone is looking to see what will now be done to quell the rebellious spirit which has been rising in the south since his election." The next period, Dudley implied, involved "looking" and waiting.[10]

The waiting period turned out to be brief. One by one, seven Southern states left the Union following Lincoln's November 1860 election, certain that the Republican victory would mean the end of slavery's expansion, and very possibly of slavery itself, in the United States. By April 1861 the seceded Southerners had formed a separate government—the Confederate States of America—and vowed to establish an independent nation, free from all ties to U.S. political institutions. Further, they vowed to eradicate all signs of federal government presence, including Union control of Southern military installations. With tensions mounting, the showdown came in mid-April 1861, when Confederate forces attempted to forcibly remove the U.S. troops stationed at Fort Sumter, located in the heart of Charleston harbor. The attack on Fort Sumter outraged and galvanized the North, leading Lincoln to call for a force of 75,000 troops to defeat the Confederate threat and preserve the Union. And the Sumter attack drove four more Southern states—Virginia, Tennessee, North Carolina, and Arkansas—into the Confederate

8

ranks, among them the most industrialized and populous states of the region.

❧

The "family quarrel" was fanned into a domestic conflagration that would last another four years and end the lives of more than 600,000 Americans. The war would also transform the lives of women, certainly in the South but also in the North, and in ways that would have long-range implications for all American women. The war brought women into a new relationship with a broad spectrum of economic, political, and even military activity. It also raised new questions about women's traditionally subordinate roles in society, including the kinds of questions Gail Hamilton addressed in her midwar commentaries. Would Southern white women seem inherently more "patriotic" because the war invaded their homes and farms and domestic lives? Would Northern women necessarily be uninvolved onlookers? Answers offered by public commentators and Northern women themselves opened up new understandings of women's relationship to civic and political life in America.

Among some women, their response to the war compelled a more forthright articulation of political independence. According to some Northerners, women's political commitment to their nation and to their government was the same as men's, and so they should be regarded as independent political actors who deserved full and equal rights as U.S. citizens. These Yankee women pointed out how the war required many of them to take on new economic and political challenges, and to assume a greater degree of autonomy in running their households and expressing their political views. Thus the war did bring Northern women more firmly into the civic sphere and into a more individualized relationship with the federal government and the nation-state.

In assessing these wartime transformations, numerous observers have read the war as a prod to feminism. The Civil War, maintained the authors of the *History of Woman Suffrage* (1882), "created a revolution in woman herself, as important in its results as the changed condition of the former slaves." To the writers of this feminist manifesto, including Susan B. Anthony and Elizabeth Cady Stanton, the Civil War became an igniting force for female activism, a step upward in the climb to full political equality. In more recent years, many historians have offered a similarly upbeat assessment. One modern historian has suggested that the economic and civic demands placed on Northern aid-society women during the war may have provided "a necessary precondition for a revitalized and enduring feminist movement." Another argues that the Civil War, for women in the North and South, was a vehicle that could "arouse their emotions, permit them to work with and not against their men, remove them mentally and physically from their narrow domestic world, and challenge them to perform great new tasks and assume new responsibilities." Conventional wisdom generally echoes these scholarly assessments. "The chaos of the battlefield," claims a popular account of American women's history, "turned out to be the ideal ground for female initiative." Indeed many probably think of Northern women during the Civil War as forebears of the Rosie the Riveters of World War II: women who seized new economic opportunities provided by the conflict and, as a result, gained greater confidence in their own abilities. And even after acknowledging that the Rosies in both wars suffered considerable gender discrimination, many would still argue that, in light of the possibilities women glimpsed during the war, they became only more determined to fight for justice and equal rights.[11]

One goal of this book is to challenge the received wisdom

concerning Northern women and the Civil War. Constituting a racially, ethnically, and economically diverse group, Northern women did immerse themselves more thoroughly in the civic life of the nation, but the climate of the war hardly made that civic sphere a hospitable and welcoming environment. While Northern women did take up new economic activities, they also faced tremendous economic burdens as they tried to make do without their male breadwinners. The obstacles, both material and ideological, that women encountered often made them feel more like victims than crusaders. Likewise, Yankee women became more astute political observers during the course of the Civil War, but because the conflict placed so much emphasis on masculine military heroics and high-level political decisions, they found themselves isolated from the tumultuous political life of the war years. In addition, the ideological climate fostered in the era of the Civil War placed a premium, for both men and women, on obedience and obligation, and less on active engagement in civic life. Northern women were admonished to be loyal and faithful participants in the war effort, ready and willing to follow the commands of government officials, wartime administrators, or male employers and superiors. Women who served in a variety of wartime support activities—as aid-society workers, hospital nurses, teachers of freed slaves—came to understand better than most that the war, and their government, demanded their allegiance more than it encouraged their critical interaction.

Yet, while I caution against reading the Civil War as a moment of female liberation, I do not see the war as offering simply an either-or proposition for Northern women, a choice between liberation or oppression. The war situated Northern women in a new civic setting and placed a higher value on their ideological commitment to the nation-state, their economic contributions to home and family, and even their partisan affiliations. Behind the story of Northern women's wartime experiences, I read the story of an expanding nation-state and the way women, in particular, were affected by that expansion. In the later stages of the war, as the nation extended its reach in a variety of directions, women were affected by a wide range of state-sponsored initiatives, including the pension program, various forms of government employment, and the imposition of loyalty oaths. At the same time, the Civil War imparted new lessons about submissiveness and subordination, making women more clearly aware of their second-class status outside the domestic realm.

On April 30, 1861, two weeks after the attack on Fort Sumter, a notice appeared in the *New York Herald* from a woman of that city who wished to rouse her female compatriots to minister "to the sick and wounded" men who were "struggling to protect the Stars and Stripes, our nation and our homes." Wishing to give aid and comfort to the "brave sons of liberty," the writer addressed her plea to the "Daughters of the Union," a group she envisioned as "ladies of respectability" who, as she did, still felt the "blood of '76" coursing through their veins. In identifying loyal Northern women as daughters of the Union, the *Herald*'s contributor articulated a view of female patriotism that spoke to both traditional notions of womanhood and a new civic relationship that would take shape during the Civil War. As "daughters," Northern women would, to some extent, remain tied to long-standing notions of family and gender hierarchy. Yet daughters of the Union, this writer suggested, also had a civic obligation to be willing to "do anything" for their country, to step outside the bounds of home and family and forge their own relationship with the nation-state. Some did so as nurses, some as teachers of former slaves or partisan activists or relief workers on the home front. During the next four years, in these and in other capacities, Northern women would discover the new opportunities and a new form of subordination that would signal the next stage in the development of American womanhood.[12]

Chapter One

Loyalties in Conflict

❦ ❦ ❦

In the fall of 1862 Josiah Dexter Cotton said his good-byes to his wife, Ann, his two daughters, Ella and Mary, and his two-year-old son, Dexter. Cotton, who would give the next two and a half years of his life to the Union army, departed from his Ohio home after enlisting as an army surgeon. From all accounts, his absence proved difficult, at times overwhelming, for his wife. While Ann had a fair amount of household help on which she could rely while he was gone, she nonetheless felt considerable anxiety about her circumstances. "How I wish this dreadful war was over & you safe at home," she wrote to Josiah in October 1862. "I would not feel so badly if I thought you felt very sorry to leave, but you know you don't feel half about it as I do, do you?" From Ann's perspective, Josiah's enlistment and his enthusiasm for the Union cause underscored how much they differed on the subject of civic obligation. "I am more a wife than a patriot," Ann confessed, "& although I do care for my country, I care for you much more."[1]

And yet, as time passed, Ann Cotton reconciled herself to the situation and seemed to gain a new appreciation for civic involvement. "I want you to come home so much," she wrote in June 1863, "but as you seem determined to stay, I hope you will be able to do so." She also came to support those political leaders who advocated a more aggressive prosecution of the war, hopeful that a victory would bring Josiah home that much sooner. "I am so anxious to have the war brought to a speedy termination," she explained in the fall of 1863, "& hope nothing will happen to prevent a vigorous & successful pursuit of Rosecrans Army after the rebels all are conquered." Soon after writing these lines, Ann Cotton began working with some of the women in her church on behalf of the Republican gubernatorial candidate in Ohio. Although certainly still a "wife," Ann Cotton began to give more attention to her position as "patriot."[2]

Ann Cotton's travails capture many of the tensions that beset Northern women during the Civil War years. As her early letters suggest, Ann at first saw the cause as something distinct from, and at times in conflict with, her home and family obligations. Her concern for domestic happiness and security made it difficult for her to support her husband's military undertaking. Yet she gradually became an attuned political observer and commentator and, in her own way, came to appreciate the importance of civic and political involvement. Indeed, by the fall of 1864 she fervently hoped that Lincoln would be reelected. "I cannot think of much except the coming election," she wrote in October 1864, "& hope it will result favorably for the north." The war had propelled even this reluctant patriot into civic life. During the Civil War years, thousands of other Northern women similarly found themselves pushed toward civic engagement as they learned to accept the demands that the prolonged conflict placed on their homes and families.[3]

Still, women of the North had trouble challenging the negative portrayal of their patriotism that was gaining prominence. By the middle years of the war, commentators remarked repeatedly on what they saw as Yankee women's lackluster commitment to the war effort. With the Union army encountering mounting obstacles on the battlefront, some even wondered if Northern women might not be to blame. Their patriotism seemed to lack substance and direction, it was said, largely because so many women of the North remained relatively untouched by the conflict. And while numerous women would mount an articulate defense of their national loyalty, the public image of Northern women suggested that their support for the Union cause was measured and tentative.

❧

The outpouring of patriotic sentiment that followed the Confederate attack on Fort Sumter prompted hundreds of thousands of Northern men, far in excess of Lincoln's request for 75,000, to enlist in the military. By December 1861, largely owing to recruitment undertaken at the state level, the Union army had more than 640,000 enlistees. By the time the war ended, more than two million men would have served the Union. Still, while this constituted the largest military mobilization in the history of the United States, significant numbers of Northerners remained relatively unaffected. Of the roughly four and a half million Northern men eligible for military service, fewer than half ever enlisted. And among the total population of nineteen million in the free Union states, there were certainly many families that had no man who was, or could be, tapped for service. In the South, in contrast, where the total population amounted to nine million people, about three-quarters of all eligible men joined the Confederate forces. These statistics offer compelling evidence of the North's wartime advantages. Put simply, the same level of home-front commitment put forth in the South was not, and never would be, required to sustain the Union side.

Nor were all classes of Northern society affected equally by wartime mobilization. Union soldiers were a youthful lot, most being under thirty, which meant that few had accumulated much property of their own. Estimates suggest that nearly 50 percent of the Union army was made up of farmers and farm laborers, with the laborers representing the bulk of that category. A slightly smaller proportion, about 40 percent, consisted of skilled and unskilled industrial workers, noteworthy because they represented a larger percentage of the army than they did of the overall population in the North. Finally, about 2 percent of Union soldiers were professionals and businessmen. Thus the vast majority of Union soldiers were clustered in the middle and lower levels on the socioeconomic scale.[4]

With the exception of a small number of black sailors in the navy, all of the initial enlistees in the Union military were white. Until the fall of 1862, the Lincoln administration did not invite black men to join up, and in fact refused to recognize the few African American regiments that were formed. But by the end of 1862, with Lincoln's pledge of emancipation about to take effect, the Union government finally rescinded its claim that the war was only about preserving the Union and was therefore "a white man's war." As the battle against slavery gained momentum, black men, including free black Northerners, joined the war effort, and they did so in impressive numbers. By the time the war ended, 186,000 African American soldiers had fought for the Union. Most came from the slave states, but 34,000 were black men of the North.

The numbers are suggestive when considering women's lot in the war. Compared with Southern women, fewer women in the North would have to give up a man to the military, whether husband, son, father, or brother. Most of the women who were affected were related to farmers, farm laborers, and industrial workers, and most were probably the mothers or sisters of young enlisted men. Estimates suggest that up to 70 percent of Union soldiers were unmarried—although many could no doubt claim a sweetheart. Still, in 1860s America sons and brothers played crucial roles in the family economy, and their absence could bring hardship. Northern black women were relatively unaffected by the first years of the war, at least from the standpoint of their domestic arrangements.

Early Union propaganda counseled women—white women in particular—to play their part in the war effort by supporting and encouraging their men to serve. *Arthur's Home Magazine,* a popular periodical, urged Northern women to look to the example of their revolutionary foremothers, to make the family and domestic sacrifices that the country required. "Our mothers," the editors declared, "are equal to their high duty, and strong enough for any sacrifice their country, in this hour of its trial, may demand." In "The Volunteer's Wife to Her Husband," a typical early war poem, a Northern woman urged her husband to enlist for the sake of "your" country:

> Don't stop a moment to think, John,
>   Your country calls—then go;
> Don't think of me or the children, John,
>   I'll care for them, you know.

Despite the relatively high proportion of bachelors in the Union army, much of the early enlistment propaganda depicted spousal separation. No doubt this was because it was more dramatic than the parting of sons and mothers or brothers and sisters, and the separation of husband and wife also provided a richer opportunity for sermonizing about patriotism. Mothers, after all, could expect to see their sons leave home, even in peacetime. It was less likely that wives would be compelled to relinquish their spouses. In August 1861 a *Harper's Weekly* cartoon reversed the imagery of "The Volunteer's Wife," suggesting that the woman who held her husband back turned him into an unmanly shirker. A large woman was shown holding a small and overly coiffed gent, and the cartoon's caption smirked, "He shouldn't go to the horrid war, away from his 'wifey, tifey.' He shall have a petticoat and a broom, and stay at home." Patriotism demanded that women allow their men to do men's work. Annie Dudley of New Hampshire observed that women seemed to take this message to heart. "Companies are being formed in small towns, and the leave takings are sad indeed," she wrote in her diary on April 15, 1861, "but everyone says go, and God keep and bless you is the prayer of mother and sister, wife and sweetheart."[5]

Yet many women soon discovered they could do more than simply bid men adieu. On April 23, 1861, Caroline White joined other women from Brookline, Massachusetts, at "Panter's Hall . . . to work for the soldiers." She brought home a shirt to sew, worked "diligently" on it for most of the day, and visited with another woman to compare her progress. Like many Northern women, White would remain intermittently involved in soldiers' aid work for the next four years. In New York City, Caroline Dunstan learned that, on April 22, ladies were "meeting to prepare lint & bandages etc to be sent to W[ashington]" and that some women were already planning to go as nurses. In May, women in Chambersburg, Pennsylvania, representing a variety of church denominations, formed a society "to supply regularly the Hospital at this place, with all the comforts necessary for the sick soldiers." In Haverhill, Massachusetts, women organized themselves to work for the soldiers, agreeing "to nominate two ladies from each religious society in town, to act as directresses." On the next day, April 23, so many of the town's women came to lend their assistance, "it was found impossible to supply the ladies with work." In Richmond, Pennsylvania, an aid society was formed in September 1861, and two men were designated as chairman and secretary. Nonetheless, as a reflection of who did most of the work, the group called itself the "Richmond Ladies' Soldiers Aid Society."[6]

In the first weeks and months of the war, many women became accomplished military spectators, visiting training camps in the North, attending military rallies, and participating in public farewells to departing regiments. With troops often gathering and training in close proximity to Northern towns and cities, women were caught up by the military spectacle. Caroline Dunstan watched the New York Seventh Regiment march off on its way to Washington, and a few weeks later she traveled with her mother to the Battery "to see the Tents & barracks there." In western Massachusetts, Susan Hale stopped to watch a regiment of soldiers, dressed in "picturesque" blue Zouave uniforms, carry out their exercises. In keeping with her political sympathies, Maria Daly of New York made a point of cheering on the New York Sixty-Ninth Regiment, an Irish fighting unit. Daly participated in a common female ritual when she presented a flag to the departing soldiers. "I thought that the poorer men," Daly explained, "should be equally cheered and encouraged." In Madison, Wisconsin, local women in July 1861 organized a huge banquet, with 6,000 people in attendance, for the men leaving for the South. Not all departures were cheerful, however. While in New York in the early stages of the war, the English observer William Howard Russell noticed a crowd of women, some with children, gazing "earnestly and angrily" at the upper floors of a large house, and learned they were the "wives, mothers, and sisters, and daughters of volunteers who had gone off and left them destitute." In Boston, one woman there observed, "mothers & sisters" could be seen "haunting the neighboring towns & the State & common for their sons & brothers who have enlisted, by stealth & gone away or are preparing."[7]

Military mobilization would have a much different effect on poor women than on those with greater means. Since the loss of a man often meant the loss of a steady income, these women showed considerable alarm at the prospect of their menfolks' departure. They became increasingly visible symbols of home-front inequities that more privileged Northerners found disturbing. Patriotic Northerners, male and female, were troubled by the notion that wealth could qualify a woman's patriotism. They preferred to think of women's patriotism as coming from a unified sense of stoic self-sacrifice and commitment. However, to address the economic reality, many supported the dispensation of state and community funds to assist women who gave up men to military service, hoping to make their patriotism less dependent on financial well-being. Most poor women could expect nothing but hardship if their men enlisted. Certainly those left destitute would need more than stoicism to get them through the separation.

Stoicism would not prove all that useful to less impoverished women either. Ann Cotton repeatedly bemoaned the trials she faced while her husband was away at war. Eliza Otis, for her part, began to panic about her lack of resolve immediately after the attack on Fort Sumter. "Could I give up my Husband if my Country should need him?" she wrote in April 1861. "God help me to do my Duty!" The wife of an Iowa surgeon called to serve in the army thought back on her anguished cry—"Doctor, how can I let you go?"—as his leave-taking had approached. "Where," she wondered, "was all my patriotism, my loyalty, my love of country? It was all gone." Maria Daly struggled with her inability to make this personal sacrifice and tried to come to terms with the possibility of her husband's departure by relying on her religious faith. "Women," she wrote in her diary in June 1861, "must trust, and only by committing their loved ones to that Divinity who shapes all ends can they ever be at peace." Rachel Cormany, living in Chambersburg, Pennsylvania, felt an "indescribable heaviness" in her heart when her husband, Samuel, told her of his plan to enlist. "We prayed earnestly over it," Cormany wrote in her diary.

"I became calmer and felt more resigned, at times still I am over-come."[8]

Although many women obviously agreed with their loved ones' decision to depart for the war, quite a few gave their consent reluctantly. "Sometimes," wrote a Michigan woman to her husband in August 1862, "I cannot feel reconciled to it at all." Others no doubt agreed only with the understanding that the separation would be brief. "Now I want you to promise me good," wrote an Iowa wife to her husband in May 1861, "that you will come back when your three months are out, will you? If I know that you will come home at that time I will try and bear it." Still others expressed outright relief when male relatives stayed behind. Gussie Kidder of Eau Claire, Wisconsin, expressed her support for the war, but when the regiment her brother intended to join was not called out of the state, she was "very glad." "I thought him too young to go," she explained to a girlfriend in New York State, "and it seemed to me that there were no more soldiers needed to crush the rebellion than we had already in the field." And then there were those who withheld their consent at first, and gave permission only when the nation, and their men, renewed the call for enlistment. In the summer of 1861 Jane Thompson and her husband, William, first broached the subject of William's enlistment. Apparently Jane resisted William's wish to go. He was angry and implied that other men's wives had been more cooperative, making particular reference to one couple, the Corbetts. Because Mrs. Corbett had allowed her husband to go to war, Thompson fumed, "Corbett could go to Congress the next Election because he was going to war," but he could not, because his own wife "always objected or interfered." Jane was holding back his career—or so it appeared to William. A year later, in August 1862, when William Thompson again raised the subject of going off to war, Jane relented. She wrote to her husband, "[I] made up my mind this time when you said you were going not to say one word against it."[9]

Jane Thompson felt prodded by her husband's ambitions, and she also did not want him to bear the stigma of cowardliness for staying home. "It was a great sacrifice to me and to you no doubt for you to leave home and its pleasures to fight for your country," she wrote in September 1862, "and I have not regretted that you went although I spend a great many lonely hours but that is nothing to what it would have been to had you staid at home and been called a coward." To this she added, almost as an afterthought: "and another thing your country needed you and why should I object to your going."[10]

In her afterthought lay the crux of the problem: how could Northerners reconcile the obligation to defend the nation with obligations to home and family? This was an age-old question, to be sure, but it was a particularly daunting one for Unionists in the Civil War. Men and women in the North were finding it difficult to delineate the Union cause as a battle to preserve hearth and home, especially as the conflict involved subduing fellow Americans in relatively far-off locales.

Confederate soldiers, in contrast, could more readily link the fight for home with the fight for the Confederacy. Since the secession crisis, their cause had been couched in terms of protecting white women and white homes, especially by politicians raising the spectre of a "black Republican" invasion. With the beginning of the war and the advance of Union troops into Southern territory, that sense of defending their home deepened and drew in more Southern white men, including nonslaveowners. "The man who loves his family the best now," wrote one Virginia soldier in 1862, "is he who is the most anxious and will risk the most and suffer the most to repel the invader." The notion of home protection made women "objects of obligation" and allowed men to cloak their duties in the familiar garb of paternal responsibility. This in turn encouraged white Southern women to understand the conflict in terms of their own protection and to make certain demands on their husbands and the Confederate leadership, to remind them that defending their women and their homes must remain central to the Confederate undertaking.[11]

On occasion northern soldiers were able to meld the cause of home security with the larger national enterprise. Samuel Cormany of Pennsylvania convinced his mother to bless his crusade to fight for "my Mother and Home and Country." But there was no way around the fact that the home commitment, for Union men, was less immediate. "We are fighting for matters real and tangible . . . our property and our homes," remarked a Texas soldier; Union men, he believed, fought for "matters abstract and intangible." Indeed Northern soldiers, as well as the broader Northern society, adopted a more abstract and state-centered nationalism as the war dragged on. Shaped in part by wartime politics, propaganda, and cultural practices, the new national view became pervasive. Fighting for a broad and undivided Union changed the way many Union men articulated their vision of the nation.[12]

In notable contrast with Confederates, Union soldiers felt compelled to rank their commitments, placing country first and home second. Perhaps to underscore the significance of waging a far-reaching national struggle, one that would take them a considerable distance from their own domestic circle, they may have found it necessary to identify the fight for "the country" as something separate from, and higher than, the fight for "home." As many suggested, a secure and stable home life was important, but they could be truly happy and contented in their homes only if the Union was preserved. "My duties to my country are of

more importance now than my duty to you," wrote Julius Skelton
to his wife, "for the reason that without a country [and] without
a home we cannot enjoy each other['s] love." Others, too, made
the kinds of calculations that one Michigan recruit made to his
sweetheart. "Duty prompts me to go," he wrote. "My country
first[,] home and friends next." Another explained, "Home is
sweet and friends are dear, but what would they all be to let the
country go to ruin." Yet another ordered his priorities this way:
"First my God, second my country, third my mother."[13]

Union soldiers and Northern women did, on occasion, stress
the need to protect homes and families, but generally only when
there was an immediate threat to domestic stability. Maria Patec,
for example, believed Union soldiers were "men who love their
homes, country, and firesides and are willing to fight for them."
Patec, though, saw the war from the vantage point of Kansas, a
region that had been besieged by proslavery rebels for years. Domestic imagery was also important to Minnesota soldier James
Bowler, on a new assignment in September 1862 to subdue Sioux
Indians who were waging war on white settlers in Minnesota. As
he explained to his fiancé, his duty was to his country "and its suffering, unfortunate people who have become victims of the enemies of God and humanity . . . Did you ever contemplate how
horrible it is that young, respectable females like Yourself and
your friends are in the hands of savages who have not the least
restraint, either moral or physical, upon their conduct toward
their victims?" Perhaps what is most remarkable is this Minneso-
tan's readiness to issue the kind of warning—and to pinpoint the
threat the enemy posed to white females—that was never used
to describe his work in the South. The fight against the Confederacy, many Union soldiers explained, did have a bearing on their
homes and families, but not so much in the immediate present as
at some undetermined point in the future. Taylor Peirce of Iowa

suggested precisely this idea when he wrote to his wife soon after being mustered into service: "Dear Catharine, the happiness and prosperity of our Children depend on the Suppression of this rebellion and although you know that I love you and the children as well a man can and will probably have more concern for your present welfare than most men yet your future prosperity is of greater importance than anything else in the world." Peirce tried to explain that, in this war, any possibility for future domestic happiness rested on the present triumph of the Union.[14]

As men left homes and hearthsides, wives and mothers, to fight for the Union, Northern women realized that their own importance had been dramatically diminished. They did not represent the cause of the hour; they were not the main focus of men's allegiance or sense of obligation. In Iowa, Marjorie Rogers felt "so inefficient, so weak, not equal to all that would be required of me" when she contemplated her own small domestic sacrifice— her husband's service—for the sake of the nation's future. It was one thing to give up men in the name of patriotism when that patriotic cause seemed intimately linked to domestic fulfillment. Now, however, Union women had to come to terms with a different kind of sacrifice: one that was grounded in the demands of national unification and national ideals. In the spring of 1862, after her husband had returned on a brief furlough from the battlefront, Eliza Otis struggled with the new priorities. "It's hard to do without him," she confided in her diary when her husband had taken his leave, "and yet I would as soon lay my head upon the block, and throw away forever my hopes of immortality, as to say one word to dissuade him from duty, or lead him to seek a life of inglorious ease at home, in this hour of our Nation's imminent peril. His country has higher claims upon him now than I have."[15]

In many exchanges, husbands and wives (and, to a lesser extent, mothers and sons) argued over priorities, as women asked

men to come home and men lectured women on the imperatives of national duty. Certainly Ann Cotton felt the tension in
her conflicted loyalties and berated herself for her "selfish" wish
to have her husband at home. A Pennsylvania woman likewise
found it difficult to subordinate the lesser claim of home to the
"higher claim" of country. "You are my all in this world," she
wrote to her husband, "and without you now my Pet I feel as
though I could not live." News of ill health could also prompt
women to urge their male kin to reconsider their objectives.
When Sara Billings got word that her brother Levi had been sick,
she wrote to him with emphatic advice from home. "We feel it is
your duty to return from the service," she urged. Other women
asked husbands and sons who had gone to war to avoid going into
battle, hoping that their menfolk could do their duty by joining
the army but also, in the end, be able to fulfill their familial obligations by returning home safe and sound. Such pleadings often
prompted Union men to again affirm their commitment to a
higher cause. After explaining how he could not yet resign his position, James Bowler in the First Minnesota Regiment lectured
his fiancée on his soldierly obligations. "I am more than ever impressed," he wrote on April 4, 1862, "with a sense of the duty
which every ablebodied young man owes to his country at this
critical period."[16]

Bowler and his intended showed an acute appreciation for the
problem of conflicted loyalties. When he initially enlisted with
the First Minnesota in 1861, James Bowler said his good-byes to
Lizzie Caleff, his sweetheart. Lizzie and James wrote often to
each other throughout 1862. She spoke frequently of her great
longing to see him; he responded with tenderness and concern,
although he also made his military commitments clear. Then, at
the end of 1862, while Bowler was home on a furlough, he and
Lizzie were married. After he returned to the front in early 1863,

she wrote letters to her "Dearest Hubbie" and confirmed news of her pregnancy. Lizzie continued to write of her desire to see him and told him she hoped that, even if the war continued past the following fall, he would come home to be present for the baby's arrival. James replied that he could not, and asked her not to insist on his return. Such demands, he explained, took on a new significance in light of their "new relation." Lizzie explained in her next letter that she would never take advantage of their altered situation by insisting on his return. "You know," she explained, "that I always told you I would never be the one that would hinder you from doing what you thought was your duty." James Bowler remained in the army until the end of the war. For her part, Lizzie refrained from demanding that he return, although she tried, for the rest of the war, to muster what she could of her domestic influence in her letters to James.[17]

While many Northern women clearly felt considerable anguish in trying to cope with conflicting demands of home and country, being called upon to give up their men for something higher than home ultimately compelled them to see themselves in a new civic light. The sacrifice they made as women was not just for themselves and their homes but for the preservation of the nation. Confederate women may have sent men to war with the expectation that they would fight to keep Southern women and homes safe, but Union women had to embrace the subordination of domestic ideals to national ones. And with so many Northern men making explicit their ranking of country over home, women also had to learn to separate and reexamine their own priorities. The evidence is subtle: a mother's growing attentiveness to local politics, a wife's heightened interest in reading war news, a sister's new concern for the plight of other soldiers and soldiers' families. As they gave up their men for the fight, many Northern women began to carve out a new political mentality in which they became aware of their own duties to the nation-state. They learned to step, albeit tentatively, beyond the domestic circle to consider the national and ideological dimensions of the conflict.[18]

More than a few men encouraged women to take that step, and praised them when they did so. Soldiers lauded their wives for their loyalty and their patriotism, for their willingness to risk domestic comfort and security, and for making the sacrifices required of a true soldier's wife. Josiah Corban wrote his wife in Connecticut that he never would have left "if you had not been the most Patriotic of women and willing to make any sacrifice in your power to save our Government from ruin." When the wife of an Ohio sergeant wrote to her husband, "Your country's cause is my cause," he replied: "I am doubly proud of you for this sacrifice." Grace Weston's fiancé likewise promoted her patriotic devotion. "I cannot tell you," he wrote, "how much I admire the spirit you have shown. I feel that you share in the sacrifice I am making and you do it as becomes one well worthy a patriotic soldier's love." And in April 1864, when Taylor Peirce wrote a letter to his son Frank to explain the circumstances of his enlistment, he gave much of the credit to Frank's mother. "Your mother," he wrote, "felt like I did myself about it. She was very loth to let me go but she thought it was the duty for every one to defend the country that was able."[19]

Catharine Peirce's own letters suggest she did indeed take the country's cause to heart. "I do not want thee to think I want thee to give up until the war is over," she wrote to Taylor. Though she hesitated about his duty in case of illness, she tried to put even that possibility in a patriotic context. If he ever became so sick that he was not fit for duty, she explained, "then I want thee to get home as soon as thee can for my sake and thy own and Uncle Abe allso." In Massachusetts, Fanny Pierce worked at rethinking her commitments when her brother Elliot enlisted in the Thirteenth Massachusetts Volunteers. She used the occasion of Elliot's departure to give herself a new identity as "a soldier's sister"—a title that required bravery and sacrifice in support of her sibling's endeavors—and to do her part for the war. Her other brother, Jesse, also felt the pull of the soldier's life, which, Fanny explained, would leave her "to defend the hearth stone." By August 1861, she expressed a strong identification with the military cause, placed herself clearly among those who would do the fighting, and aligned herself against those who stayed home. "I wonder sometimes," she wrote to Elliot, "how it is that so many able bodied men can stay at home, quietly at such a time, and think, if I was a man I should seize a gun and run."[20]

Grace Weston, whose fiancé found her "worthy a patriotic soldier's love," also made clear her understanding of sacrifice. Weston's husband-to-be, Walter Allen, did not enlist until the end of 1863. He signed up for service from his (and Grace's) hometown of Worcester, Massachusetts, while Grace was working as a governess in Chicago. In November 1863, with his decision to enlist imminent, she wrote to him about union. "Union of body should ever be secondary to the nobler union of soul. But enough of union now. There is no doubt but that we are true Unionists. I think we know what should be the foundation of a Union." Grace neatly conflated their marital goals with their political ones, and thus implied her support for his military objectives. She emphasized her belief in the cause, which was not just his but hers as well. "I can never weary of good and noble purposes and have never for a moment doubted that you were sincere in your desire to serve your, our true country." Perhaps for Grace and Walter, the fact that they had not yet established their home made it easier to meld the fight for the country with the goal of securing their future domestic happiness. "If you do your duty to your country," she wrote in January 1864, "we shall have a right to such a home under the 'starry banner,' and we cannot but be happy in the consciousness of duty faithfully performed."[21]

Eliza Otis, who lived in Louisville, Kentucky, when her husband, Harrison, enlisted in April 1861, vowed she would not prevent Harrison from serving. In May 1862, when Harrison had returned to the front after a brief furlough at home, Eliza began an extensive correspondence with some of the other soldiers in Harrison's regiment. She corresponded with Mr. Lutz, Mr. Fornshell, and Mr. Matsen, writing of her concern for them, reminding them that the people at home had not forgotten them. She asked Frank Fornshell, in particular, to send her word in case her husband was wounded on the battlefield. But her concerns were not simply practical; in each letter she reiterated a certain theme: that those who fight for the Union fight with the support of all the homes and hearts in the land. "I expect I feel only as every true American woman feels," she wrote to Mr. Lutz, "that *all* who have taken up arms in this hour of our Country's need and peril, who taking their lives in their hands have gone forth to strike for the defence of Freedom and all the sacred rights of man, have a *claim* upon our sympathies, and should be loved and cherished by every loyal heart in the land." Feeling bereft at the breakdown of her own home circle, Eliza Otis created a new circle, a circle of fellowship with other soldiers, a circle that embraced a broader, national polity. A Wisconsin woman articulated a similar sentiment. "In light of the war," she explained, "I view every loyal soldier as my brother." Like Eliza Otis, she in effect imagined, and made herself a part of, a vibrant, national community.[22] The process of giving men up for the cause increased women's investment in the national struggle, prompting them to see their sacrifice of husbands and sweet-hearts as a sacrifice for the national good.

❦

As the Civil War conferred a moral legitimacy on an increasingly powerful nation-state, Northern women, just like Northern men, came to accept the importance of committing themselves to that morally energized state. These feelings apparently intensified as the war continued and as Northerners became more invested in a forcefully articulated national agenda. "For any thing else I could not let you go," wrote one navy officer's fiancée, "but . . . I am glad dear that I can give something for my country, and will try and be as brave as many others who too have sent their dearest ones." As the war persisted, and the soldiers' sacrifices grew more demanding and the war's objectives more all-encompassing, some women felt their own patriotic impulses more keenly. On January 1, 1863, the day the Emancipation Proclamation took effect, Sophia Buchanan reminded herself of the importance of the contest. Although she could not always feel fully reconciled to her husband's absence, the war, she wrote, was "no slight struggle, [but] a matter of life & death, to the most glorious nation, the sun ever shone upon." By August 1864, Emeline Ritner was apologizing for her earlier insistence on her husband's return. Her demand, she explained, was based only on her concerns about his health. Now, though, she was resolved about his commitment and, by extension, her own. "I feel it is a duty I owe my country," she explained, "to give up my dear friends to fight and even this in her defense." Finally, as the war dragged on, some women wrote that they wanted to do more than send their men into the fray. "We wish to do something for our Country," one young woman wrote to Abraham Lincoln in September 1864, speaking on behalf of herself and fifteen others in her small Ohio community. "We have been wanting to do something Ever since this Cruel war broke out but Circumstances will not permit it. but we cannot wait eny longer we must do something We have sent all that is Near and dear to us and we must help them in some way We are willing to be sworn in for one year or more eny lenght of time it makes No difference to us."[23]

Even the significant number of Northern women who remained relatively untouched by the conflict had to consider the manner and means by which their patriotism would be expressed. New York socialite Maria Daly, for example, never had to witness her husband's enlistment, but she devoted considerable effort to preparing herself for that possibility. Others contemplated possible financial burdens and declared themselves willing to bear such hardships for the sake of the country. Wrote Helen Grinnell, another well-to-do New Yorker, in her journal, "I have felt very little unhappiness with regard to being poor"— although the fact that no male relatives were going off to fight, and that "being poor" was a relative concept, may have allowed Grinnell to rank her own priorities more easily. "I pray God," she wrote, "that the Constitution and the Federal Government may be sustained and that the union may be preserved." Mrs. A. C. Hinckley in Northampton, Massachusetts, no doubt found it easier to declare her patriotic beliefs with her son safely far from home, and out of the country, when war broke out. "I rejoice that you are not shouldering the musket in a wicked war," Hinckley wrote. "I am loyal to the Stars & Stripes but pray most sincerely that they may not fight."[24]

While such women counted themselves a part of the patriotic home front, theirs was precisely the type of problematic patriotism that made critics complain of Northerners' lackluster support for the Union cause. In the face of repeated obstacles to the war effort, especially by the summer of 1862, when the Union army suffered several defeats and calls went out for more soldiers to join the fray, women's prayers seemed increasingly insufficient. Many in the North hoped that women, families, and a broad array of civilians—not just male enlistees—could be counted on to demonstrate their patriotic commitment. And many felt that not all had yet contributed equally. Despite the mounting human and material costs of the war, some Northerners—especially those of the more privileged classes—seemed to be underpaying. Generally, men of property had managed to avoid military service, which meant that privileged women had endured far less hardship. As military recruitment efforts intensified, these social inequities came into sharper relief.

Military mobilization, as many Union officials began to realize, required organizing everyone for the fight, not just men. Given how difficult it was to merge the struggle for the Union with the defense of home and family, it may have been especially important to direct particular attention to women and their concerns. If the government hoped to bring more men into service, suggested a writer for the *United States Service Magazine,* men must "be assured that those who may be dependent upon them shall not suffer in their absence." One type of assurance came in the form of the bounty system, in which the federal and state governments offered cash payments to new enlistees so that their families would not be left destitute. Further inducements were offered, in the summer of 1862, with the revamped pension system that guaranteed payments to soldiers' kin in the case of an enlisted man's demise. Both developments helped press poorer families, and women especially, into service through monetary incentives. When bounties and pensions proved insufficient, the government exerted other kinds of pressures. In March 1863 the U.S. Congress passed the Conscription Act, empowering the federal government to draft men into service, but also allowing wealthier men to avoid conscription by buying a substitute or

by paying a $300 commutation fee. As a result, the new enlist-
ment and conscription procedures instituted by the state and
federal governments only increased the impression that privileged Northerners were avoiding their patriotic duty, for they
had no need for bounty payments and had the means to avoid the
draft. The midwar crisis made it clearer than ever that some
wealthy Northerners, including women, remained almost unaffected by the traumas and troubles of war.[25]

Wartime literature began to reflect these social tensions, perhaps most starkly in the growing rebukes against the North's
"shoddy aristocracy." Once a technical designation for reconsti-
tuted wool products, the term *shoddy* increasingly referred to
the tendency of some wartime merchants and manufacturers in
the North to produce inferior military goods—uniforms, blankets, even weapons—while reaping enormous profits. Those who
enjoyed the fruits from this commercial fraud, the "shoddy aristocracy," were often portrayed as a class of men and women,
once poor and struggling, who were now wallowing in their ill-
gotten wealth. While many raised a hue and cry against the crass
and corrupt manufacturers, some of the strongest condemna-
tions were hurled at the female beneficiaries of the shoddy economy. A story in *Harper's Weekly*, for example, depicted the self-
aggrandizing escapades of "Miss Clementia Shoddy" and her
mother, "Mrs. Shoddy," who demonstrated their appalling lack of
patriotism by "dancing and making merry, and throwing away
fortunes on diamonds" while "our brothers and sons are dying
on battle-fields." Indeed, women's distance from military service
made them particularly prone to the charge that home-front luxury and extravagance captured their attention far more than wartime sacrifice. "Mrs. Shoddy," in the view of some Northern commentators, pointed to an inherent flaw in women's capacity for
patriotic enthusiasm.[26]

Other writers hoped that by appealing to traditional notions of feminine sacrifice they could arouse the nobler instincts of Yankee ladies on behalf of the war effort. Writing at the same time that the new conscription law was enacted, Gail Hamilton's strategy for promoting patriotism revolved, to a great extent, around setting aside feminine luxury and indulgence and encouraging women to embrace poverty and deprivation in urging men to fight. Impoverishment, Hamilton believed, demonstrated the depth of Southern sacrifice: the rebels, she insisted, fought "bare-headed, bare-footed, haggard, and unshorn, in rags and filth," but did so "bravely, heroically, successfully." To emulate their Southern counterparts, Northern women must "not only look poverty in the face with high disdain, but embrace it with gladness and welcome." Hamilton insisted on understanding female patriotism from the standpoint of women's capacity to abstain and forbear, sentiments that were far nobler than luxury and indulgence.[27]

Like other women writers of the war years, Hamilton envisioned Northern women not fractured and divided by class and social conditions—as they often were—but united in common bonds of suffering and sacrifice. Fanny Fern, writing for the *New York Ledger* in November 1862, hoped to stimulate women's patriotism by lauding their sacrifices as a unified expression of devoted womanhood. She described the poor soldier's wife who "in giving her husband to her country, has given everything; who knows not whether the meal she and her little ones are eating, may not be the last for many a hungry—desolate—day." Yet, Fern suggested, this role was not reserved for poor women exclusively; even officers' wives, she noted, had to spend hours in "dreadful suspense and anxiety" as they waited for news from the battlefield. In fact, she implied, even women who had no men at war had to endure the agony and isolation of the home front, while men could at least enjoy the fellowship of military life. In this way, Fanny Fern tried to erase the very real and troubling class distinctions that had begun to intrude on the question of Northern female patriotism.[28]

Increasingly, writers and speakers hoped to rouse their sisters by acknowledging that the war demanded a different and more ideological kind of patriotism from all its supporters. By 1863, female authors began to take note of the new demands the war imposed on Northern women and to articulate the content of Northern female patriotism, moving it beyond the traditional sphere of domesticity and into the "higher" realm of nationhood. Hoping to foster "a healthy, intelligent patriotism, in the social and domestic circles of our land," Mrs. O. S. Baker pondered the war's demands on Northern women in the pages of the *Continental Monthly* in July 1863. Acknowledging the class antagonisms that had now seeped through the Northern home front, Baker spun her argument from a story about a poor, suffering soldier whose family was ridiculed by aid-society women because of their lower-class status. Baker made it clear that the real challenge of patriotism was not for poorer women, who had already made enormous sacrifices, but for wealthier women, who had avoided them. To fully embrace the meaning of the Union struggle and help defeat the Confederacy, Baker explained, women must cultivate "a true understanding and appreciation of the principles of our democratic institutions." Baker hoped to push Northern women, even slightly, into a broader civic sphere in which they would embrace not just their own domestic obligations but also the political ideals of the nation. Women, she argued, could and should become a force for democracy and thus fully embody the Union cause.[29]

The anonymous author of an 1863 Union pamphlet made a similar argument. The tract, *A Few Words in Behalf of the Loyal*

Women of the United States by One of Themselves, took direct issue with the assertion that Northern women had been less patriotic than Southern women. To some extent the author seemed
to argue for a very traditional feminine role, one in which Northern women would clearly reject the overly demonstrative displays of their Southern sisters and perform their support tasks in
more quiet and unassuming ways. But the writer also confronted
the question at the heart of the female patriotism debate: was
women's patriotism simply an expression of their homebound
commitments, or did women have the capacity to grasp the
larger demands and the "higher claims"? "It is no virtue," the
pamphlet argued with respect to Southern women, "to wear a
coarse dress if you can obtain no other, or to live poorly when
good living is too costly for your means." This was not patriotism
but merely the by-product of Confederate women's support of an
immoral cause.[30]

The undesignated "loyal woman" went on to explain: "We
know that women usually adopt the political views of their husbands and we profess no surprise that Southern women should
have done so." Thus rebuking the notion that Southern women
behaved out of their own sense of patriotism, the author considered whether Northern women, as well, might simply be following "the political views of their husbands." Yes, she said, but only
those women whose husbands sympathized with the South and
so refused to act on behalf of the Union. True Unionist women,
in contrast, acted not out of familial devotion but out of a deep
and reasoned understanding of the contest. The Unionist cause
compelled women to do what women "usually" did not do: to put
their patriotism at the service of not just homes and husbands
and families but a higher claim.[31]

With the war prompting Northern men and women to disentangle the demands of home and country, a number of women began to embrace a form of patriotic expression that stepped away from immediate domestic concerns. These Yankee females increasingly recognized their own relationship to the "higher claims" of nationhood. Some expressed this in the support they showed for their male relatives in the military; others entered the public discussion of female patriotism and countered the accusations that had derided women's commitment to the Union cause.

Still, over the course of the war the public perception of Northern women's patriotism remained mixed. There were, of course, numerous celebrations of the devoted and sacrificing wives and mothers who willingly yet tearfully bade their husbands and sons adieu. And there were also, especially as the war dragged on and the Union suffered severe military setbacks, frequent public outcries about Northern women's lack of patriotic fervor. Sometimes the attacks were aimed precisely at the wealthier women of the "shoddy aristocracy." But perhaps even more often commentators criticized Northern women generally for their weak expressions of loyalty, frequently drawing unfavorable comparisons with women of the Confederacy. While some women did their best to rebut these charges, Northern women would repeatedly find themselves scrutinized for any indications of wavering loyalty or dubious commitment.

The Union struggle forced Northern women into a new ideological predicament. Because the fight for the nation was seen as something separate and "higher" than the fight for home, Northern women became aware, in new ways, of their secondary status in the nation-state. To a great extent their perceived position as guardians of home and hearth made them vulnerable to charges of faltering patriotism, precisely because their homebound commitments seemed to divert their focus from the larger political struggle. Yet as growing numbers of Yankee women embraced the Union struggle, they also learned new lessons in nationalism. Giving up their men to fight for something outside the domestic sphere would lead them to learn about, embrace, and interact with that higher and more abstract plane of civic life.

Chapter Two

The Economic Battlefront

❦ ❦ ❦

In 1859 Mary Austin married well. Having moved to rural Michigan at the age of eleven with her parents, Austin no doubt had an intimate familiarity with farm living and with the grueling demands placed on farmers' wives. Still, she must have expected a certain degree of comfort and security from her union with Bruce Wallace, one of the lucky few who had joined the California gold rush and returned with something to show for his efforts. With his new-found wealth, Wallace bought a 160-acre farm that would offer both home and livelihood for himself and Mary when they set up housekeeping in Girard, Michigan.

At first the outbreak of the Civil War seems to have had little effect on the Wallace family. Then, when renewed calls came for Union enlistment in August 1862, Bruce Wallace joined the Nineteenth Michigan Volunteer Infantry. Mary remained on the farm with their two children: a two-and-a-half-year-old boy and a six-month-old baby girl. During the ten months of her husband's service, Mary fared reasonably well, certainly better than other farmers' wives who had fewer resources on which to draw. She had a considerable amount of livestock that could be sold for income, and she was also willing—and able—to apply her own labor to keep the farm running. In early September Mary was hard at work cutting corn; in November, as winter began to descend, she did not shy away from chopping her own wood. Once, when a neighbor's pigs got into her corn field, Mary managed to get them out and back to their rightful owner.

Yet for all her triumphs, Mary Austin Wallace faced tremendous challenges in running a farm on her own in the 1860s. More than anything, her account of her life during Bruce Wallace's absence speaks to her dependence on men. Although she was fortunate in having livestock to sell, she found herself selling animals not for cash but in exchange for neighboring men's labor. For example, she "sold Mr. Hitchcock the calf" to get some help, perhaps a little more than a day's worth of labor, around the farm. The need to pay men for labor often cut into her earnings. When she decided to sell her pigs, she had to find a man who could deliver them to market. In the end, her husband's stepfather did the job, but it meant turning over a dollar of the proceeds to him in exchange for this service, a pecuniary loss she certainly would not have incurred had her husband been home. And help was sometimes hard to find. When she needed someone to do carpentry work on the house she and Bruce were building, she scoured the neighborhood—apparently without success—in search of men who could lend a hand. "Mr. Green had so much to do," Austin wrote in her diary in October 1862, "that he could not come." Green suggested she try Mr. Wilson, but Wilson's wife said that he, too, was too busy to work for Mary.

Mary Austin Wallace managed to keep her Michigan farm running, although her success certainly had something to do with her relative wealth, and perhaps with her husband's relatively brief term of military service. Her story compels us to reconsider some of the traditional tales that have been told of Northern women's Civil War experiences, tales that emphasize their great accomplishments and enhanced personal satisfaction. Mary Wallace had to negotiate an economic battlefront that brought her into a new set of commercial relationships, some of which were enriching and empowering, but she also learned frustrating lessons about her economic dependence and vulnerability, and how difficult life could be without a man around the house.[1]

❧

On the eve of the Civil War, Northern society was undergoing a profound and dramatic transformation brought on by the early development of factory production, an emerging transportation network, and an ever-expanding commercial nexus. But all this novelty operated in tandem with long-standing traditions shaped by economic habit and ideology. When the Confederacy attacked Fort Sumter, most Northerners were still tied to a rural livelihood, working on farms and following the same rhythms and patterns of agrarian life that they had for generations. True, as of 1860 a sizeable group of Yankees already had had several decades of experience with the expanding industrial system. In that final antebellum year, mills and factories provided employment for 1.1 million Americans, most of whom lived in parts of New England, the mid-Atlantic, and the old Midwest. Yet antebellum mill life was no sweeping system of industrialization. Most mill hands worked in small and relatively unmechanized shops. The most significant shift in the industrial process at this point was not to large-scale factories and mechanization but to less reliance on an apprenticeship system of training skilled artisans and more reliance on wage-earning labor. Even greater numbers of workers, including many women, served as "outworkers" who contributed to commercial production by performing piecework in their own homes, often far from the urban and industrial hubs of the antebellum North. In this way many rural Northerners combined an agrarian life with a wider range of market activity, carrying out both agricultural and industrial tasks—such as piecework, hiring out to other farmers, and producing and selling marketable commodities.[2]

Northern women stood right at the wedge of antebellum change and stability. In many parts of the North women and children were among the first to be brought into industrial work. Through the relatively cheap, unskilled labor provided by female workers, critical labor and technological innovations were introduced in a number of crucial industries, most notably textiles and shoemaking. Growing numbers of Northern women were taking up work in factories, even if only for short periods of time. In 1860 nearly one-quarter of all manufacturing jobs, about 285,000, were held by women. At the same time, industrialization was pushing other women more firmly into the domestic sphere. With men, and even older children, spending more time away from home—either working or in school—more and more unpaid domestic labor fell on women's shoulders. Driven by an intensified cult of domesticity that placed heightened value on household care, working-class and middle-class women were finding it necessary to devote more time to domestic tasks, including shopping, child care, and cleaning.

A similar process affected rural women. Northern farm women had long participated in a variety of commercial activities—generally, selling surplus goods such as butter, eggs, and homespun cloth—to supplement the family income. But over the course of the antebellum period, they became less connected to the world of commercial exchange. By the 1850s, Illinois farm women, for example, devoted less time to income-producing tasks and more effort to household responsibilities—making soap, sewing clothes, preparing food—that were now deemed necessary for proper home maintenance. Northern women were certainly part of a commercializing and industrializing society, but they often experienced the economic changes in the form of greater domestic burdens.[3]

One indication of women's ambiguous economic status could be seen in changes occuring in the American legal system. Although married women's status was still, for the most part, governed by the legal restrictions of coverture, even this doctrine had been somewhat modified by the eve of the Civil War. For the most part, married women's access to property and wages acquired after marriage remained under the sway and control of their husbands. However, a number of states, in the South as well as the North, had enacted legislation granting married women control of the property they had brought into a marriage settlement themselves, in some cases protecting women's property from their husbands' debt collectors. The New York State Earnings Act of 1860, the most advanced measure along these lines, gave married women the right to sue and be sued and to retain control of their wages and earnings in their own names. By 1865 twenty-nine states had passed some type of legislation granting married women control of their prenuptial property. Nevertheless, when the war began, married women in many states lacked explicit, legal property rights, while those who had such rights often could do little without extensive prenuptial documentation, significant assets, and considerable legal support. Even more, the changing legal climate left many women confused and uncertain as to what their rights and liabilities were at any given time. Changes governing married women's legal standing, observed two scholars in 1862, "are still in progress, and for many years to come the law on the subject will no doubt be in a 'transition state.'" For most Northern women, especially the vast majority who lacked significant financial resources, this "transition state" encouraged families to rely on long-standing customs and traditions that placed economic power in the hands of husbands and fathers.[4]

Women's work and their economic contributions also remained clouded by a mystifying ideology of domesticity. Because industrialization had placed a higher premium on men's income-earning activities, women's work was more and more removed from the economic realm. Northerners on the eve of the Civil War celebrated women's work (by which they almost always meant domestic housework) not for its economic value but for its moral, spiritual, and calming contributions. Women were seen to nurture, to dispense their womanly influence, and to uplift their homes and families; they did not, however, work, toil, or sweat. And while most of their work clearly affected the family economy—in terms of their ability to scavenge or save or produce household necessities—antebellum ideology did not in any explicit way acknowledge the effect women had on the economic status of their families and households.[5]

The war came, then, at a point when some tentative changes could be glimpsed in women's status, but when few fundamental challenges had been mounted against traditional notions of patriarchal authority and male economic dominance. If anything, predominant beliefs and practices continued to keep women marginalized in terms of earning wages or negotiating other economic transactions, which meant that men made most of the economic decisions while women generally had little or no experience conducting their families' financial transactions. Few had put their names on contracts or leases; many had infrequent contact with banks and other financial institutions; most had little income or property that they could claim exclusively for themselves.[6]

When their men went to war, Northern women suddenly came into contact, and conflict, with what was often a disturbing world of commercial transactions. Indeed, in the wartime setting, the commercial world proved to be especially troubling. The war was barely under way before stories of profiteering and speculation were rampant. Inflation sent prices soaring to levels not seen since the time of the American Revolution, while wages, especially wages of those working on war-related contracts, often lagged behind. Estimates suggest that prices increased throughout the period of the war by about 100 percent, while wages rose only by about 50 to 60 percent. Somewhere in this maelstrom, Northern women had to learn to negotiate their economic position: to settle debts, pay mortgages, acquire incomes. In light of the legal and ideological limitations imposed on them, they usually did so with inadequate training, diminished confidence in their abilities, and insufficient tools for the job. By and large women felt badgered and harrassed, hardly empowered, by their new wartime economic responsibilities. Public discourse paraded images of impoverished home-front women and suffering soldiers' wives as the victims of wartime profiteering.[7]

Beset by economic difficulties, Northern women increasingly turned to the government for support—for help finding jobs, for help in securing fair wages, and for various forms of economic assistance. By war's end they had been drawn into a new economic relationship with the government, becoming the beneficiaries of state support payments, federal pensions, even federal employment. This development, in part, led many women to feel a new level of economic empowerment. They became more articulate and accustomed to expressing their economic needs in a political context, and more insistent about those needs. At the same time, however, the government response was shaped by a paternalist concern for women's dependent status, especially their relationship to Union soldiers. At the end of the war women had a new economic relationship with the nation-state, but it was one that reemphasized their subordinate status, if not to male kin then to male public officials.

❧

From the time when men first left for the war until the moment they returned, financial concerns were a central preoccupation in their wartime exchanges with the women at home. "Keep a good account of your money matters," Frank Lincoln advised his wife, Rebecca, shortly after his enlistment in the fall of 1862, "and don't think because you have a little extra money that it will always last." Even seemingly minor money matters, especially for less prosperous families, took center stage. "Did Warner pay you that dollar he said he did?" Anne Saylor asked of her husband, Captain Phillip Saylor, in April 1865. "And I want to know did Rogers pay you what he promised on that cloak?" "you wrote that if you had a dollar that you would send it," Benjamin Morse, a member of the Eighth Vermont Volunteer Regiment, wrote to his wife, Rosina. "You mustent do that for if they wont pay me I cant send you any & to think that you cant have a dollar for your own use it is to bad." After she fixed a well that had collapsed, Louisa Phifer wrote to her husband, George, a corporal in the Thirty-Second Illinois Volunteer Infantry, "It took 8 dollars less than I expected it would."[8]

Such remarks suggest economic hardship as well as an important shift in the roles of women and men during the Civil War. Despite the emphasis before the war on men's financial responsibilities and breadwinning capabilities, the war increasingly compelled an acknowledgment of women's economic contributions as men had to surrender certain financial responsibilities. Rebecca Lincoln, for example, was now charged with keeping track of the family's financial transactions. Other women, too, had to sort out bills and debts and a wide variety of monetary obligations. Yet as Frank Lincoln's warning implied, women lacked experience in such matters and, at least as some men saw it, ran the risk of destabilizing their families' financial status. Worried about women's ignorance, men and women both looked for ways to keep a careful, and male-directed, check on home-front finances.

From the outset few Northerners were inclined to make drastic changes in the way they conducted their business. Local communities sought to create conditions that would prevent a dramatic reconfiguration of men's and women's economic positions. When the war began, Union privates received a somewhat steady salary of $11 per month, later increased to $13 and finally to $16 for the last year of the war. This was by no means extravagant (a Union private made about the same as an Ohio wage worker in the early 1860s) but it did provide a crucial base income. To make sure that the money got to those who needed it, several states made arrangements for a portion of the soldiers' pay to be regularly delivered to their families at home. The state of Wisconsin, for example, employed a corps of "allotment-commissioners" who arranged to send the soldiers' pay home so that women and children would have the benefit of their earnings. Many states and local communities authorized additional payments to the wives and children of soldiers, to be delivered directly to families while the men were away. Some of this was in the form of bounty payments for enlistment—as high as $1,200 per soldier by war's end—that were paid to soldiers but often turned over to families and relatives. Besides distributing such bounties, the state of Wisconsin also made monthly payments to a soldier's wife ($5) and his children ($2 each). In April 1861 the city council of Philadelphia appropriated $125,000 for payments to the families of volunteers, with the average distribution per family amounting to $1.50 per week.[9]

Still, such institutional supports were far from reliable, for payments—including soldiers' salaries—were often delayed. As a result, families had to take their own steps to maintain economic, and personal, stability. The departure of the male breadwinner prompted many women to move in with other kin—parents, in-laws, siblings—to avoid becoming suddenly and drastically self-reliant. Abby Hood of New Bedford, Massachusetts, returned to her father's house when her husband, James, left for war. Although James preferred to have his wife reside at a local boarding place, Abby—with a child on the way and perhaps uncertain of James's continued support—opted for the seemingly more stable circumstances of her paternal home. Catherine Peirce and her four children moved in with her husband's sister and brother-in-law in Des Moines, Iowa. In Michigan, Sophia Buchanan arranged to lease the house she shared with her husband, Claude, residing instead with her parents during the war. William Thompson advised his wife, Jane, to leave Iowa while he was away and stay with his family in Pennsylvania. Such household shifts often caused women considerable stress. Inevitably there was friction over how to share chores and how to allocate resources. Sarah Pardington moved out of her brother-in-law's residence in Trenton, Michigan, after some unspecified tensions emerged, declaring she would "never make joes Plase [her] home again." In New York State, Semira Merrill hoped to allay any interfamilial friction by preparing her own food for herself and her three daughters while they lived in her parents' house. For Jane Thompson, being with her husband's family in Pennsylvania only heightened her sense of loneliness. After two and a half months there she returned to Iowa, anxious to have her own household duties to attend to so that she "would not have so much time to think about being left alone." Thus, despite moves and adjustments to avoid living alone, many women still faced the predicament of managing on their own.[10]

Families in rural areas sometimes moved into towns to minimize grueling farm chores and to be closer to neighbors who could lend assistance. Rhoda Southworth reported on families in rural Minnesota who were struggling "to take care of their stock and get wood and water" without their sons. "I think," Southworth observed, "they will move into town if they can get some family to move into their house and take care of the cattle." Others stayed put but looked toward particular men to fill the void. Emeline Ritner did not leave her Mount Pleasant, Iowa, residence and urged her father, who was investigating various business propositions around the country, to move back home. "Everybody is going to war," Emeline explained soon after her own husband reenlisted in 1862, "and you must come home to stay with us poor women." In some families, men decided to enlist on the condition that other male relatives would stay behind to watch out for mothers and sisters. Union soldier Levi Perry was thus considerably distressed when he got the news that his brother Chandler had enlisted, because, as Levi told his mother, "he promised me when I left home that he would stay and take care of things at home now there is no one to look to things but you."[11]

When he or his male relatives could not be present, there were other ways in which a soldier could continue to play the part of family provider. Evidence suggests that many soldiers regularly sent most of their pay home—whether through an allotment system or simply in an envelope sent personally from the front. The reams of testimony deposited in pension files attest to countless wives and mothers and sisters who were utterly dependent on the pay from soldiers. When her son went off to war, Catherine O'Donnell was a widow living in New York City, and she relied on the money sent by her son prior to his death in 1863. Nancy Batson, because of her husband's infirmities, "was compelled to wait until her" soldier son sent his wages "before she could purchase the necessaries of life." When home on furlough, Matthew Bates brought cash to his mother, Elizabeth, and instructed a neighbor for whom he had worked to pay his mother the wages still owed to him. The grief each mother experienced at the death of her son was no doubt laced with the fear each felt about the threat of looming impoverishment now that her male provider was no more.[12]

Sometimes soldiers sent their money not to female relatives but to men—relatives or neighbors or local merchants—who were entrusted to dispense it according to their wishes. Soldiers no doubt hoped that such arrangements would give them greater control over financial transactions and minimize women's entanglements in business dealings. This practice served to perpetuate women's second-class status in commercial and monetary matters and underscored men's lack of trust in their financial abilities. Lyman Gray of New York State chose to send his wages not to his wife but to the man who held their mortgage. "The reason of my sending my money to John," he explained to his wife, Theresa, "is that I want him to have all the money that you don't use." When the mortgage holder died in 1863, Lyman Gray chose a different male surrogate to whom to send his money. John Benton, also in New York, sent his money to the village storekeeper and had his wife, Rosella, draw from that. Samuel Potter of Pennsylvania told his wife that after his last payday he had sent $50 to his father. "If you dont get along for money," he advised, "you had better draw some from him." John Beatty sent his money to a man named Andrew, although he eventually directed him to let his wife, Laura, have as much as she needed of the $500 in his keeping. Taylor Peirce of Iowa, suggested that his brother-in-law, who was now providing shelter for Peirce's wife, Catharine, fatten and sell the livestock that Taylor and Catharine owned. He said Cyrus could then use that money to pay his debts and give some to Catharine for her own needs. Nonetheless, with Cyrus suffering from frequent bouts of asthma, Taylor Peirce recognized that some of the responsibilities had to be taken up by his wife. "I now trust in thy good judgment," Peirce wrote to her in September 1862, "to see to our things and when thee is at fault consult either Cyrus, Ingersole or J Sumpter and whenever the[e] asks my advice I will give it."[13]

Taylor Peirce, perhaps more quickly than other men, began to realize his own limitations in overseeing the business affairs of his family and how much he had to rely on the judgment of those who best understood the immediate circumstances at home, including his wife. Decisions would have to be made about the mill that Taylor owned and any property the Peirces might wish to purchase in the future. Even more, Taylor Peirce realized that the future of his wife and children might depend on her ability to manage the family business. "I want thee," Peirce advised Catharine in September 1862, "to take hold and do for thyself and use thy own judgment about matters and lirn to lean on thyself so that If I should be called away thee will have a knowledge of business to make a living for thyself." Certainly the threat of death compelled him to give greater attention to his wife's economic skills. And while Peirce may have been more open-minded than many, his sentiments point to a trend evident in the correspondence between many soldiers and female kin over the course of the war: a growing awareness, on the part of both men and women, that women had to assume greater responsibility for business and other economic concerns if they were to see to their (and ultimately their men's) survival and well-being.[14]

Women stepped into the economic breach, albeit with some reluctance. Many felt frustrated by a lack of basic information. Distressed at her inability to manage the renting of her husband's mill, Ann Cotton adopted a self-deprecating approach. "I see that I know nothing at all about business affairs," she wrote to Josiah in February 1863, "& am tired of it already." Certainly she was not the only one to feel that her inexperience and ignorance confirmed just how unprepared she was for the commercial sphere. Rebecca Lincoln of Brimfield, Massachusetts, although relatively well-off, may have been frustrated by her husband's insistence that she keep a careful record of money matters despite the fact that he still withheld vital information. "I have let the town have $150," she wrote to her husband, Frank, early in 1863. "Who takes care of your money from the government. You have never spoken of it." Like Rebecca Lincoln, other women pressed their menfolk for a more accurate economic picture so that they could better fulfill their home-front responsibilities. Theresa Gray, who was compelled to get her money from the mortgage holder to whom her husband sent his pay, asked for more precise data so she could get a clearer picture of their economic prospects. "I wish your business with money," she wrote in July 1862, "might be settled up so that I might know how it stands. I wish things could be managed so as to clear this place from all encumbrances, for a little home is a great help you know." Anne Saylor in Illinois also wanted more complete accounts from her husband in order to manage more efficiently. "What did you charge for fixing the schoolhouse pump?" she asked her husband, Phillip. "Tell me when you write. I can't settle with Jacobs till you do." Even if they were not always successful in managing their new commercial activities, many women gained a clearer understanding of the obstacles they faced, and then, in some cases, demanded that those obstacles be cleared away.[15]

Other women sought assistance from men even as they realized that the men simply could not help them in ways they once had. Writing from Weymouth, Massachusetts, Fanny Pierce advised her brother of some of their financial woes. Her words suggested her ambivalent assumption of economic authority. "The interest on the mortgage of the estate," she explained in December 1861, "is due the first day of January. I think I can raise ten dollars of it in time and perhaps a little more, but feel a little anxious about the rest and thought I had better mention it to you, knowing you would like to help if it was in your power." More rarely, Northern families worked out an affirmative and encouraging arrangement regarding women's financial responsibilities. "I feel willing for you to do all business," Rosella Benton's husband wrote to his wife in August 1863, "and make shifts as you think best, especially in minor transactions, for it is not possible for me to know all the circumstances." In February 1865 he even encouraged her to use her own judgment in closing a sale on some of their property.[16]

Few women, though, enjoyed either the financial resources or economic independence of Rosella Benton. In isolated rural settings, women confronted the fact that they had depended on male relatives for their very survival. George Shepherd worried that his wife in Wisconsin would "freaze to death doing the chores" and asked her to write to him as to "how you gett a long for choping." Richard Tebout, a black soldier from New York, appealed for a furlough by making specific reference to helping his old mother who "has not any one to get Wood for her next winter." Without the words of George Shepherd's wife or Richard Tebout's mother, we cannot know for certain just how these women managed. Like others without their menfolk, they may have recruited neighbors to help with the most demanding chores. Farm families often relied on day laborers—when they could find them and afford them—to fill in for absent kin. When the well on her Illinois farm collapsed, Louisa Phifer had to grapple with a task that had not fallen to her before, and she scouted for neighborhood men who could assist her. Some women recognized their need to move beyond their dependence on men and determined to do things themselves. For Emeline Ritner, it was hog butchering that forced her to cross the gender divide. Although she found someone else to do the killing, Emeline herself faced the chore of turning the dead animal into food that she and her family could consume. She and her husband's cousin, Lib, "went to work and cut it up ourselves." "We done it up just right," she told her soldier husband. "We just had to do it. There was not a man on the hill that we could get." Rosella Benton in New York took pride in doing chores usually done by men, although she also recognized her limits. "I have thought this winter that it was well for me that I knew how to fodder a horse or a cow in my young days. I wish I had the strength to chop or split wood, we would be almost independent of all the men about here."[17]

Women in both rural and urban areas generally tended vegetable gardens, and some may have expanded their efforts in that regard, both to produce their own food and to sell their surplus. "I have got squashes cucumbers beets beans peas onions corns turnips and cabbage," wrote Diana Phillips of Maine to her soldier husband, "all up planted on that small peice of ground below the stable." The line that separated, albeit imperfectly, men's cash-crop work from women's home-oriented gardening became even more difficult to draw during the war years. In May 1863, Emeline Ritner and her cousin Lib "planted the corn & potatoes ourselves. We didn't know where to find anybody to do it for us so we pitched in and planted it ourselves." When the fall came, she found herself nervously contemplating the low price corn was fetching in the local market. Marjorie Rogers also grew corn, but she had better luck in the marketplace. When her husband, a surgeon, left for the war, Rogers moved from her family farm in

Tama County, Iowa, to live with siblings in a nearby town. She returned to the farm, though, to see that the corn was brought to market. "If there had been a man to do me the favor of driving down the hills, I would have appreciated it but men were scarce and especially when needed." As she came through town at harvest time, seated high on a mountain of corn, the townspeople looked at her in surprise. Two men came to help her down, but she "declined their kindness and said I would get down the same as a man did if I could do a man's work." When the local merchants saw the good quality of her crop, she got a high price for her corn.[18]

Financial incentive and sheer will power seem to account for Marjorie Rogers's advance into the sphere of men's work and business. Other Northern farm women managed to do men's work thanks to the wonders of technology. Tens of thousands of new machines and agricultural implements enhanced Yankee farm women's productivity. During the 1860s, reapers, harvesters, hay rakes, and other machines filled in for the labor of thousands of farmers who had left for the war, allowing a reduced farming population to meet and even exceed the agricultural demands of Northern society in the 1860s. Between 1860 and 1870 the average farmer's annual investment in new equipment jumped from $11 per year to $20 per year. Given the overall lack of ready cash in the South, far fewer farm machines made their way there, leaving Southern women without this technological advantage. In her postwar memoir, Mary Livermore recalled traveling through the farm districts of Wisconsin and eastern Iowa, where she saw women hard at work, driving "the horses round and round the wheat-field, diminishing more and more its periphery at every circuit, the glittering blades of the reaper cutting wide swaths with a rapid, clicking sound, that was pleasant to hear." Advertisements and editorials in agricultural journals confirmed Livermore's recollections, suggesting that many women had assumed tasks, especially mechanized ones, related to commercial farming. *Prairie Farmer* magazine advertised a hay rake by showing a young woman driving the new invention above the caption: "My brother has gone to the war."[19]

Farm machinery, however, was no magic bullet for Northern women or for Northern agriculture. For every farm family that invested in a shiny new reaper, there were many more that could not afford to mechanize. At least one study of Northern agriculture during the Civil War suggests that the dramatic increase in farm labor productivity during the 1860s stemmed not so much from mechanization as from "an increase in the labor of women and children devoted to market production." In other words, agricultural strides may have come less from women driving reapers and more from women taking larger quantities of milk and butter and eggs to the marketplace, to bring in more cash income. It seems likely that Northern farm women worked harder and intensified their commercial interactions to fill in the economic gaps left by men who had gone to war. Rosella Benton sold butter, and Emeline Ritner offered canned blackberries and her garden potatoes for sale, although the market conditions for both were poor. Lydia Watkins reported to her son Benton that she had raised 300 cabbages in her garden and expected "to glut Gran Rapids market this time." Rachel Cormany, who grew tired of having to depend on the kindness of strangers in Chambersburg, Pennsylvania, sold her produce in the local market in the fall of 1864. "I find," she wrote her husband, "I will get along better by being a little independent."[20]

Women found countless other ways to bring in cash. Some took in boarders. Catharine Peirce and her in-laws gave room and board to Iowa soldiers on their way to camp. "We are haveing a good time working for soldiers all this cold time," she wrote her husband in January 1864. "There has been some here now for five weeks and sometimes as high as thirty and forty." Susan Eaton's home in Mattapoisett, Massachusetts, was, in the fall of 1864, apparently overrun with boarders. To Eaton, the presence of a "good many strangers" suggested new commercial possibilities for her seaside New England town, which, she remarked, "may become quite a watering place if people will open their houses."[21]

Taking in boarders offered the obvious advantage of keeping women close to home and children and domestic chores. The same was true for many of the informal sewing and knitting tasks women assumed, working for friends, neighbors, and relatives. During the Civil War years, countless women sewed shirts, or knitted hats, hoping such modest offerings would improve their cash-flow situation. Here, though, they confronted the limitations of their domestic confinement. Few people in rural communities had cash available to pay for such mundane tasks, and instead they offered other goods and services in exchange. "I have been making a silk vest this week to pay a man for chopping wood," Samary Sherman explained to her cousin Lucretia Sibley. "I cannot get much sewing to do here. The women about here make all their mens clothes . . . The children have worked out considerable for molasses and potatoes, but they cannot get any money here for work." Semira Merrill tried knitting women's gloves and mittens in her upstate New York community, but many found the price of 25 cents per pair beyond their means. Anne Saylor in Shelbyville, Illinois, got a sewing machine in the spring of 1865 so she could earn more by her stitching. Still, when her husband needed money that June she had nothing to show for her efforts. "I do not see how I can help you if I could get money for all my sewing I could send you some but I cant." Rachel Cormany took in sewing for her in-laws, and when she was not paid in cash she decided to keep the butter they had loaned her.[22]

The war also created new types of employment opportunities for women that pushed them beyond the accustomed boundaries for female economic activity. Women gained a more visible presence in a number of professions both because fewer men were on hand and because employers quickly seized the opportunity to employ a cheaper work force. Emily Elliot of Wooster, Ohio, for example, continued to work as a schoolteacher while her husband, Denton, served as an officer in the 103rd Ohio, a practice she may well have discontinued had she been a married woman with a husband living at home. Already a largely feminized profession, especially in New England, teaching was a more lucrative career than many other forms of employment available to women in the 1860s. Although they almost always received less pay than male teachers, female instructors—like their male counterparts—enjoyed a 20 percent increase in wages during the war years, no doubt because the workforce was constricted. Unlike other jobs, the foothold women secured in teaching during the war persisted, and even expanded, in the postwar years. In Illinois, for example, 4,000 more female teachers were employed in 1865 than in 1860, while the total number of male teachers had decreased by 2,000. Following her brother Benton's enlistment, Genie Watkins took a teaching job in the Whitney School District in Michigan, happy to earn $2 per week. Charles Ingersoll's sister secured a position as a schoolmistress in upstate New York when the schoolmaster there became a soldier. Knowing that teaching, especially in Massachusetts, offered better money than many other jobs available to her, Julia Underhill wrote from Menosha, Wisconsin, to ask her aunts what "good female teachers" there were earning.[23]

Mill and factory jobs also opened up to women when men left

for the war, although many of those opportunities would disappear when the men returned. Women worked in traditionally female occupations such as shoemaking and textiles, where wages had always been low and the working conditions less than ideal. One young Massachusetts woman moved to Northampton during the Civil War and got work in a hoopskirt factory. Her employment was brief, however, for she found that the money was a meager compensation for the grueling labor she performed. "I have just about made my board," she observed in her diary, "but working all the time as hard as I could." A few women found new and apparently more lucrative avenues available to them. When she wasn't looking after boarders, Susan Eaton had begun to learn a new trade, making halters for horses. The experience impressed Eaton with the fact that "the women can do it as well as the men."[24]

Of course the industrial demands of the war itself—the need to quickly produce everything from army blankets to bullet casings—brought thousands of women into new manufacturing jobs. The massive Northern army required a vast array of goods that would have to be manufactured by workers on the home front. With the government granting numerous contracts for wartime production, thousands of jobs were created, more than could be filled by male workers alone. More than 100,000 new factory, sewing, and arsenal jobs became available to Northern women during the war. Demand for seamstresses, in particular, skyrocketed during the war years, owing to the increased need for bedding and uniforms and other textile goods. Civil War seamstresses, however, may well have been some of the most downtrodden employees of the era. Most worked for government subcontractors, who generally ignored the government's recommended pay scale and sought to economize with minimal wages and inadequate production space. The tent-making indus-

HARPER'S WEEKLY.
A JOURNAL OF CIVILIZATION.

VOL. V.—No. 238.]　　　NEW YORK, SATURDAY, JULY 20, 1861.　　　[SINGLE COPIES SIX CENTS.
[$2 50 PER YEAR IN ADVANCE.

Entered according to Act of Congress, in the Year 1861, by Harper & Brothers, in the Clerk's Office of the District Court for the Southern District of New York.

try, for example, relied considerably on subcontracted female labor. One employer in Philadelphia, a subcontractor for the U.S. Army Procurement Office, began his business by renting a room and hiring thirty "girls" from the city and suburbs. Described by one newspaper as "mostly Americans, some of whom have seen better days," the girls complained when, after ten days, their employer failed to pay them the promised $1.50 per day. Seamstresses in New York City saw a decline in their wages from 17.5 cents per shirt in 1861 to 8 cents per shirt in 1864. Cincinnati women complained that while contractors took in $1.75 per dozen gray woolen shirts, they paid their stitchers only $1 per dozen.[25]

Yet, as exploitative as this arrangement was, these were jobs that were generally available to white women only. Black women had far fewer employment opportunities, even during the war years, although a few made inroads here and there. Twenty-four-year-old Catharine Dodson became a government employee, working first in the U.S. Senate and then, with a recommendation from Senator Charles Sumner, as a doorkeeper in the Treasury Department. She earned $1 per day. Dodson's earnings were extravagant compared with the economic resources of most Northern black women. Because they generally lacked property from which they could draw an income and were often denied entry into the more lucrative female occupations, African American women had meager opportunities for economic stability, let alone advancement, during the war. Yet their need for money

The tremendous demand for munitions created employment opportunities for women, although the jobs were often dangerous and underpaid. The top image shows women performing some of the more routine tasks at the United States Arsenal in Watertown, Massachusetts. Credit: Library of Congress, Prints and Photographs Division [LC-USZ62–96445]

was even more pressing than that of white women, especially if they had male wage-earners in the military. Although black men could not join the Union army until late in 1862, eventually 34,000 free Northern blacks did enlist. But because black soldiers initially received less pay than whites, and often received their pay only after considerable delay, black women on the home front confronted significant economic obstacles. David Demus, a farm laborer from Pennsylvania who enlisted in the Massachusetts 54th Regiment, chided his wife for doing field work for a local farmer. But the fact that the government had yet to pay him the $90 owed for his military service had no doubt exacerbated his wife's financial need. Mrs. John Wilson, whose husband served in the 102nd U.S. Colored Regiment, wrote to Secretary of War Stanton requesting a furlough for her spouse. Since her husband had received no pay, she was "compleatly distitute," she explained. "I have no support except what I earn by my own labor from day to day." In New Jersey, Rosanna Henson found that racial prejudice deprived her family not only of her enlisted husband's wages but also of state support. "I being a colored woman," she explained in a letter to Abraham Lincoln, "do not get any State pay." Lavinia Brown, an elderly widow living on the outskirts of Delaware, Ohio, had relied on the wages her son earned, prior to his enlistment in the Massachusetts 55th, as a plasterer. After he left for the war, she explained in her pension claim, "she was wholly dependent on him, and what little she was able to earn herself by hard work, for her support." Just how Mrs. Wilson and Lavinia Brown earned a living is not known, but Mrs. Wilson's reference to her "own labor" and Lavinia Brown's description of "hard work" suggest employment that was not necessarily steady or highly paid.[26]

As the war progressed, women were increasingly drawn into,

or further involved in, the world of commercial transactions. Whether they took eggs and butter to market, sewed shirts and jackets, or sold property to pay off debts, women stepped into a somewhat unfamiliar economic space in which they had to sell or exchange something they did or something they owned. And while some women certainly took pride in their economic accomplishments—learning a new trade, for example, or successfully exchanging crops for cash—most encountered considerable frustration on entering an arena in which their sex placed them at a noticeable disadvantage. As teachers, they were routinely paid less than men who did the same work. If they sewed, they found that so many other women were sewing their own families' clothes that they could earn only minimal pay or no cash at all. If they had to settle a loan or negotiate a business deal, they felt hampered by their ignorance of such affairs. If they had produce to sell, they faced the challenge of transporting it to market. For every Mrs. Rogers who proudly rode her wagonload of corn into town, there must have been countless women who had to find men to help them, and then had to pay those men a portion of their hard-earned income. Rosella Benton complained to her husband that she had to sell her butter at a less than opportune time because she could get the work done only when the neighborhood men were free to assist her. In Iowa, Emeline Ritner hoped to make some money by selling their two old cows. Although she might have earned more by having the cows fattened and then slaughtered, Emeline knew this would be "a great bother . . . to get [them] butchered and sell the beef and hide and everything." And even after she decided to sell, she still couldn't find anyone willing to buy. "I have the poorest luck in the world doing business," Emeline wrote to her husband. "This winter I can't make it go at all." As Emeline Ritner saw it, the problem lay not with her dependence on men, whom she needed for some of the difficult farm chores, but her own poor "luck" in "doing business."[27]

The Civil War propelled Northern women into an exploitative exchange system in which their sex was a significant obstacle to their economic success and even survival. Consider, for example, one woman's tragic story. After Julia Underhill married her schoolteacher in 1858, her father disinherited her, convinced she had made an ill-advised choice at far too young an age. Undeterred, Julia and her husband, Leemon, moved to Wisconsin, where Leemon took up work as a cooper and Julia gave birth to two daughters. By the fall of 1863, Leemon had left for the war. Now Julia tried to renew contact with her father, hoping his anger might have softened enough since the wedding that he might be willing to help her and Leemon acquire some government land in Minnesota. He wrote back offering nothing but abuse and insults for the couple. The rebuke apparently made Julia even more determined to support herself and her children while Leemon was away. In December 1863 Julia contemplated moving east to stay with her aunts in Massachusetts. "My husband," she explained, "says he would feel more contented if I was there staying with you than he does now when I am alone." She explained that she should be getting five dollars per month from the state of Wisconsin as a volunteer's wife and, while she had not received her money yet, she hoped to get it soon. The lack of state aid, though, worried her less than the constant harassment she received from the local men each time she went out alone in public.[28]

Soon after, Julia made the move to Massachusetts, where she left her daughters in the care of her aunts while she went in search of employment. She found it difficult, however, to secure good pay and decent work, even in Massachusetts—at least so long as she presented herself as Julia Underhill. The opportunities improved significantly for Henry Goodwin, the young man Julia Underhill decided to become. In her disguise as a teenage boy, she soon got work in an iron foundry in Lanesboro. "I have got a good place to work," Julia wrote to her husband, "and am my employers pet boy. I am verry lonesome but I must bear it, times are so hard that I must work in this way to support the babys." Although the circumstances were trying, Julia took some comfort in having steady work and being free from sexual advances. "It is the easiest way," she explained, "to support myself and now I am free from insult. my employer says I am the smartest best boy he ever saw."[29]

Before Leemon returned to his wife and children, though, Julia Underhill died. Her health had no doubt been ruined by the demands of her work in the foundry. Such a tragic demise underscores the economic vulnerabilities of women like Julia Underhill. Finding it difficult to support herself and her children while her husband was at war, she had relocated in search of security and work and found that only by becoming a man could she, even temporarily, attain these goals. If Julia's life resembled a nineteenth-century melodrama, it was nevertheless an indication of just how precarious the situation was for women when they had to fend for themselves.[30]

Julia Underhill, like many others, found herself forced to make a living in an expanding Northern economy that had generally drawn on women as a cheap source of labor. But in the context of Civil War America, tales of economic woe such as hers aroused public sympathy for women's economic troubles, propelling women into a more forceful public discussion of their economic rights and also imposing new conditions of economic subordination. Many came to see women as victims who required men to salvage their financial circumstances for them. Some believed women were inherently less fit to handle the complexities of the commercial sphere. And more than a few came to believe that allowing women to suffer economic harm, especially women who had soldiers at the front, represented an unpatriotic act that required government correction. Civil War Northerners observed women's financial misery and saw the need for a new civic relationship between women and government.

Massachusetts prison officials offered a variant of this analysis when they surveyed the rising female prison population during the war years. Many Northern states registered a noticeable increase of female inmates, especially in local prisons housing those convicted of petty crimes and misdemeanors. Reformers and prison officials, too, noted that the majority of women in this new prison class were the mothers, wives, and daughters of Union soldiers. Interestingly, prison officials believed the source of the problem was not poverty but in fact ready cash and a lack of male assistance and supervision. A special Massachusetts report gave particular attention to "the distribution of State Aid and bounty money," declaring that "the possession of more money than usual makes these women idle and exposes them to temptation; they drink, and from this are led on to worse offenses; while the absence of their sons, husbands, and fathers leaves them without restraint or protection." Given the delays and difficulties women faced in securing state money, the problem of increased crime among women no doubt stemmed more from a lack of money than from unfettered access to it. Nonetheless, the prison officials offered a revealing insight into wartime perceptions of women's economic incapacities. In various ways, women suffered from the economic irregularities of the period and from their inexperience in assuming financial responsibility. But as they concluded, the real source of women's wartime economic problems was the lack of male protection.[31]

Obviously female criminals represented an extreme case in the story of women's economic troubles. Most women did not go to jail—but they did find it difficult, if not impossible, to navigate the heartless world of capitalist exchange. As she had in much of the early war propaganda, the figure of the "soldier's wife"—and sometimes the soldier's widowed mother—again appeared in letters and stories and magazine illustrations, where she embodied a sort of "everywoman" of the Civil War era. But this time she was not the woman who sacrificed her home for the higher claim of the country, but the woman who suffered at the hands of an expanding and changing Northern economy. She offered a symbol that soldiers drew on to curse those who stayed home and cheated helpless women instead of serving their country. She also provided an image that newspaper and magazine editors used to call attention to the tragedy of wartime profiteering. This wife or mother figure stood as a warning of economic victimization that became all too familiar to many Northern women. And in many ways she became a stand-in for a more generalized perception of how women confronted the marketplace.

Although many soldiers came to depend on women's economic capabilities at home, they remained uneasy about the new demands placed on their wives and mothers and sisters, continuing to see themselves as the natural providers and reluctant to have women immersed in the family's breadwinning. Three days after Frank Pierce returned from the army, in January 1865, he told his wife, Harriet, that her days of doing piecework for a local New Hampshire mill were over. He felt so strongly on this point, in fact, that he stated his views emphatically on the pages of his wife's diary. "Finished drawers today," wrote Harriet. "Frank says I shant do any more." "Yes, and I mean it," Frank wrote underneath Harriet's entry. John Pardington of Trenton, Michigan, had refused to even consider having his wife "work out" while he was away. "What a wife of mine working out with that little darling," he wrote with respect to his wife and child. "Why it almost makes me crazy to think of it." To forestall this possibility, Pardington immediately sent his wife $7 of his savings.[32]

While some women certainly derived satisfaction from working and contributing to the family economy, others seemed wary of expanding their sphere of commercial activity, reluctant to become involved in a world in which they had little experience. They worried about the uncertainties of the marketplace and were strongly suspicious of men's questionable economic motives, especially in a period of wartime speculation. Ann Cotton, for example, was exceedingly hesitant about signing a lease that would allow a local man to rent her husband's sawmill because, she said, it would "make me responsible for the debts." "I wish you would have it all arranged with the assistance of a lawyer, without my having to sign that lease," she wrote to her husband in February 1863. In Iowa, Emeline Ritner worried that her husband had not been straight with her about all of his economic troubles. She asked him for a full accounting of his business affairs but also wanted to keep her own name free from entanglement. She rejected his suggestion that some of his property be placed in her name.[33]

In seeking to keep themselves free from economic burdens, both Ann Cotton and Emeline Ritner hoped to maintain a comfortable distance from the economic chaos that seemed to loom on the horizon. For many women, the wartime world was a threatening economic battlefront, peopled with unscrupulous men ready to prey on their financial vulnerability while their kin were away. Enlisted men sounded this theme repeatedly in their letters home. Time and again, soldiers ranted against cads who cheated and manipulated their wives. "I believe you wrote that you paid Kidder 10.30," Benjamin Morse warned his wife, Rosina. "If so, he has cheated you the raskall." Sylvester McElheney advised his wife in Franklin County, Pennsylvania, to watch out for a man to whom they owed money. "I dont wont you to pa him for I think he has got [enough?]." From afar, soldiers tried to bring their personal influence to bear against the cheaters. John Pardington bemoaned the wretch doing business with his wife and promised to intercede on her behalf. "Tell me in your next letter," he wrote his wife, Sarah, "if luke Covil has Paid you or not . . . I will write him a note which I think will make him Pay for I think he has acted a mean peice of Business." A note would have been too delicate a solution for George Shepherd, who raged against the rogue trying to extract money from his spouse for an account that George had already settled. "Tell him," Shepherd wrote his wife in Eau Claire, Wisconsin, that if he tries it again, I "will just shove my foot up his Ass." Perhaps the soldiers' frustration and outrage was best expressed by Taylor Peirce, who pinpointed the particular problem of the economic vulnerability of the "soldier's wife." Although generally encouraging of his wife's business dealings, Peirce denounced the new owner of their mill, who was refusing to make the mortgage payments. "If Mr. Granston," Peirce wrote to his wife in July 1864, "wishes to take advantage of a soldiers wife while her husband is absent defending that that he has not the courage to defend himself just tell him to go to hell. I think it dammd small for such a man as him to try and draw fifty dollars out of a woman who has a family of little children and no certainty of her husband ever being again with her." Peirce, in effect, had transformed Mr. Granston's swindling of his wife from a routine act of money-grubbing into a larger political problem of disloyalty.[34]

Although many men, including Taylor Peirce, thought their wives were capable financial managers, they still believed that the materialistic and profit-oriented economy of the North could be a hostile world for unsuspecting women on their own. If nine-teenth-century Yankees had misgivings about their capitalist system and its lack of human compassion, they were even more concerned when women became entangled in it. With the war providing so much opportunity for profiteering, many soldiers came to believe that untutored women would become the easiest targets and the likeliest victims of those trying to make a profit from the war. In the most public accountings of this drama, those who in any way benefited from soldiers' wives' distress were denounced as unpatriotic. As the war progressed and more Northerners became aware of home-front suffering, magazine stories and illustrations told tales of rich industrialists and so-called "shoddy" contractors who enjoyed a new-found wealth at the expense of other people's misery. The October 24, 1863, issue of *Harper's Weekly* offered a series of scenes depicting "service and shoddy," in which the most prominent figures were not the soldier, nor even the wartime contractor, but "the soldier's wife" and "the contractor's wife." While the latter donned silks and spent money furiously, the former could not pay her creditors and lived in poverty. The message, with respect to both women, was telling: the wartime economy put undue pressure on women—turning one into a reckless spender and the other into a suffering indigent—because they were ill-prepared to cope in the commercial world.[35]

Northern women often echoed this sense of economic victimization. While many handled their finances ably, they still worried that they might not be sharp enough and knowledgeable enough to cope with inflated prices, the complex market, and double-dealing mortgage holders. As a result, women came to believe themselves inadequate and to feel more dependent on men's financial abilities. With inflation rates soaring, women felt particularly burdened, being both deprived of a man's wages and

Public discussions highlighted the troubling effects of the wartime economy on Northern women, as featured in this Harper's Weekly *cartoon contrasting the impoverished soldier's wife with the dissipated contractor's wife.* Credit: Harper's Weekly, October 24, 1863

forced to pay exorbitant prices. Distressed by the high price of apples in the fall of 1864, Emeline Ritner wrote to her husband, "How I wish you could be here to buy things for us." Jake Ritner agreed, implying that he would, in military fashion, keep things running smoothly. "I would like to be at home," he wrote, "and act as quartermaster and commissary for you a while." After she returned to Iowa, Jane Thompson felt overwhelmed by the economic demands on her. "Mr. Risker," she explained to her husband, "says we have a meat bill there and he wants the cow. I wish you would tell me what to do . . . Oh dear, I do wish you were at home."[36]

Because of inflation, women had to lay out considerable amounts of cash right when they seemed most incapable of bringing it in. "I so hate to use your money," Emeline Ritner explained in a letter as she detailed the high price of wood and molasses, "that you have come by such hard work and I at home not making anything at all." Although she planted and raised crops and butchered pigs, Ritner still felt as if she were "not making anything at all," certainly not in comparison to her own husband's efforts. Emily Elliot took some comfort in the fact that she brought in a little bit of money as a teacher, although it still seemed insufficient. "O dear," she told 'ier diary, "how everything costs. Three dollars for a calico dress, and every thing else in the same proportion . . . I'd feel as if it was pretty bad for me to be spending so much if I was not making something." Realizing how limited her economic intake was because of her husband's absence, Rachel Cormany bemoaned her lot as a "soldier's wife," a term that implied financial vulnerability, especially compared with her wealthy (and selfish) relatives. "If I were not a soldiers wife," Cormany observed, "and had plenty—I would not mind it—but they are rich and know my circumstances as well as I do."[37]

By the latter part of the war, public commentators wrote frequently on the subject of women's wartime victimization, with many middle-class observers voicing concerns for working women in particular. The descriptions often gave prominence to the notion that, as soldiers' wives, such female laborers were particularly deserving of public sympathy, perhaps even public relief, because they had sacrificed their menfolk. The war in effect recast women's private economic suffering into a topic worthy of public discussion. Economic aid and assistance, for example, were cloaked in the mantle of loyalty and patriotism, prompting more privileged women to intensify their charitable efforts. Such sentiments no doubt inspired Caroline Dunstan who, when she was not preparing lint for the bandages of wounded men or shopping for patriotic souvenirs in New York City, spent considerable effort in aiding a local soldier's wife. In December 1861 Dunstan first became familiar with the troubles of Mrs. Ross, identified throughout Dunstan's diary as "the soldier's wife," and began offering her assistance. Unable to secure aid for Mrs. Ross from her Bible society, Dunstan gave her food and money directly. She may, in fact, have experienced her own personal Civil War drama through the Ross family's miseries. In August 1863, at the end of a furlough for Mr. Ross, Dunstan gave money to him and to his wife, and she was there for the emotional moment when "Mrs. Ross & her husband the soldier . . . bid goodbye." When she learned of Mrs. Ross's untimely death a few months later, she made a final attempt to aid the family by helping the Ross children get properly situated.[38]

Caroline Dunstan went beyond the standard charitable practices, giving aid when aid societies did not, and even, at one point, giving money to Mr. Ross so he could buy tobacco. Her relationship with the Ross family suggests the power of sympathy, now given a patriotic overlay, to motivate middle- and upper-class women to provide for soldiers' wives. Other benefactors directed their energy toward working women who were earning less than subsistence wages. Sewing women, many of whom were forced to live on shrinking wages paid by greedy subcontractors, particularly engaged the sympathies of more privileged Northerners. A few well-to-do women even initiated their own social welfare schemes during the war. In April 1863 Elizabeth Rogers Cabot attended a "mother's meeting" in Boston where she and others discussed the possibility of creating institutions "to help the poor." By January 1864 she was working as an inspector in a sewing room where poor women made soldiers' clothes. As Rogers explained, with "ladies" like herself able to offer "free work & time" in overseeing the contracts, the seamstresses could "receive better pay for making soldiers' clothes, than from Contractors." Caroline Kirkland undertook a similar project in New York, where she paid seamstresses twice what the contractors paid for sewing "a shirt or a pair of drawers." Maria Daly and her husband, Judge Charles Patrick Daly, likewise lent their assistance to seamstresses and other female wageworkers in New York when they helped form the Workingwomen's Protective Union in November 1863, an organization that did not win concrete reforms so much as it educated the public about the plight of working women. Even labor leaders like William Sylvis lent assistance to seamstresses, encouraging them, late in the war, to form a union that would establish a standard price schedule for their sewing tasks.[39]

Such schemes, though, generally had little effect on the women's actual earning power. Slightly more effective were the public appeals made by workers themselves. As the war wore on, female stitchers broadcasted their plight with federal officials and other prominent Northerners. Many called attention to their status as soldiers' relatives, recognizing that this would emphasize the patriotic component of their position and make it more likely that officials would intervene on their behalf. By the fall of 1863, seamstresses in a number of Northern cities began publicizing their exploitative circumstances, formulating petitions and memorials that they presented to President Lincoln and other representatives of the federal government. When the sewing women of Cincinnati wrote to Lincoln, they sought to go beyond the "soldier's wife" label but made it clear they were still linked to the men in blue, identifying themselves as "the wives, widows, sisters, and friends of the soldiers in the army of the United States, depending upon our own labor for bread, [and] sympathizing with the Government of the United States." Philadelphia women made a similar appeal but were challenged by a protest from other seamstresses in the area who opposed discrimination in favor of soldiers' kin and against the many other women who needed the work. Yet when the Philadelphia women later presented their grievances to the federal government, they returned to familiar ground and proudly claimed kinship with the country's enlisted men. A Philadelphia minister pressed the seamstresses' case in his own missive to President Lincoln. "These women," explained the Reverend Harris, "are, very many of them, the wives or widows of American Soldiers; & all they need is the show of fair play at the hands of the government for which their husbands are fighting or have died." New York seamstresses, writing to Secretary of War Stanton in September 1864 with similar grievances, presented themselves as "delicately-reared women whose husbands, fathers and brothers have fallen on the battle-field." In New York, Cincinnati, and Philadelphia, as well as elsewhere, women called on the federal government to issue work (and pay) directly to them, to circumvent the profit-squeezing subcontractors. Patriotism, they implied, demanded such government intrusion in the marketplace.[40]

In effect, seamstresses sought to expand women's civic claims and civic power, appealing to the government to extend its reach to the women who had already demonstrated their allegiance to the Union. No doubt the seamstresses assumed that identifying themselves as soldiers' wives and kin would more likely gain them their goal of better pay—and in many cases they were probably right. But pitching their appeal in this way also had the effect of muting the power and potential of their civic involvement: by focusing more on their sacrifice as soldiers' kin than on their own painstaking labor, they weakened their claim to an independent female voice in public affairs. They called attention not so much to the exploitation of their labor power, but to the unscrupulous manipulation of their status as soldiers' relatives in need. They were, in other words, women who under better circumstances would not have entered the marketplace at all.

The seamstresses' appeals did win some short-term gains. In early 1865, Philadelphia sewing women went to Washington, where they met with Lincoln in person. Although no legislation emerged from their discussions, Lincoln promised to monitor the seamstresses' circumstances more closely and to order higher wages for women working at the federal arsenals. The meeting earned the women more public sympathy and attention. It also highlighted a new type of protective governmental policy taking shape in Civil War America. Government employment for women and pensions for wives and mothers of Union soldiers were geared toward those who could claim a relationship to an enlisted man, or toward those who under "normal" circumstances might have relied on a male breadwinner who had enlisted. These initiatives drew on the wartime notion that allowing women to suffer because their men had gone to war was disloyal, and officials could portray the government's economic protection of women as an act of patriotism. The proposed solutions helped to foster a new type of relationship between women and the federal government, one that acknowledged a greater civic role for women but also gave them less room to maneuver as independent political actors.

A similar dynamic took shape for women who were hired by the Union government during the wartime expansion of the federal bureaucracy. Taking jobs as clerks and office workers in various branches of the federal government, these "government girls" were among the most visible of the new wartime female employees. Before the war began, a scattering of women could be found in a few government departments, such as the Patent

Office and the U.S. Mint. But as the war persisted and the government bureaucracy expanded, increasing numbers of women joined the federal payroll. The most notable expansion occurred in the Treasury Department. Following the initiative of U.S. Treasurer Francis Spinner, Congress passed the Deficiency Act, which authorized the hiring of women by the Treasury Department at one-half the salary given to men. By the end of the war, 447 women were Treasury Department employees, most of them working as copyists and currency counters. The U.S. Post Office and the War Department also first hired women during the war years, again in various clerical positions. While female employees in government service generally earned less than men, their wages were often considerably more than those earned by women in other professions, such as teaching or sewing. Full-time female workers in the Treasury Department, for example, received a relatively generous $600 per year.[41]

No doubt a foremost reason for the government's hiring of female workers was the savings it enjoyed by paying women half as much as men. But the public justifications for employing women also stressed political imperatives—frequently referring to the support rendered to wives and mothers who had lost men in the war—despite the fact that a significant portion of the women hired did not suffer from such circumstances. Government officials suggested that patriotism required heightened government involvement in women's economic lives. Lincoln himself, in supporting a woman over a man for a post office appointment in Rockford, Illinois, noted that, as a soldier's widow, the female candidate had "the better right" to the position. The Treasury Department, in its new employment practices, likewise gave special consideration to soldiers' relatives. When they could, those who recommended women for employment stressed an applicant's status as a Union soldier's relative. "Mrs. Anne Gentry," wrote that woman's advocate, "whose husband while in the service was killed . . . is in very indigent circumstances." Iowa representative John Kasson emphasized his candidate's marriage to a Union soldier. "This only case from my district is, I believe, especially meritorious," he wrote in an 1863 recommendation for Mrs. M. J. M. Clark. "The husband, a soldier without means, the wife intelligent, competent." Moreover, as Kasson suggested, such an appointment could improve the feelings of his local constituency toward the government, as they would no doubt look favorably on this paternalistic patriotism as practiced by the Lincoln administration. Even a few black women benefited from this form of governmental favoritism. In 1867, Ulysses Grant wrote to the secretary of the treasury on behalf of Mrs. Lionel Booth, whose husband was killed at Fort Pillow, to see if a position could be secured "which will support her." The new hiring practices gave the impression that the U.S. Treasury Department, in particular, had become a special government refuge for needy soldiers' relatives. When, in 1864, the department became the focus of a congressional inquiry into allegedly immoral behavior on the part of its female workers, the committee ultimately dismissed the charges against the "government girls" as being "exceedingly unjust and cruel," particularly given that "a majority of [the department's women workers] are wives or sisters of soldiers who have fallen in the field."[42]

Of course, not all women could claim to be a soldier's relative, nor did all wish to make that their most significant point of identification. A number of female applicants for government positions stressed their own worthiness and personal loyalty to the Union, rather than the unfortunate loss of a male provider. In an atmosphere that linked politics to economic rights, they emphasized their own independent expressions of Unionism. Jane Seavey of Maine was teaching at the State Female College in

Among the most visible new female employees during the Civil War were the clerks hired by the U.S. Treasury Department in Washington. Credit: *Harper's Weekly,* February 18, 1865

Memphis, Tennessee, when the war broke out. In her December 1862 letter of application to the U.S. Treasury Department, Seavey explained how she had been caught behind Confederate lines "but seized with joy the opportunity [to] escape from an atmosphere rankly poisoned with the most violent secession principles," even though it meant suffering severe financial losses. Mary Clark found herself in similar circumstances, although she managed to leave the South soon after the war began. "Upon the break out of hostilities," she explained in her December 1865 application for a job, "I returned to my loyal home and have endeavored to find similar occupation in the loyal states." Jennie Gaughran wrote to Abraham Lincoln in July 1864, also hoping for a government position. She cited no male relatives in the Union army but did stress her mother's position as the matron of a local military hospital and the fact that she and her mother hoped to support the education of her younger sisters. "Should there be a vacancy in the Treasury or Post-Office Departments," Gaughran wrote, "I should be pleased to obtain it & will promise to make every effort to give full value for the Compensation of the Same."[43]

The federal government's wartime employment of women, although significant, was a relatively minor component of the newly expanded relationship between women and the state. One year after the Civil War began, the federal government undertook an extensive overhaul of the federal pension program, creating a system that would dramatically extend its embrace of Northern women and signal a new level of state-sponsored assistance. In July 1862 the U.S. Congress passed a new pension law that widened the circle of those eligible to receive pensions and increased some of the payments for widows and orphans. Replacing an earlier, outmoded system by which local measures and special legislation provided for soldiers' widows, the new law mandated a regular, uniform dispersal of eight dollars per month for every widow who filed a legitimate pension claim. Successful applicants received pensions for the duration of their widowhood. Children were also included in the new system, receiving two dollars per month for their support. Widows who remarried forfeited their widow's claim but could continue to benefit from child support payments. In an even greater change, for the first time the government provided pensions to soldiers' dependent mothers and sisters in cases where there were no widows and orphans. By the end of the war, the pension program was the most extensive social welfare system yet enacted by the national government; by 1893 it took up 40 percent of the federal budget. Its focus was turned overwhelmingly toward women and their dependents. By 1865 widows and orphans—as opposed to soldiers themselves—were collecting three-fourths of all pension payments.[44]

Without question the new system reflected the prevailing public focus on how the war victimized the figure of the soldier's wife. Simultaneous with the new pension law came other government measures—an increase in bounty payments and a decrease in the standard term of military service—designed to ameliorate the suffering of soldiers' families. The new legislation revealed a recognition on the part of the Republican Party that support for the Union war effort would come not just from men who served in the military but from Union families as well. The 1862 pension law seems to have been directed specifically at soldiers' kin, especially female relatives, as the pension rates for sick and wounded soldiers were not increased, at least not initially. But in reaching out to families, the Republican-sponsored pension legislation further confirmed the status of husbands and fathers as breadwinners and underscored women's status as dependents. Indeed, a mother who hoped to draw a pension was required to prove her financial dependence on her soldier son and to demonstrate explicitly why her husband had not been, and could no longer be, the family provider.[45]

The pension law established a new standard for government paternalism and created a new relationship between women and government. With this significant expansion of its bureaucracy, the federal government confirmed the notion that the nation-state must bear some responsibility for the care of soldiers' female dependents—that this was, in fact, an essential act of patriotism. In making the government the surrogate breadwinner for soldiers' wives, the pension legislation enhanced the moral power and legitimacy of the nation-state. It also drew women into what was often a complicated bureaucratic process in which they had to appear before courts of law, deliver testimony, present witnesses, and, in the case of widows, demonstrate the legality of their marriages (not always an easy process in the relatively unbureaucratized world of Civil War America). For American women in the middle years of the nineteenth century, this represented a far greater degree of civic activity than most had ever known.

In debating the new pension system, both political parties demonstrated a new awareness of women's civic role. Democrats and Republicans agreed that women and children must be protected from the suffering that would befall them if they were left without a source of support. Still, the debate surrounding the pension bill reflected some of the social tensions, and party strife, of the era, indicating somewhat divergent views of how government policy should evolve and the nature of the female constituency. While Republicans pushed for a graduated pension system that would provide increased benefits for officers' dependents, Indiana Democrat William Holman berated his opponents for giving "less consideration" to the wives and children of privates "than is to be received by the wives and children of those who occupy a higher position in their country's service." Philip Johnson, a Democrat from Pennsylvania, agreed, maintaining that the pension was not "a compensation for talents" but a protection from want. Democrats, in this regard, were not so much interested in protecting different degrees of female privelege as in playing up social tensions and class antagonisms that could weaken Republican authority. The Democrats in effect tried to play the patriotism card by suggesting that a higher value was being placed on the patriotic service of the military elite than that of the rank and file. "Are the wants of an officer and his family," Johnson argued, "supposed to be greater than those of a private and his family? Does it cost more to maintain the widow of an officer than it does to maintain the widow of a private soldier?"[46]

Apparently, at least in Republican eyes, it did. While few congressional Republicans would have disputed Johnson's point that the pension was meant to be a protective shield for women, as opposed to a monetary replacement for the soldier, Republicans, perhaps bowing to the power of their more well-to-do constituency, believed they could not offer officers' wives the same pension as privates' wives. In the end, while Democrats championed a path of paternalism geared more specifically to the needs of less well off white families, the Republican Congress committed itself to a program that differentiated among women based on their husband's military status. Under the Republicans' system, the more recognition a man received from the army, the more his female kin would benefit. The system ultimately placed greater emphasis on male service and female sacrifice than on women's individual needs or wartime contributions.

The patriotic imperative of the wartime era even made it possible for Republicans to extend government assistance to black women. Following the massacre of African American soldiers that took place at Fort Pillow in 1864, the pension law was amended so that the wives of black soldiers, too, could receive benefits. However, the new legislation came with a somewhat more complicated set of rules for evaluating the marital status of former slaves. In fact the inclusion of black men and women in the pension system allowed the federal government to undertake a more intrusive investigation into what it considered "proper" and "improper" marriages, for white women as well as black. In this way, the federal government began to assume responsibility not only for women's economic condition but also for their moral standing. The pension system became perhaps one of the most significant vehicles for drawing women into a new civic role, and

85

it subjected their private lives and economic circumstances to increasing government oversight.

In countless ways, the Civil War complicated the lives of Northern women. Wartime circumstances compelled women to compete for jobs, negotiate wages, manage household accounts, and file pension claims. Through these trying and demanding situations, some Northern women developed a more articulated sense of their own economic potential. Some took pride in learning new skills and occupations. Some called on government officials to respect them as loyal and hard-working American citizens, not simply as soldiers' relatives, when they asked for financial assistance or for help in securing a government job. But the war also gave rise to stories of women's economic victimization, especially their vulnerability to cheaters and scoundrels determined to derive a profit from poor and unknowing soldiers' wives. The merging of financial need and patriotism created a powerful vehicle used by many to demand greater government involvement in Northern women's economic circumstances. Catherine Speilman used it in June 1864 when she wrote to Abraham Lincoln as "a pore widder wumman whose husband fote in your army," asking the president to "see if you cant git me a plaice in one of your hospittles." As an unfortunate soldier's wife, Speilman had become—at least from the standpoint of public discourse—one of the Civil War's most sympathetic victims. She symbolized the women of the Civil War era; hers was the image of womanhood that Republicans had in mind as they crafted the government's evolving social welfare policies. She was the "everywoman" who, because of her status as a soldier's wife and an economic dependent, was drawn more closely into the civic sphere, where she became the focus of a protective and paternalistic government.[47]

Chapter Three

Domesticity under Siege

🌿 🌿 🌿

In the North in the 1860s, few institutions were as hallowed and celebrated as the middle-class home. It offered an orderly and peaceful refuge. It revealed the loving and wholesome influence of virtuous mothers. It was the source of upright moral virtues and molded the character of its own inhabitants, as well as the less fortunate in the community. With her home as her base, a virtuous Northern woman could extend her influence beyond her own domestic sphere, reaching out to orphaned children, poor families, or "fallen" women. "Be it ever so humble," middle-class Northerners often sang, there was just no place like home.

Few, of course, lived in such an idealized shrine. Poor families, including black and immigrant Northerners, lacked the economic means that might allow the home to become a woman's exclusive, nurturing preserve. Many Northern homes, of course, were plagued by instability and change, illness and death, factors that compromised the blissfulness of idealized domesticity. Nonetheless the ideal home was a noble and worthy objective, a home worth striving for. In this regard, many Northern women were influenced by the books of Catherine Beecher and followed her directives for creating order and comfort in the home. Likewise they read the voluminous literature of popular sentimental fiction, comforted by images of domestic harmony and distraught over depictions of disorderly and abusive households. Perhaps no home offered a better approximation of the ideal than the domestic quarters of Rachel Halliday, the kindly Quaker mother in

Uncle Tom's Cabin, written by Catherine's sister Harriet Beecher Stowe. Stowe described a maternal enclave from which Rachel dispensed "loving words" and "gentle moralities" while offering protection to downtrodden runaway slaves.[1]

Harriet Beecher Stowe's novel suggested that the Northern home was not just restful and restorative but also held political power. The virtuous home, overseen by a morally upright woman, could be a powerful weapon in the battle against slavery. While Southerners called slavery their "domestic institution," many Northern women believed that slavery only destroyed domesticity, and that everything about Northern middle-class life sanctified it. Catherine Beecher, too, saw political significance in the Northern domestic ideal. The protected home, she argued, offered a refuge from political antagonisms and partisan conflict and thus could be a site for the proper uplift and education of the American family. In a period of democratic and economic change, it offered a crucial model of order and stability.[2]

The Civil War had dramatic effects on this sanctified domestic realm, and especially on Northern women's ability to draw on the domestic sphere as a source of feminine authority. The war, after all, separated husbands from wives and fathers from children. Men returned with horrendous wounds and debilitating illnesses, and some did not return at all. Moreover, as we have seen, when Northern men went to war, many self-consciously identified with a cause and objective that they ranked higher than home. The pull of the home would, of necessity, take on diminished significance in their lives. Northern men's new identity as soldiers decreased the relevance of their prewar identities as fathers and husbands. "A soldier must not be fainthearted or babyish nor tied to a woman's apron strings," explained one recently married Vermont soldier, "for it is unmanly and unworthy." Certainly, all wars compel men to make similar judgments. But in the Northern states in the mid-nineteenth century, the powerful and pervasive image of domesticity meant that this challenge to home influence took on heightened significance and prompted many Northern women to redouble their efforts, often unsuccessfully, at exercising moral power and authority.[3]

The Victorian ideal of the home was not unknown in the states of the Confederacy, but it never possessed the power it had in the North. The imperatives of the plantation economy meant that Southern white men did not relinquish their domestic authority to the extent that Northern men often did. The Southern home—so entwined with the farming and plantation economy of the region—was not the same kind of domestic refuge and retreat because it was more visibly involved in the world of business and production. And since the Confederate home had to accommodate slavery, it was not so much the site of virtuous endeavors as it was of slave mastery and patriarchal authority. Thus, when Confederate men left for war, Southern white women expressed fewer concerns about their weakened domestic authority and more anxiety about their assumption of men's patriarchal role.[4]

Northerners were more strongly attached than ever to their domestic ideals when the Civil War began. Although some initial recruitment efforts emphasized the need for men to free themselves from women's apron strings, few questioned the importance of women's home-based assignments. Men had military business now, and women would tend to home and hearth. "Don't think of me or the children, John," the "Volunteer's Wife" recounted to her husband. "I'll care for them, you know." Yet wartime separations, especially those of husbands and wives, and unmarried lovers, were fraught with tension. In their correspondence, men and women struggled over what their responsibilities to each other should be in light of the rupture in their traditional relationship. Wives wondered what, precisely, their womanly identity was, with no husbands at home on whom to focus their undivided love and soothing influence. And when men paid little heed to their feminine directives from home, Northern women felt increasingly uneasy about their ability to exert any significant moral influence, especially in combatting the potential pitfalls of the soldier's life.[5]

Although some used the occasion of the war to exert an intensified moral influence on their menfolk, Northern women also sensed that their domestic and moral authority had been superseded by the demands of war. Quite a few, in fact, hesitated about dispensing advice or admonishments—about anything from card playing to sexual promiscuity—to absent men, feeling uncertain of their place in the strange and very masculine world of the military. Even more, men, and some women, accepted the idea that men at war were entitled to a certain moral leeway, given the demands and trials of the soldier's life. The experience, in effect, reinforced women's perception that the Union cause must rank higher than home, that the work of saving the country had to be disentangled from the work of protecting domestic life. In this regard, Yankee women were forced to acknowledge the fiction of the antebellum ideology that had raised domesticity to a high plateau of private and public significance. If apron strings and other forms of womanly influence only hindered the work of saving the Union, just how significant, some may have wondered, was Northern women's domestic authority? Such questioning certainly encouraged Northern women to doubt the influence of the domestic sphere and to recognize the importance of exerting influence through different, and more public, channels.

Not only did the war begin to show women the falsehood of their domestic power, but it also demonstrated how porous the public and private realms could be. During the war, women's private lives, more so than men's, received intense public scrutiny. This was especially true in the later stages of the war, as more women assumed visible wartime roles, especially as nurses, government employees, and teachers of former slaves. In these public contexts, women's private acts assumed broader significance; even harmless flirtations could be linked to the fortunes and failures of their men on the battlefield. The Civil War era saw a new level of public and governmental intrusion into women's private lives, ranging from more persistent public gossiping to government directives regarding the personal appearance of female nurses to federal investigations into the sexual activity of the newly employed "government girls." The private domestic realm was no longer the source of women's unique moral authority; it was instead the site of new entanglements for Northern women in their broader civic roles.

❧

Although at the start of the Civil War Northern women were charged to keep the "home fires burning," many women quickly realized that domestic life, in wartime, was hardly a scene of considerable interest or excitement. Unlike the Southern home front, which faced repeated threats of Union invasion, Northern homes were generally far removed from the conflicts and dramas of the war. As a result, Northern women often felt a sense of purposelessness and emptiness when their men left for war. Many believed that they, their homes, and their families were just not interesting enough to the departed menfolk. "You do not miss me half so much as I do you," Ann Cotton wrote to her husband, Josiah, serving as a surgeon with an Ohio regiment. "You are all the time surrounded by so many & do not get time to feel lonesome while I am alone most of the time & have nothing to do but think of you & wish you back." In fact Ann Cotton had quite a lot to do, what with caring for her children, including one young son with developmental impairments, and maintaining her home, but the comparison with her husband's position made her life feel empty and unfulfilling. Without her spouse's presence, Ann Cotton did not derive the same solace and comfort from the domestic scene. The war made domestic life a source of anxiety and loneliness. "You have something exciting all the time," Elizabeth Caleff wrote to her fiancé with the Minnesota First, "but you never can imagine how lonely I feel when I think of you being away." Mary Baker likewise felt bereft with her fiancé's departure. "Am so lonely," she wrote in her diary in July 1861, "miss Elliot every minute. Dont know what I shall do so long without him."[6]

Letter writing helped, to some extent, to reestablish intimacy and some sense of domestic purpose. Sophia Buchanan saw her moments of correspondence as a time to talk with her husband, Claude, to "hold a few minutes converse; commune with my only loved & absent one." She pressed him for more details about his life in the army. "I'de love to know at what hour you have to drill, &c, so that in imagination I can be by your side at those hours." Like Sophia Buchanan, Clara Wood tried to make contact through letters. "I have got your pictures in front of me," she wrote in 1862 to her husband, Amos, "I write a few lines & then look at them & think & even say how I wish how much I wish he was here." Others made allusions to their sexual desires. "Oh, how I wish I could sleep with you tonight," Jane Thompson wrote to her husband in September 1862. "Would you like to sleep with me?" Lizzie Bowler (formerly Caleff) teased her newly wedded husband after his brief furlough home. "Be a good hubbie," she admonished him, and "dont say naughty words."[7]

Some women managed to address their loneliness and anxiety by visiting male relatives in military camps. Generally, visits took place while troops remained encamped in their Northern quarters, before they departed for battlefields in the South. Once regiments moved South, camp visits were less likely for enlisted men, unless medical circumstances compelled a woman to come and attend to a soldier's needs. Officers' wives, however, often stayed with their spouses for extended periods, even in Southern camps, so long as the military situation allowed and the women could cope with the inconveniences. Some women, in fact, made semipermanent homes at their husbands' military posts. Throughout the war, Julia Grant was her husband's nearly constant companion, prompting many to wonder if her persistent presence served as a restraining influence against the Union commander's drinking. Many other women made frequent and prolonged visits, so much so that the Union's Army of the Potomac was described by one female observer as "teeming with women."[8]

While they offered comfort and welcome diversion, camp visits could also create tension, and could compound women's uncertainties about their domestic role. Many women eagerly embraced the prospect of reunions with their loved ones but found it difficult to adjust to the military environment. Women were out of their element in the camps and could not be the same wives or mothers they were at home. Many had to live within the military encampments and eat the soldiers' fare, rather than live and eat separately as husband and wife. Emily Elliot felt "comfortable and happy" to be living with her husband, a captain in the 103rd Ohio Infantry, while his regiment was stationed in Nashville, Tennessee, in January 1864. She was especially pleased when they no longer boarded with a local woman and "ate dinner of our own cooking." "We are keeping house," she reported triumphantly, clearly happy to have her own domestic space. Yet even under these circumstances, she felt uncer-

GOING TO THE BALL

BALL ROOM.

THE SUPPER ROOM   THE GANDERS.

tain about her abilities and responsibilities. She frequently commented on her own "ignorance"—perhaps with respect to military etiquette—and found that "the sun" did not "always shine" on her marital union. The experience of living in a military setting seemed to reinforce a sense of inadequacy on the Ohio schoolteacher's part, a feeling that there, on her husband's turf, she had to learn to abide by his wishes. "It seems," she wrote in her diary, "as though I am not half good enough for him." Although tempted to visit her husband while he was encamped at Little Rock, Lizzie Bowler declined, largely out of concern for her newborn's health. Mothering and a military visit, the Minnesota soldier's wife sensed, would not mix. Sarah Butler, who expressed considerable anguish and grief about her husband's absence, also felt ambivalent about prolonging her stay with the celebrated Union general in camp. "I do not know how I can leave Mr. Butler," she wrote while with him during the occupation of New Orleans in the spring of 1862, "with the summer before him . . . [but] if I stay and get very sick it will be ten times worse for him." Clearly, as Sarah Butler and Emily Elliot realized, military obligations and domestic concerns did not always fit neatly together.[9]

Men likewise had mixed feelings about having their female relations in camp, and were suspicious of the kind of feminine influence that womenfolk might try to bring to a military setting. One Union soldier—certainly not the only one—fought with his wife over whether or not she should visit. "You say I don't want

As these illustrations of a military ball suggest, officers' wives were occasionally present in military camps, although the relative scarcity of women also prompted the "ganders" to dance with one another. Credit: *Harper's Weekly,* February 20, 1864

you 2 come & see me," he wrote, "that is not so, I should be as glad 2 see you as anybody would 2 see their wife but . . . it is not a fit place for any woman, for there is all kinds of talk, songs and everything not good for them 2 hear." Eunice Tripler's husband, who was the medical director of the Army of the Potomac early in the war, expressed outrage when his wife unexpectedly arrived in camp. "I could scarcely eat anything," Tripler recalled, "for my husband was ashamed of me and I felt it." In part, soldiers and officers felt uncomfortable about exposing women to the rough talk and harsh conditions of army life. Perhaps more important, they worried that women's presence might impair their own masculinity, constraining them from participating in the "kinds of talk, songs, and everything" that virtuous ladies should not hear. A domestic influence, so many men seemed to feel, could hamper military morale. To women like Eunice Tripler the message was clear: a woman's presence, once celebrated as a softening and harmonious influence, now, in wartime, became a source of shame.[10]

Not that women abandoned their role as moral guardians. It was, after all, women's business to bring a restraining influence to bear on their loved ones' behavior—whether "talk" or "songs" or "everything"—and even from home, many women tried to do what was expected of them. If they could not be with their menfolk, many reasoned, they nonetheless had a responsibility to remind them of domestic duties and moral obligations. Mothers wrote frequently to remind sons of the religious principles with which they had been raised. "I wish to impress upon your mind," Lucinda Ingersoll wrote to her son Charley from upstate New York, "the importance of trusting in God and striving to obey his commands." In a subsequent letter she added, "We do hope you will never attempt to play cards or practice whatever is wicked." Rhoda Southworth worried about the lack of religious feeling in

Wives who made extended visits to military camps no doubt spent con-siderable time performing demanding domestic chores. Credit: Library of Congress, Prints and Photographs Division [LC-USZC4-7983]

the Fourth Minnesota Regiment in which her son Eli had en-listed, but took some comfort in knowing that he had been "so early taught the language of prayer." When Lizzie Caleff referred to demoralizing influences that her fiancé, James Bowler, should avoid, he was amused that his sweetheart had assumed this ma-ternal responsibility. "You desire me to be a good little boy," Bowler wrote in January 1862. "I'll try, mother."[11]

After several months in the military, James Bowler probably

seldom thought of himself as a "good little boy," and his bemused retort suggests that it might be difficult for wives and sweethearts to command the level of authority they hoped to assert. Jane Thompson, for example, tentatively broached the subject of her husband's drinking, recalling how he had resented her intrusions before. "You are just as apt to get in that habit as anyone," she wrote of his imbibing inclinations, "Now do not be angry at what I have said for it is all in kindness." Mattie Blanchard worried that her husband, Caleb, would, in his loneliness, turn to card playing, and she prayed that he would not "use them any more for the sake of yourself and for your friends." Like Thompson, she worried that, although she thought only of his welfare, her spouse would still "feel hard towards me for what I have wrote." Other women may have found it easier to express their concerns indirectly. Catharine Peirce addressed the issue of her husband's possible moral failings by speaking through her daughter's voice. "Sallie," she explained, "wants thee to try to quit swaring before thee comes home again." Emeline Ritner sensed it was better to applaud her husband's moments of restraint than to reprimand him for his weaknesses. He must, she explained, "persevere" in resisting his officers' pleas to join in the drinking, "and never be tempted from the right by any set of officers or anybody else." Since their husbands had intentionally placed military obligations above domestic ones, and repositioned themselves in a world that could be brutal and fierce and intensely masculine, women like Emeline Ritner, Mattie Blanchard, and Catharine Peirce, while compelled to offer moral advice, sounded noticeably uncertain about how it would be received.[12]

Indeed, the military world tended to be unreceptive to female admonishments. The very act of seeing men off to war compelled women to give up some of the moral clout they had previously asserted. Some soldiers said as much when they explained how they could not press for a furlough or seek a reassignment in military duties, even if it would give their wives a sense of peace and security. "You know when I was your man I would come when I could and see you," wrote George Shepherd, an English immigrant farmer from Wisconsin, to his wife, Mary. "But now I am Uncle Sam's man & can't come only just when he pleases." In the military world, Shepherd made clear, a wife's directives could go only so far. And given the demands of war, men, and some women, thought it best to cut their loved ones some slack. When Mary Pierce visited her husband, Elliot, a captain in the First Army Corps, in Culpeper, Virginia, she wrote the folks back home of the many parties and entertainments enjoyed by the soldiers. "We are very dissipated here in the Army," she explained, "the officers and men mean to have a good time, as long as they can and I don't blame them they see hardships enough." Not that Mary Pierce encouraged a climate of debauchery; rather, she reflected a point of view that others no doubt shared: that because men endured unparalleled difficulties at war, women should not pull too hard on the domestic strings.[13]

With the wartime climate generating ambiguity and uncertainty about women's domestic authority, it is hardly surprising to find women, while their men were away, reflecting on their failures as wives. Faced with the emptiness of the home front, wives often thought about how poorly they had played their domestic parts in the past. "When I think over our Married life & think of the many ways I have irritated you I almost wonder that you can love me at all," remarked Clara Wood in a letter to her husband, Amos. His departure, she maintained, served as a lesson for her "disagreeable disposition," a quality she promised to correct if he ever returned. Experiencing the absence of the steady companionship of their spouses, many women felt they had not fully appreciated their domestic responsibilities when they had them and wondered how successfully they had carried them out. Following a brief visit from her husband, a soldier in the Eleventh Michigan Infantry, Melissa Wells worried that, during the quick reunion, she had not lived up to her wifely duties. "I know that it is the duty of every wife to make home as pleasant and attractive as possible for her Husband," Wells wrote in January 1864, "but I fear in many instances I have fell far short of my duty." Indeed, without being able to work through the day-to-day dilemmas and conflicts of married life, how could Wells not feel domestically inadequate? More important, if women had little opportunity to demonstrate their wifely abilities, would their husbands feel the same ties of love and devotion for them? Rachel Cormany, living with her husband's family in Chambersburg, Pennsylvania, confronted this worry directly. "The question sometimes come to my mind," she wrote in her diary in March 1863, "Does he really love me?"[14]

Because women's identities were so closely bound up with domestic life, many left on their own could not help but feel neglected and unloved. In a sense, men's temporary abandonment of the domestic front, and their apparent disregard for wifely attentions and affections, provided negative reinforcement for the broader civic message of the wartime North: that country took priority over home and that the truly demanding issues of the hour stood far outside women's domestic purview. While this message could propel women to think more broadly about their own civic responsibilities, as we have seen, it could also undermine the authority, and comfort, they derived from the domestic realm. As they grappled with feeling alone and unwanted, women gave voice to the sense of belittlement that the war had imposed. While they shouldered their familial duties, they also feared that their menfolk now viewed those duties with a certain apathy and indifference. Surrounded by screaming babies, Me-

With the war forcing the separation of sweethearts, couples felt increasing pressure to marry. Some—as depicted in this illustration—exchanged vows in Union army camps. Credit: Harper's Weekly, April 4, 1863

lissa Wells wrote to her husband, "Such things are any thing but pleasant, that is true . . . But never mind, you may have all the fun at my expense that you like and I will comfort myself with the thought that when you get home you will have to take a part in some of those interesting scenes." The "fun" that she perceived her husband as having at her expense could not help but compound Melissa's sense of neglect in what was now a disregarded domestic sphere. Clara Wood experienced similar frustrations regarding her husband's absence from the family. Writing from South Hadley, Massachusetts, she explained how she felt, since her husband's departure, being called on to care for their son

Freddie without him. "Oh I do feel so anxious about him," she wrote, "if you was only here I would be so glad I should have someone to help me do & I feel now as if I was alone." In Trenton, Michigan, Sarah Pardington wrote her husband that she was distressed that he had been signing his letters simply "Jack." "I do not laugh at you for Wanting me to Write Husband and Father," Jack replied. "More like I ought to be shamed of my self for not doing it in respect to that dear little angel and yourself." Jack's wife keenly felt the loss of his familial role, apparent to her even in his missing signifiers.[15]

Although women living in 1860s America certainly accepted their primary responsibility for caring for children, many could not help but resent the extent to which the war diminished the pull of family and offspring on absent menfolk. After James Bowler received word of his baby's arrival, he suggested to his wife, whom he sometimes called Libby, that she might want to move the baby to another bed before his return, so that nobody would "come between Libby and me." Soon after, Libby dreamed that, while the baby was napping in her cradle, James returned and "passed right by her and never looked at her." Libby Bowler bristled at James's apparent lack of interest in his child. So did Abby Hood, apparently to an even greater extent than Libby Bowler. Married in 1856, James and Abby Hood of New Bedford, Massachusetts, had their first and only child in 1862, after James's enlistment in October 1861. When James left for the war, Abby moved in with her father, despite James's objection that her father might turn her against him. And indeed, when James returned from the army in July 1865 he was rebuffed by Abby, who also refused him permission to see his son. In April 1866 James went to court to get access to his child. He did receive occasional visitation rights, but Abby Hood retained full custody. As she told the court, James "has not cared for the child or shown or felt any affection or duty in relation to it."[16]

Such resentments could make pregnancy an undesirable experience rather than, as it might have been under more secure circumstances, a welcome womanly obligation. In Mankato, Minnesota, Laura Beatty experienced her first pregnancy on her own, and was also distressed that her new husband seemed unable to appreciate the burdens of childbearing. "I tell you, John," she wrote in the hope that he might be able to come home for the birth, "this baby business isn't always very funny." Many women were probably grateful to avoid the kind of anxiety Laura Beatty felt. In 1864 Rachel Cormany expressed relief that, during her husband's recent furlough, she had not become pregnant. Emily Elliot, too, was happy to find that a possible pregnancy, during her extended stay in camp, was only "a false alarm." In the context of war, pregnancy stood no longer as a symbol of domestic bliss but as a possible source of domestic suffering.[17]

The war weakened women's sense of self and security as men's military participation alienated them from their traditional domestic roles. Perhaps the most effective tool available to Northern women who hoped to reconnect their men to a sense of family and domestic responsibility was religious admonition. When they spoke about their men's Christian duties, women believed that they spoke from a higher order of moral righteousness. Many thought it was particularly important to remind their male relatives and companions about their religious obligations because the chaos of war not only held the possibility of death but also threatened to turn men's sights too much in the direction of worldly affairs. Reflecting on the horrors of war, one soldier's wife in Wisconsin found comfort in prayer. "I pray God constantly that He will take our affairs into his own hands," she wrote her husband, "—& let the right speedily prevail and peace be restored. Oh Cassius I hope you too will not fail to pray to Him who alone can protect us and ours in this world." Lucinda Ingersoll likewise reminded her son Charley to pray "that God who rules in wisdom may in His own good time deliver our country from the troubles which now hang over it." Issuing such religious directives may have helped women regain some sense of the control they had lost when men left their domestic sphere and entered the military. Lizzie Bowler acknowledged that she could not and would not compel her husband to desert his national duties in favor of his domestic ones, but soon after their marriage she wrote, "There is one request that I am going to make of you, and I want you to take into serious consideration, that is that you will become a christian." Christian duty, she believed, would make him "care less for the things of this wicked world and pay more attention to heaven and heavenly things." She may have hoped that by directing his "attention to heaven and heavenly things" he would turn his thoughts not only to the afterlife but also to his earthly home—where a new wife and baby waited for him patiently and devotedly.[18]

Thousands of Union soldiers did heed the call of God during the war, and pledged themselves to become more devout Christians. Revivals occurred in some Northern regiments, although far less often than in the Confederate army, and many soldiers regularly attended religious services and prayer meetings. Nonetheless, most Union soldiers seemed to take a more practical approach to their religious beliefs, seeking comfort and solace in God when their fears of battle were most intense. Many, too, were skeptical of their chaplains and the various organizations that sent preachers to proselytize among the enlisted men. And Northern women, despite their awareness of God-fearing ministers within the Union military, remained concerned that the mili-

Among the Northern couples who married during the war were Eliza-
beth and James Bowler of Nininger, Minnesota, shown here shortly af-
ter their wedding. Credit: por/16904/r3, Minnesota Historical Society

tary setting was hardly conducive to religious uplift. "You know,"
wrote Ann Cotton to her husband, Josiah, in October 1862, "that
the *greatest* objection I had to your entering the army was the
fear that you would not lead a truly Christian life while there, & I
know you will find it hard to do so." Like Lizzie Bowler, Ann Cotton tried to marshal her authority and offer her admonitions
through the voice of Christianity; still, she feared that no amount
of strenuous preaching could fully counteract the immoral influences of army life.[19]

Immoral influences, many worried, were legion. And high on

the list of wartime wickedness, of course, was sexual misbehavior. The Civil War, as all wars, tested traditional notions of romance, sexual fidelity, and marital obligation. If the war made men less concerned about their domestic obligations, it also made women worry about how seriously their absent husbands were adhering to their marital vows and romantic pledges. They wrote often about the possibility that mens' attentions might wane and their attraction to other women might increase. Men, however, usually treated the subject lightly, even flippantly, and sometimes humorously. Quite a few believed certain types of sexual encounters were among the "privileges" earned by hard-working enlisted men. Lucius Mox of Franklin County, Pennsylvania, wrote to his sweetheart about "some very pretty ladies" he met while stationed in town. Those ladies, he wrote, "will likely get acquainted with this chicken before many weeks role around But now Jennie you must not get jealous for I am resolved not to fall in love with any of them, only just for the ocasion." James Bowler likewise seemed aware of this romantic privilege when he responded to his fiancée's query about the ladies who greeted his regiment as they passed through Indiana. If, as the newspapers and wartime propaganda implied, it was "patriotic" for young, unattached women to offer their kisses, was it not also "patriotic" for the men—regardless of their previous commitments—to accept them? "You want to know," Bowler wrote back, "if I got a kiss from any of those ladies. I did not though I might have done so if I had stepped forward but I kept back as I did not feel much like kissing any one I saw." Eighteen months later Bowler and his fiancée, Elizabeth (Lizzie), had married, but he continued to jest about his romantic prerogatives and chastised his wife for seeking to deny him "what few little privileges" he was "able to secure." Those "privileges" included keeping company with black women, who, in the eyes of many Union men, seemed to be the most readily available sexual partners in the South. In Lizzie's eyes, this was "not to be tolerated among respectable people." James quickly backed down and argued that he had written "a jesting, frollicking letter" only to see how she would respond. James Beatty, in a less jesting tone, seemed resigned to the idea that he, like other upstanding fellows, might give in to "some kinds of temptations to evil" that "will be much stronger in me now than ever before." This, Beatty implied, was an inevitable result of war and would be little affected by women's home-front counseling.[20]

"Temptations to evil" seemed to plague Union men at every turn. Not surprisingly, in cities throughout the North, and especially in areas where Union soldiers clustered, prostitution increased dramatically. Certainly Union officials did not welcome this traffic in sexual activity, but they were relatively tolerant of their troops' promiscuous adventures. Military officials worried more about the debilitating effects of venereal disease. In two noteworthy cases, where Union troops were stationed in Southern cities, Union commanders tolerated the prostitutes, although they tried to contain the public health risks. In Nashville and Memphis, the occupation army initiated a policy to legalize and regulate prostitution, hoping to ensure that when Union men visited with "ladies of the night"—as they surely would—the possibility of contracting a disease would be minimized.[21]

While men at war were granted a certain amount of moral leeway, the same could not be said for the women they left behind at home. If anything, the women's sexual behavior was now subjected to more intense public scrutiny. Women left without male companionship or acceptable male protection were examined and judged for sexual misbehavior in a more public setting. Because soldiers' wives and sweethearts were engaged in a public and patriotic enterprise, their private deeds and attitudes became admissible subjects for public discussion. Even the smallest departures in appearance or behavior, especially on the part of soldiers' wives, brought them into the glare of public criticism. A new frock, a fancy hat, an unguarded comment to another man: all these could be, and often were, taken as indications of the unchaperoned wife's depravity. Eliza Otis did something to arouse her family's suspicions, although it may have been nothing more than traveling frequently without a male escort. Her husband, Harry, had nothing but contempt for those who leveled slanderous accusations against his wife. "They," he wrote in a private reference to her family members, "who would ruin her pure name say she is not true. Palsied be the tongues of slander. Her unwavering constancy gives the lie to their every calumnious tale." Eliza Otis's relatives no doubt saw "unprotected" women like Eliza in a new light of sexual availability, which put added pressure on them to guard their moral reputations. James and Lizzie Bowler, when not exchanging barbs about his dealings with freedwomen, wrote frequently about the misdeeds of a mutual acquaintance, Rose Stone, a Minnesota woman married to a man in James's company. The stories may have served to ease tensions in the Bowler marriage, allowing them to focus on Rose in the part of the unfaithful soldier's wife. As evidence of her "loose" ways, Lizzie related to James that Rose had allowed another man to take her to a party where she "got to flirting so that" the poor fellow's mother "had to talk to her." James, for his part, used Rose as yet another humorous foil for his own misbehavior. "If R—e were here I might be tempted to give you cause for jealousy," he wrote to his wife in November 1864. "Do you not feel as though you ought to be here to watch me?" Rose's case revealed how a woman's behavior could be read as a barometer of her commitment and support for a man's wartime sacrifice. John Pardington of Trenton, Michigan, was shocked when he heard the stories his wife had to tell about her own sister, Mary. To John, they offered moral lessons not only about proper wifely behavior but also about the intermingling of sexual and political loyalty. "How did she know," he exclaimed in reference to his sister-in-law and her husband, "but What When she was enjoying herself on the floar to the sound of the fiddle he might have been Laying on the Battle feild wounded or dying. Shame on a Woman with no more feeling tha:: that. She do not deserve the sacred name of Wife. I thank God that I have such a Wife as I have got."[22]

Because women's most private actions were now linked, in the minds of many, to a broad set of political and military consequences, the public assumed it had a right to know about and intervene in such matters. Even an inappropriate wink or wave could imply the dampening of home-front support for the Union army's efforts. Certainly Ellen Horton found herself scrutinized in this context. While her husband was off fighting in Virginia, Ellen became the subject of malicious gossip in her Vermont community. Although generally inclined to trust his wife, Edwin Horton worried that his mother would continue to spread malevolent talk about her and that, as a soldier's wife, Ellen could not help but appear in a negative light. "Now Nell," Horton insisted, "since their is so much said about Soldiers wives I was in hopes you would carry yourself strait enough to avoid all stories but Nell I dont care what she says about you or me but as long as I am away a good many will believe her." Just how "strait" one had to be is suggested by Emeline Ritner's problems with a neighbor who disliked Ritner's new hat. "Old Mrs. Burnett," Emeline wrote to her husband, Jake, from her Iowa home, "just raked me right before the people after meeting was over" because Emeline had spruced up her old hat. "She said when people talked of soldier's wives dressing, she always held me up as an exception, but now I was as bad as any of them." Emeline Ritner became the target of abuse for apparently dressing in a way that attracted too much, and clearly inappropriate, attention: the kind of attention that soldiers' wives had to be particularly careful to avoid.[23]

Rachel Cormany discovered that some men did cast their unwanted gaze in her direction, now that she was on her own. Her neighbor Mr. Plough berated her for wearing a slightly lowered neckline, but he also made it clear that he had not passed up the opportunity to look at her youthful body. "It is enough to make any man's courage rise," he told her, "to see girls with their shoulders bare and you ought to know that Mrs. C." Cormany had made herself more visible as an unchaperoned female, even if her only crime was a slight exposure of skin, and she correctly perceived her neighbor's remarks as both rebuke and unwanted attention, calling him an "old scamp to think of such things and to speak of them." Julia Underhill had also felt herself caught in a battle against lewd men, on one side, and heightened public scrutiny, on the other. With men preying on her in public, she found it increasingly difficult to maintain a respectable reputation, as well as her sense of independence. Indeed, unwanted sexual advances in part pushed Julia Underhill to relocate to Massachusetts and then to dress as a man when seeking employment there. "Every time I go out," she wrote her husband from Menosha, Wisconsin, "there is a set of loafers standing around that most eat up every woman with their eyes . . . There is no danger but what any soldier woman can get help as long as she tries to do what is right . . . but let her get a bad name and decent folks wont help her."[24]

Clearly, Cormany and Underhill could distinguish between invited and unwanted sexual attention. But the broader Northern society found it more difficult to determine the extent to which unchaperoned women could be considered instigators, as opposed to victims, of inappropriate behavior. In St. Paul, Minnesota, James Beatty was shocked by the level of licentiousness he found among the city's female inhabitants, including "wives and mothers & sisters." "How many women in this city," he remarked, "seem to have forgotten that [purity and truth] are everything to women." The New York Prison Association, in surveying that state's growing female prison population, adopted a more ambiguous approach, seeing soldiers' spouses as both victims and perpetrators of sexual misconduct. "Wives, whose husbands had gone to the army," the report explained, "were left unprotected and exposed to the arts of the designing and the vicious of the other sex. Some of them . . . have lapsed from virtue, and naturally desire to obliterate the evidence of their guilt." A more sympathetic portrait, one that implied a link between women's economic and sexual dependency, appeared in Henry Morford's 1863 novel, *The Days of Shoddy: A Novel of the Great Rebellion*. In the book, the shoddy contractor, Charles Holt, encouraged his clerk to enlist, with the promise that the clerk's family would receive Holt's assistance and protection. But once the clerk was away at war the evil Holt tried to seduce the young soldier's wife, who—though she might fall victim to poverty—remained true to the principles of romantic fiction and kept her virtue intact. Having failed at his seduction attempts, Holt met his death in the end at the hands of a Union sentry. *The Days of Shoddy* attributed no evil intentions to the innocent soldier's wife, but Morford's novel did carry a darker message: that the virtue of even the most upstanding of soldiers' wives would be sorely tested and embattled in this period of prolonged military conflict.[25]

Evidence does suggest that the war severely tested the marital stability of many Northern couples. During and immediately after the war, the divorce rate, although still minuscule with respect to rates today, increased significantly. Whereas in 1860, 1.2 of every 1,000 marriages ended in divorce, by 1864 this number had increased to 1.4, and in 1868 it was up to 1.8. Public commentators found the number of divorces, by 1867, to be "very considerable." And because grounds for divorce in the 1860s were often limited to physical abuse, desertion, or adultery, divorce trials called more attention to the problem of the unchaperoned soldiers' wives who, during their husbands' absence, were sexually unfaithful. Thomas Rodman, for example, sued his wife, Ann, for divorce in November 1865 in Bristol County, Massachusetts. Rodman asserted that in December 1862, when he was called to his regiment in Louisiana, he left his wife "with ample provision for her comfortable maintenance and support." But, he said, "during his absence in the military service of his country," she made "his home the resort of divers lewd persons and did commit the crime of adultery therein." Allen Howland of Fall River, Massachusetts, likewise argued he had been the victim of his wife's sexual duplicity. After Howland had enlisted as a soldier in 1862, his wife, Sarah, had engaged in adulterous affairs. The story was virtually the same for Alexander Duckworth, who divorced his wife, Mary Jane, after fourteen years of marriage, including three years when he had been in the army and his wife had been unfaithful. Throughout the country, similar tales were told, with wives cast in the part of the cheating spouse and husbands as the virtuous upholders of marital and national honor. Although there is no reason to believe these wives did not in fact cheat on their husbands or seek out sexual companionship during their absence, the cases against them were clearly reinforced by the widely rehearsed tale of soldiers' wives' sexual availability. These divorce cases, and the rising divorce rate, further underscored the danger of leaving soldiers' wives unsupervised, and confirmed the need for greater public scrutiny of women's private behavior.[26]

꧁

In the latter part of the war, even greater attention was focused on Northern women's sexual behavior. As increasing numbers of women stepped into public wartime roles—as nurses and as other representatives of the Union administration—they, too, became subjects of more conspicuous investigation. Although such scrutiny was not an assault on women's domestic privacy, it did represent a challenge to the domestic ideal that celebrated female purity and virtue. Whenever women entered a new public (and male-dominated) arena—whether as nurses in military hospitals, as teachers in Union-occupied areas, or as employees in government departments—their sexual behavior became a point of public discourse. Often the intensified scrutiny and criticism came from those with political motivations, especially those wishing to challenge programs and policies of the Union administration. Nevertheless, as with soldiers' wives, the private lives of working women were seen as an acceptable topic of public discussion because their behavior could be linked to military effectiveness. In the end, the wartime discourse about women's roles and sexual behavior compelled women to live by a stricter code of behavior, and also offered an opening for keener government oversight of female morality.

From the outset, white women who hoped to serve as nurses for wounded soldiers came under unusually close inspection. Soon after the war began, Dorothea Dix, a well-regarded medical reformer, became superintendent of nursing for the War Department. Not all nurses received their appointments through Dix's Army Nursing Corps, and indeed many nurses—especially black and working-class women—were not even regarded as such because they were classified as laundresses or cooks. But for the nurses that Dix did hire, white, middle-class women in the Florence Nightingale mold who drew from an array of domestic skills to care for sick and wounded men, there could be no hint of sexuality. "No woman under thirty need apply to serve in government hospitals," her nursing bulletin explained. "All nurses are required to be plain looking women. Their dresses must be brown or black, with no bows, no curls, no jewelry, and no hoops." Dix wished to keep romantically inclined women out of her hospitals, and she also knew that her appointees, many of whom would be subjected to male advances, would be carefully scrutinized for signs of moral weakness by those who hoped to deride this experiment in female nursing. Touring the Washington hospitals in September 1861, Dix found that there was not a woman there "who is not constantly watched for evidences of favor to individuals and for grounds of scandalous suspicion and . . . talked to with a double meaning." It was women's vulnerability in this new position that compelled Dix to impose her restrictive policies. For women to succeed in this new role, there could not be even the slightest hint of impropriety, even if the impropriety stemmed more from male attitudes than female impulses.[27]

Women who entered these new public arenas found their sexuality was one of their main points of identification, and they were forced to take extra steps to prove their skills and ability. "I have no doubt that most people think I came into the army to get a husband," remarked Cornelia Hancock, a nurse who attended wounded soldiers after the Battle of Gettysburg. Hancock seems to have removed much of her aura of sexuality by approaching her work as a soldier, as one in the fray who simply did the work that had to be done. Maria Daly, a society matron in New York City, assumed that women who took up nursing had ulterior motives. "There are single women who want something to occupy their minds and hearts," she declared. When her own friend Harriet spent time as a nurse on a hospital transport ship during the 1862 campaign up the Virginia Peninsula, Daly's husband advised Harriet to quit. Although many onboard improprieties could be attributed to male surgeons, rumors of scandal did the most damage to the female nurses. "So much is said about the nurses who have gone," Maria Daly explained to Harriet. "Some of the men say that they are closeted for hours with the surgeons in pantries and all kinds of disorders go on." Young women, in particular, found the job's obstacles severe. "It would not do for you to be here," Hannah Ropes wrote to her daughter from the Union Hotel Hospital in Georgetown, where she served as matron. "It is no place for young girls. The surgeons are young and look upon nurses as their natural prey."[28]

To avoid being seen as young and available, many nurses adopted a maternal demeanor in their work, even if they were not much older than the soldiers they cared for. They encouraged their male patients to call them "mother," while they in turn called soldiers their "boys." In the view of Mary Livermore, a well-known leader of the Sanitary Commission in the Midwest, the maternal strategy was a natural component of women's caregiving responsibilities. When encountering wounded men on a Mississippi River transport boat, Livermore recalled, the female nurses "fell into maternal relations with them, as women instinctively do when brought into juxtaposition with weakness." Livermore may well have been right that women instinctively grasped at the comfortable and traditional role of mother. Mothers, after all, could touch young men's bodies, while young single women did so at their own risk.[29]

Women who became teachers of freed slaves also encountered intense moral scrutiny. The aid and missionary societies that began sponsoring educational efforts among the freed people during the Civil War were, like Dorothea Dix, anxious to choose women who would not only keep their own impulses in check but also not invite improper advances from military officials. "Women of the right character," wrote one female observer, "could and doubtless will be very useful . . . But they should be selected with care from those whose position and character would command the respect of the military and civil officers of the Government." Preference, she concluded, should be given "to ladies of maturity" and those of "strong practical common sense." But despite such advisories, female teachers, too, invariably came in for investigation, especially from opponents of the administration's emancipation policies. Some schoolmarms, a Boston Democratic newspaper maintained, are more intent "upon flirting with the officers, in a manner not entirely consistent with morality." Such charges of indecency offered another opportunity to question both a new avenue of female independence and a new and somewhat controversial government experiment.[30]

Charges of impropriety, of course, were not all fabricated. Quite a few women did form romantic attachments while nursing, or teaching, or visiting men in military camps. Engaged in work that involved close and intimate relations with men, numbers of women inevitably explored the amorous opportunities. Cornelia Hancock kept an eye on several ladies who, apparently, had skirted Dorothea Dix's hard-line directives. "There are many good-looking women here," she wrote from Gettysburg in August 1863, "who galavant around in the evening, and have a good time." During her tour of duty, nurse Harriet Whetten encountered the daughter of a Union officer who dressed in fancy clothes and did nothing "but flirt with one of the medical cadets." In the South Carolina Sea Islands, Esther Hill Hawks learned that one teacher had taken her romantic pursuits too far. Miss

Garland's "flirtations," Hawks wrote, "have reached the ears of the prim ladies at the 'Rooms' and they decide that she is too young to be sent so far without a protector." Certainly some flirtations involved extramarital affairs. One biographer of Clara Barton has found evidence of Barton's attachment to a married Union officer, and another scholar speculates that Charlotte Forten, a young black teacher in the Sea Islands, developed romantic feelings for a Union official who was both white and wedded. Eliza Otis, for her part, was no adulterer in actuality, but she indulged in fantasies regarding an unmarried doctor in her husband's regiment. When the doctor managed to secure permission for her to extend her visit with her husband, Eliza wrote in her diary that she wished to cover "those tempting looking bachelor lips of his with genuine, heartfelt kisses." Since she and her female companion could not do that, they kissed their own husbands instead, "fancying all the while that we were kissing the doctor, which made the thing unusually delightful."[31]

Of course Otis, Barton, and Forten expressed only discreetly whatever illicit longings they may have had. Women nurses and teachers generally had no interest in publicizing their own, and others', seemingly improper actions. As Northerners learned, especially in the final years of the war when female propriety came under public scrutiny, misbehavior could provide an excuse for challenging even the limited steps women were taking toward independence. Perhaps nowhere did the tempest surrounding women's sexual behavior swirl as fiercely as in the area of women's newest wartime breakthrough: government employment. As with teaching and nursing, there were some political figures who raised questions about allowing women onto the government payroll in the first place. Fearful that women would have a "corrupting" influence on the moral climate, critics worried that government work would be compromised if women were employed. Concerns reached an apex in the beginning of 1864, when one New York congressman ordered an investigation into the foremost employer of women in the U.S. government: the Treasury Department. Congressman James Brooks leveled charges "of gross immoralities on the part of the superintendent and the female employees of the printing division of the Treasury Department," based on rumors of illicit relations between Spencer Clark, a Treasury official, and a number of young women in his employ. In the lurid investigation that followed, several young girls were forced to sign confessions documenting their liaisons with Clark, another young woman told of indecencies occurring in the ladies' "bonnet room," and another spoke of sexual innuendos uttered by her supervisor. At a low point in the proceedings, officials directed that the funeral casket of one young woman be opened to ascertain if she had died as the result of an abortion (her virginity was intact). To a great extent the investigation had originally been motivated not by fears of women's sexual indecency but by a political desire to derail the Treasury's Spencer Clark (Congressman Brooks was a Democrat). In drawing on the specter of female immorality, Clark's political opponents sought to attack the Treasury Department where it seemed most vulnerable, by targeting the promiscuous mingling of men and women in government employment, just as those who opposed education for the freed slaves chose to question the morality of female teachers. "A Treasury bureau," claimed one of Clark's chief attackers, "where is printed the money representative . . . of all the property and of all the industry of the country" and where "upon the faith and good conduct of which depends, more or less, every man's prosperity—is converted into a place for debauchery and drinking." The lesson was clear: women's increasing visibility in public spaces—whether as soldiers' wives or "government girls"—made their private behavior a subject for intensified investigation. Particularly where money was at stake—the currency that increasingly served as the lifeblood of the nation—female licentiousness had to be held in check.[32]

In the end, the committee reporting on the investigation exonerated Clark and his female employees, but the aura of impropriety continued to linger in government circles. Nurses continued to work under clouds of moral suspicion, and female civil servants remained tainted by the Treasury Department scandals. One applicant for a Treasury Department position still felt compelled to distance herself from the earlier wrongdoings, even after most members of the congressional committee had taken pains to clear the names of the accused. "I know that the ill-reputation & conduct of former attaches of this Department have cast a certain odium upon its female employes as a class," wrote Sallie Bridges in her September 1865 application, "but as I know of many others who have placed there whose names are as untainted as my own . . . I think you may have no hesitation on this score in forwarding my wishes." Moreover, in various branches of the government officials felt compelled to issue directives to closely monitor the behavior of women workers, and to keep them carefully sequestered from public contact. In June 1864 the Quartermaster General's Office issued "Rules of the Ladies Branch," which called for the appointment of female supervisors, the barring of all visitors from the ladies' rooms, and the refusal to allow women to leave their posts during working hours "without the special approbation" of the supervisor.[33]

In effect, to promote the success of new lines of employment for women, the federal government began to cast itself in the part of moral supervisor as well as paternal provider. At the Federal Arsenal in Allegheny, Pennsylvania, female employees could receive their supplies only by remaining at their work stations, an order designed to ensure that "no excuse may exist for the disorder arising from leaving their seats." The government's pension policy also came to encompass a greater degree of moral oversight of female recipients. Officials increasingly took the position that, in offering economic sustenance to dependent women, the government was obliged to monitor the morality of female pensioners. White women applying for pensions could not just claim marriage but had to produce documentation to prove it. When the widows of African American soldiers were admitted to the pension rolls in 1864, the government had to allow for the circumstances of former slaves, who had never been permitted the legal right to marriage. Subsequent pension legislation required black men and women who had lived in the former slave states to provide evidence of cohabitation rather than formal marriage, and officials had to decide when men and women had entered into committed unions and when they had simply been involved in brief romantic interludes.

Tolerance for "irregular marriages" did not lessen the government's scrutiny of both black and white widows' intimate lives. Increasingly, government investigators looked into the nature of widows' later amorous attachments, to determine if they still merited pension assistance. Because widows had to relinquish their pensions upon remarriage, congressional representatives worried that war widows—white as well as black—might cohabit rather than remarry, and thus continue to receive their aid duplicitously. Slowly, steps were taken in the federal government to bar women who "by reason of immoral conduct" were deemed unworthy of a pension.[34]

During the Civil War years, marriage itself began to look less like a private, localized arrangement and more like a public and nationally standardized institution, one increasingly subjected to the oversight and intrusion of the federal government. Even before the war, with Republicans crusading against the Mormon practice of polygamy, politicians had begun to establish their right to construct a standard system of legalized and faithful monogamous marriage. Now, with Union officials focusing attention on establishing legal marriages for former slaves, they extended the marriage campaign. Still, there were limits on the extent to which government could intrude on interpersonal relations, at least for white women and families. Some of the resistance to government interference was, perhaps ironically, a product of wartime and postwar debates about emancipation. Democrats in particular argued that government disruption of one "domestic" institution—slavery—must not provide an opening for government monitoring of other domestic relations. As a result, officials were loathe to impose too many moral restrictions on female pensioners, being anxious to keep some distance from their constituents' private domestic affairs.[35]

In various ways, Northern women found their domestic roles under assault during the Civil War years. In part this was the result of wartime tensions and dislocations. With enlisted men now removed from the domestic realm and relocated to the more intensely masculine world of war, home-front women often felt less confident about offering moral guidance and projecting a voice of moral restraint. The war in fact created a climate that encouraged some men to ignore or even belittle women's domestic duties and familial responsibilities, making women feel inadequate in their roles as wives and mothers.

Not only did women find it more difficult to assert their domestic and moral authority in their correspondence with absent male kin, but they also found their assertions of domestic and moral authority challenged in the public arena. Women's position as the upholders of moral virtue faced repeated challenges now that their private behavior was seen as explicitly linked to the fortunes of war. During the years of conflict, Northern women found their personal, intimate relationships subjected to intense public scrutiny, not only from neighbors and kin but also from state and federal officials. Ultimately, the climate of economic paternalism that the Civil War helped to create, in which officials accepted the need to provide for dependent women, edged Northern society toward a moral paternalism in which the personal habits of women, particularly those who relied on the government for support as they would have once relied on a male breadwinner, became a matter for public attention and regulation.

Chapter Four

From Patriots to Partisans and Back Again

❦ ❦ ❦

In February 1863, Jane Swisshelm was a woman with a mission. Setting out one day to talk to Abraham Lincoln about confronting the Sioux uprising in her home state of Minnesota, the newspaperwoman ran into Secretary of War Edwin Stanton, whom she had known slightly when they had both lived in Pittsburgh. Although she was dismayed by Lincoln, the outspoken journalist and abolitionist was impressed with Lincoln's feisty cabinet member, especially with his hearty support for married women's right to control their own property and his appreciation of "the many efforts of ladies to aid our soldiers." Stanton "acknowledges woman as co-laborer in preserving the Government," she later wrote in a letter.[1]

First in Pennsylvania and later in Minnesota, Swisshelm used her newspaper writing to champion Republican principles, making no secret of her allegiances. She reported on Republican Party politics in her state during the 1860 campaign, initially expressing skepticism about Lincoln but later giving him qualified endorsements. Her support wavered, however, in the fall of 1862, when the president, in her eyes, failed to respond effectively to the Sioux uprising that had led to the deaths of 800 white Minnesotans. In the beginning of 1863 Swisshelm came to Washington to lecture on the subject, hoping to lobby congressmen who were about to consider a bill that would provide money to the white survivors of the Sioux attack. When Edwin Stanton met Swisshelm, he no doubt recognized her as a woman who could influence public opinion as well as the opinion of prominent men in his party. Perhaps Swisshelm's prestige even encouraged Stanton to extend his patronage to the Minnesota-based journalist: four months later he had secured Swisshelm a clerkship in the War Department.[2]

An influential politico, Swisshelm herself, of course, could not vote. Except for a few, very limited suffrage provisions in specific states, no woman in the United States could. In general, nineteenth-century Americans scorned the notion of women as political actors, believing that the coarse and unmannered world of party politics was an inappropriate place for female participation. With the exception of a small band of female suffragists, most Americans believed that husbands and fathers were the natural representatives of women's political views in the polling places: votes for women, they maintained, would be superfluous. This meshed with the prevailing Anglo-American view that a woman's most natural state was wedlock, which offered her no legal identity separate from her husband's. Although women were praised for exerting a moral and uplifting influence on political life, few thought that influence should translate into concrete political rights or partisan responsibilities.[3]

Yet even before the Civil War, the logic behind this way of thinking was beginning to unravel. Women, particularly in the reform and abolitionist movements of the 1830s, 1840s, and 1850s, had found new ways to voice their political opinions, most often through petitions and public appeals directed at elected officials, sometimes even through private lobbying and backroom politicking. The Whig Party, which emerged in the 1830s, incorporated many of the moral reform impulses of the period and lent legitimacy to women by sanctioning women's political

clubs. In the 1850s, with all Americans experiencing an intensified sense of political engagement, the sectional crisis acceler-
ated these activities. Drawing on Whig and antislavery traditions, the emerging Republican Party enjoyed the support of
increasing numbers of women, who thronged its public events.
Their presence lent moral weight and legitimacy to the upstart
party and its platform. In the 1856 presidential campaign, when
Jessie Benton Fremont, the wife of Republican nominee John
Fremont, emerged as a spirited and independent proponent of
Republican views, women showed an even keener interest in the
party's affairs.[4]

With Lincoln's victory in 1860, many of the party's female
supporters saw themselves as more closely invested in the affairs of the government, and a significant number—like Jane
Swisshelm—publicly supported the party's endeavors and developed closer ties with government officials. Even abolitionist
women, many of whom had previously shunned the compromising nature of the political sphere, became staunch proponents of
Republicans, especially as the party moved in a more decisively
antislavery direction. In Pawtucket, Rhode Island, in June 1861,
a young Lillie Chace wrote to her friend Anna Dickinson that she
had, somewhat surprisingly, become an ardent defender of the
government, something that "one year ago I could not have been
made to believe [I]" would do.[5]

The Civil War had a dramatic, albeit complicated, effect on
Northern women's political life. The war did not bestow suffrage
on American women, nor did it transform them into political
candidates. It did, however, bring Northern women more clearly
into the political arena, and it compelled a keener awareness
and expression of their political views. Northern women pushed
beyond traditional notions of female loyalty and patriotism and
made political, and partisan, choices in their patriotic expres-

sions. They gave detailed reports on local politics to absent men-folk and wrote letters declaring their political sympathies, not only to soldiers but also to public officials. With Union men away on the battlefields, women who supported the war came to believe that having some type of political influence was necessary to counter the political power of anti-Unionist Northerners. And as members of the party responsible for waging an all-consuming war, Republicans realized that women could not be ignored if the Northern home front was to be effectively mobilized for the conflict.

In other ways, however, the war posed significant obstacles to women's political action. Because they had little experience in the political realm, women often felt insecure about their political opinions, and especially about asserting partisan positions. In addition, the war itself seemed far removed from women's political reach. Wartime events seemed less susceptible to their urging, their prompting, and their petitioning than to activities over which women had very little influence: presidential pronouncements, the 1864 presidential election, and the success or failure of the Union military machine. As the war continued, the Republican Party increasingly redirected partisan energies into notions of unswerving and unquestioning loyalty to the nation-state. In promoting "Union" clubs and "Union" candidates, the Republican Party encouraged Americans, women in particular, to avoid partisan squabbling and to focus their political vision on the single imperative of national loyalty.[6]

❦

Even before the onset of hostilities, the developing secession crisis and the election of 1860 had begun to propel many Northern women into a more active and visible political life. On the eve of the 1860 election, women in Keokuk, Iowa, participated in a Republican parade, representing the states of the Union. They were all dressed in white except for one woman, adorned in black, who symbolized the contested state of Kansas. At other Republican rallies and lectures, women attended and lent their support to the cause, sometimes appearing in pageants and sometimes coming as themselves. By the 1860 campaign, the party had begun to call on female speakers to elaborate its message to the public. Other women, like Jane Swisshelm, began disseminating partisan views in Republican newspapers. With its greater focus on male privilege and patriarchal authority, the Democratic Party generally gave less emphasis to women's participation, but even Democratic females began to show their party colors more openly with the onset of the sectional crisis. To show their dislike for Lincoln, they wore pins displaying the traditional butternut hue associated with midwestern Democrats, a muted but noticeable public statement that could generate attention and hostility. At the Terre Haute Female Academy in Indiana, two Hoosier women came to blows when one, a Republican, tried to remove her fellow student's Democratic adornment. Throughout the North, in fact, newspapers reported on political squabbles among women as evidence of how intense the conflict had become. A report in the *Kingston Argus* in New York explained that two of that town's more privileged women had ended a long friendship after one referred to Lincoln as "a vulgar man." The reports tended to cast a skeptical eye on women's political involvement, suggesting a certain political immaturity, but they also indicated a growing intensity in political feeling, even in quarters where political sympathies had not been so forthright before.[7]

Whether they engaged with fists or with words, Northern women were part of a strongly partisan and divided wartime political scene. Although both Republicans and Democrats initially supported the Lincoln administration's effort to end the rebellion and bring the Southern states back into the Union, there were, from the beginning, clear differences in the two parties' approaches to prosecuting the war. Democrats were from the outset suspected of collusion with their fellow travelers in the South, a suspicion that occasionally had some merit. In addition, Democrats mounted a more vocal opposition to the war, which grew stronger as the war continued and eventually culminated in the formation of a significant faction of antiwar Democrats, known to their enemies as "Copperheads." Even Democrats who supported the war made clear their partisan differences with the Republican administration and resisted any move to broaden the struggle's goal beyond restoring the Union to its prewar condition. Most Democrats consistently opposed efforts that might move the war in the direction of a "total war" that would include emancipation. They objected, too, to Republican efforts to crack down on Northern opponents of the war effort, believing those actions to be—as they often were—part of an anti-Democrat crusade. As the war persisted, the division between Democrats and Republicans became ever more contentious, especially in states like Indiana, Illinois, and Ohio, where the parties fought bitterly for state control.[8]

The divisive political climate inevitably forced women to take sides, sometimes placing them at odds with family members and neighbors. Whereas women in the antebellum period had tended to connect their political views to long-standing family preferences, the war forced women to make political choices that did not flow so easily or readily from family traditions. As Eleanor Bereman observed from Mount Pleasant, Iowa, women could easily be caught in a political bind. When Bereman's son Jont went to war, Jont's wife, Sarah, found herself ostracized by her Democratic parents, who objected to their son-in-law's service. "She can't stay at home," Eleanor Bereman explained in a letter to her husband, "and her father and mother are such hard-headed Democrats, they don't think Jont ought to go so she cant stay there." Eleanor observed that other local women also suffered for their political independence, including one who filed for a divorce "on the grounds that her husband was a secesh." Republican women who lived in strongly pro-Democratic or secessionist enclaves likewise had to reckon with deeply felt political allegiances. "There are many advocates of the South here," wrote Maria Patec from St. Joseph, Missouri, "and it renders it unpleasant to one so radical the other way. I can not feel the least sympathy for them in any form." For some women, their Democratic leanings grew stronger as they fretted about loved ones who had gone to fight a war that they only partly supported. "Oh Ben," Martha Jane Smith of Hendricks County, Indiana, wrote to her brother in the fall of 1862, "you was so silly for going into this awful war . . . It is outrageous scandalous and ridiculous how this war is carried on and it never will be any better until you have new officers and we have a new president elected." Ben Smith's continued military service seemed to propel his sister into the ranks of the Democratic opposition.[9]

Not surprisingly, women often became more politically engaged after a male friend or relative enlisted. When her fiancé, James Bowler, first went to war, Lizzie Caleff began—somewhat to Bowler's surprise—reading the prowar newspapers. "I read Tribune and all other kinds of war papers," Caleff explained in February 1862. "I think I am as much interested in the war as you used to be when I used to make fun of you." In Michigan, Sophia Buchanan's concerns about her husband encouraged her to look favorably on a more vigorous prosecution of the war. "I am getting very fierce in my feelings toward the rebels," she explained to her husband, Claude, in September 1862. "It is too bad you are not allowed to subsist on them as you pass through their country."[10]

For many women, especially those with men at the front, it was difficult to sort through personal emotions and political leanings. Few found it easy to support a position that seemed to prolong their loved one's sacrifice, and many found their support for the Republican administration wavering as their separations dragged on. "My patriotism," wrote Jane Thompson in November 1862, "is nearly all exhausted. I am so lonely." When her new husband became ill after more than two years away from home, Lizzie Caleff Bowler took the opportunity to remind her husband that, as a Canadian by birth, her own allegiance was naturally somewhat qualified. "You cannot expect me to love this country as you do," she wrote from their rural Minnesota home in September 1864, "nor feel willing to sacrifice that [which?] I would not be willing to sacrifice for my own country." She concluded, "I do not want to be any more patriotic than I now am." When Laura Beatty asked her husband in the summer of 1864 if he would be stumping for Abe Lincoln in the fall election, she noted that they probably differed on their opinions of "the old fellow." "Tell him," Laura suggested facetiously, "that I think he should let you resign."[11]

Men at the front had difficulty accepting such sentiments. Many soldiers believed that women had an obligation to openly support their defense of the nation, especially if they had men in the armed forces. Relying again on an ideal notion of "the soldier's wife," they imagined a model woman who did more than make quiet sacrifices for the nation. As envisioned by male soldiers, and by a growing number of women as well, this soldier's wife would not voice disloyal political sentiments, or even stay on the sidelines of the conflict. Rather, in light of the intense partisanship that accompanied the war, this woman had an obligation to move beyond simple patriotism to an understanding of unfolding political developments. Distressed to hear that his wife was "on the fence" regarding the 1864 election, James Beatty insisted that "no intelligent man or woman should say so." James Bowler likewise worried about his wife's hesitance to support the Union administration, especially in a public setting. "I would not like to have my little wife," he explained, "say things which might discourage the patriotic, or associate her in the least degree with the peace traitors [Copperheads] of the north." Robert Hubbard, a surgeon with the Seventeenth Connecticut Volunteer Regiment, provided a lengthy interpretation of Connecticut politics in a February 1863 letter to his wife. Noting that he had not intended to be so verbose, he explained that his desire to see a Republican victory had led him to preach politics to one whom he believed generally had a more casual interest in these affairs. "I know ladies are not usually interested in such matters," he explained, "but the time has come when they as well as the sterner sex must put a shoulder to the wheel." This, he said, meant not just feeling privately disgusted at the Democrats but frowning "upon such tendencies as are now being exhibited & if that is not sufficient spit[ting] upon those who manifest them if indeed they are worthy to be spit upon by their respectable female acquaintances." Iowa soldier Taylor Peirce had a far simpler request: he hoped his wife would pass along his political opinions to family members at home. In July 1864 he urged her to tell his brother-in-law "to stick to old Abe through this Presidential Campaign and his Election Closes the War."[12]

In her own way, Ann Cotton sought to give meaning to the idea of being a more politically informed soldier's wife. The Marietta, Ohio, housewife's husband, Josiah, served as an army surgeon. Cotton longed for his return and had declared herself, in January 1863, "more a wife than a patriot." Still, she supported her husband's wish to remain at war, and she gradually began taking an active interest in Ohio state politics, particularly the movement against the Democratic peace candidate Clement Vallandigham. "It is true," she wrote her husband, "that Vallandigham has been nominated for Governor, a most disgraceful proceeding . . . I will send you Brough's [the Republican candidate's] speech. I wish he could be our next Gov." By the following October, Ann Cotton could count herself as an active member of the Republican Party community, and she was helping to organize a "Brough Festival" with other ladies in her church and planning to cook an oyster supper to follow an evening political procession. A significant number of women found themselves more deeply invested in local and national politics as the war dragged on and as partisan splits became more pronounced. Not that they failed to express concern for their husbands' or sons' personal well-being; nor did they refrain from calling for their return. But they also saw themselves enmeshed in a new political dynamic, one that obligated them to the broader community as much as to their own family. As many came to see it, by personally sacrificing the presence of family members and loved ones, women had earned the right to speak out and register a political point of view.[13]

Some of the most vociferous expressions of this newly politicized womanhood can be found in the voluminous correspondence between Northern women and Abraham Lincoln. No doubt those who composed letters to the president were already predisposed toward politics. But women's letters to the commander in chief reveal that women's political beliefs and activities were moving in new directions. Some spoke to Lincoln as fellow partisans; some asked for political appointments. Quite a few expounded on matters of policy and partisanship, assuming a fundamental right to political expression. "I think a woman has all the rights of a free american sitisen," Mary Herrick wrote to the federal government, "and I want the american as it was without slavery." For Mrs. L. C. Howard of Macon County, Illinois, in September 1861, it was President Lincoln's reversal of Fremont's emancipation edict in Missouri that provoked her to write. Pointing to women's sacrifice of their menfolk, Mrs. Howard asked, "Havent we sent our Fathers; our Brothers; our dear Husbands to support you?" If women lent their support to the government, she reasoned, did it not then mean that the government must be accountable to its women? "We did look forward to a speedy termination of this war," Howard intoned, "but now what can we expect." Three and a half years later, with the war nearing its end, Mrs. A. A. Moor of Washington County, New York, made a similar point in urging Lincoln "to issue a retaliatory order" to see that rebel prisoners in the North received the same dismal treatment as Union soldiers in the South. "This cry for retaliation," she explained, "comes from all loyal mothers wives sisters and daughters of the north." Others, too, linked women's personal sacrifice with their right to demand a more vigorous prosecution of the war. Numerous black women, for example, urged a more far-reaching commitment to emancipation. Hannah Johnson, the mother of a soldier in the Massachusetts Fifty-fourth, wrote to Lincoln to see that Confederates would be prevented from "sell[ing] our colored soldiers for slaves" if they became prisoners. Mrs. Johnson, like Lincoln's white female correspondents, reasoned that personal sacrifice gave her the right to make certain political demands, even political decisions. Mattie Blanchard of Foster, Connecticut, pushed this point to its logical conclusion. "I think," she wrote to her husband in March 1863, "they had ought to let the soldiers wives vote while they are gone dont you?"[14]

Most women did not press their demands as far as the vote, but many certainly recognized how immersed they had become in the political vicissitudes of their communities. One of the most basic forms of wartime political involvement for women entailed chronicling local political life for their men far from home. Because men had few other places to turn for news of elections and candidates, women provided reports, sometimes with considerable detail, on the local political scene. Increasingly, they not only observed but also positioned themselves as participants. "Racine County held a Union convention for electing county officers," Sara Billings reported to her brother Levi in September 1864. She gave the names of the nominees as well as those who presided over the proceedings. Catharine Peirce gave her husband, Taylor, frequent updates on Iowa politics, highlighting the triumphs of local Republicans. "Des Moine," she wrote in May 1863, "has shone herself for the Union by the City election the other day." Sophia Buchanan exulted over Republican victories. "You cannot think how we are rejoicing over the election's," she wrote to her husband in November 1863. "A death blow to copperheadism, surely, & those against the Gov, & Union." Like many others, Lydia Watkins, a farmer's wife in Kent County, Michigan, took a particularly keen interest in the 1864 presidential contest and the reelection of Lincoln. Asked by her son in the army if the town would be voting for "old Abe," she replied with enthusiasm: "I answer yes head and ears if it did not I would move out of town." In New Hampshire, Lizzie Corning did not chronicle the political scene for an absent man, but her diary observations nonetheless suggest a closer scrutiny of partisan politics. "Gilmore was elected," she wrote in reference to the 1863 governor's race, "or rather the Republicans had more votes than the Democrat." Mattie Blanchard kept her attention fixed on political news in the spring of 1863. "I feel very much interested in the spring elections," she declared, "the democrats in this state have not decided upon who they will run for Governor yet and the town meeting is next Wednesday."[15]

Republican women viewed local politics with new interest and anxiety, especially in areas where a strong pro-Union position was undermined by the absence of Republican men serving at the military front. They became acutely aware of the open field that now existed for local Democrats, many of whom spoke brazenly of their desire for a Southern victory. Indeed, the sharply divided political scene seems to have intensified Northern women's political education, compelling them to choose sides in ways that Southern women did not, and could not. Without a coherent antiwar political party on the Confederate side, Southern white women felt no compulsion to either formally support or oppose such a position. Northern women, in contrast, had to reckon with organized antiwar parties, and an atmosphere of intense partisanship, in sorting out their political views.

The presence of antiwar Democrats in many Northern communities pressed Unionist women to develop a more definitive affiliation with the Republican Party. In October 1862 Jane Thompson reported to her husband, William, that she felt "quite anxious to get the next paper to see how the Election went for I am afraid it will go Democratic for there has been so many Republicans gone to war and but very few Democrats." Mary Parmelee was disgusted by the disloyalty expressed in Killingworth, Connecticut. The people of that town, she told her brother in a Connecticut regiment, "are all rebels, calling 'old Lincoln' a tyrant, opposed to the draft, some openly asserting their preference for Jeff. Davis' sway. I only wish they were subject to it—every soul of them!" Inevitably, women in such communities saw themselves inhabiting a hostile environment, a scene of conflict that at times resembled the battlefront of the South. "I begin to think the South will overpower us yet," Ruth Whittemore wrote to her soldier brother in September 1862 from her home in upstate New York. "They are gaining ground every day. The stinking Secesh here see it and are not so affraid to show their colors as they was one spell." Two months later Whittemore detailed the "stinking Secesh" victory in their town, making sure to name names so that her brother would know who the traitors were. "There are men here," she wrote, "that have said they hoped every man would be shot that went to fight against the South. Rod Curtiss for one." Whittemore's understanding of local politics informed her assessment of the larger military conflict, leading her to challenge her brother's largely sympathetic view of General George McClellan. While she was glad to know that "Little Mac" had treated his soldiers well, she felt certain that, from a political standpoint, he stood on the wrong side of the divide. "The strongest argument I have against him," she explained, "is the fact that every sympathiser with the rebels is ready to crown him king." Ruth Whittemore, in short, viewed McClellan in a political context, and dismissed him as the Democrat he was.[16]

As the war continued, Ruth Whittemore was prepared to jump into the partisan fray. By November 1863, the political battle in her upstate New York town raged more fiercely than ever: "A real war," Ruth called it, "carried on in the northern states between the Copperheads and the Union men." Yet even as she identified the combatants as "men," Ruth had already transformed herself from observer to participant. In June 1863 she had spoken openly against the disloyal statements made to her by a "miserable" Copperhead. Refuting his contention that "there was never a more unjust war on this earth," Whittemore defended the war and the right of the "government to assert its power" in subduing the traitors—no doubt including him.[17]

While women like Whittemore became more attuned to partisan politics, their political sympathies also encouraged them to embrace the wartime growth of national power. For Republican women, this included their generally enthusiastic support, after 1863, for the federal government's decision to initiate and implement a draft. Democrats, they believed, had shamefully rallied against conscription, thereby weakening the political and military support that could be extended to their own menfolk, who were shouldering more than their share of the wartime burden. More important, a draft—one that treated all party affiliates the same—might have the effect of leveling the political playing field. "I am glad that the draft has taken place," Addie Fowler wrote to her brother Henry in July 1863, "only it had ought to before now for one man ought to go as well as another." Emeline Ritner likewise exulted over the draft, and hoped it would solve some of the political difficulties in Iowa by removing those men who had gained the political upper hand. "I do hope," she wrote to her husband, Jake, "every drafted man will be a Copperhead." In Des Moines, Catharine Peirce expressed nearly identical sentiments. Although the governor downplayed the possibility of a draft in the beginning of 1864, Peirce hoped that conscription would proceed. "If the draft would only take the Cop[perhead]s out of the community," she wrote to her husband, "and place them in the front or some place where they would have to fight for the old flag."[18]

If the calls for the draft helped cement Republican women's partisanship, the same was true for women on the opposite side of the political spectrum. Because the draft had such tangible and personal implications, and because it provoked such fierce partisan divisions, Northern women registered strong political reactions in both directions to the conscription question. "Will the President have the face to call for another draft?" wondered Anna Ridgely in Illinois in June 1864. "Can he ask more men to lay down their lives for nothing? . . . Our only hope is in a Democratic President, or an uprising of the people to demand their rights as free men." Poor Northern women, a group Anna Ridgely did not belong to, had already been drawn into such an "uprising." In a few heavily working-class and immigrant districts in the North, women rose up against the draft, fearful that conscription would aggravate their economic burdens by depriving them of a male wage-earner during already difficult times. In the summer of 1863, when a federal draft was initiated, antidraft hysteria culminated in riots in Northern cities among working-class men and women. The women, observers noted, were mostly older and thus probably married, "roused to fury by the fear of having their husbands taken from them by the draft." The largest and most violent disturbance occurred in New York City, where for four days the predominantly Irish rioters looted and destroyed property, assaulted New York African Americans, and created a citywide upheaval that ultimately resulted in the deaths of 105 people.[19]

Women participated in the New York conflict, apparently with equal brutality, as well as in the smaller and considerably less devastating disturbances that occurred in New England, Pennsylvania, and the Midwest. While the violence appeared at times to be insensible, the targets were clearly political: women and men attacked the homes of prominent Republicans and the representatives of the Republican government sent to enforce the draft. The women, one observer in New York explained, "vow vengeance on all enrolling officers and provost marshals and regret that they did not annihilate the officers when they first called to procure the names for the draft." In the later stages of the New York riot, the wives of industrial workers tried to turn their neighborhoods into protected enclaves, free from the influence or interference of Republican authorities.[20]

Although extreme, female participants in the 1863 draft riots indicated women's intensified engagement with wartime politics, and their potential as champions of the antiwar and anticonscription sentiments of the Democratic Party. Outside the riot zone, other women proclaimed their Democratic sympathies. Marjorie Rogers in Iowa recalled her efforts in canvassing the countryside to generate support for soldiers, and the abuse she encountered from some families. "I was oftener insulted by women than men," she remarked, observing that the men had been warned by the Democratic sheriff to lay low so as not to seem like traitors. The intensity of the fall 1864 elections may have encouraged the Democrats to look toward their feminine supporters to counter the female Republican presence across the North. At an October 1864 rally for Democratic candidate Clement Vallandigham in Marietta, Ohio, "women and children helped form the procession that marched him through town."[21]

Certainly numerous Northern women sympathized with the antiwar tendencies of the Democrats, but these inclinations never emerged as dramatically as Republican women's partisan proclamations. In part this stemmed from the more male-oriented culture of the Democratic Party, as well as from the party's ability to rely on its strong male constituency on the home front, now more visible given that many Republican men were away at war. In addition, public events that invited female participation tended to be those with a prowar focus. Women who supported the Democrats' antiwar views may have had fewer opportunities to express their views publicly. A war meeting in one Maine community in 1862 prompted Persis Black, a Democratic sympathizer, to withdraw from public activity. "I did not go of course," she explained. "There is no need of my going anywhere."[22]

In contrast, the Republican Party offered more opportunities for women to show their support for the policies and mechanics of the organization. The party's need for higher enlistment in the military encouraged it to pay more attention to women, both in its policies—like the new pension law—and in its organizing tactics. At Republican rallies throughout the North, party leaders relied on a strong female turnout—given the lack of Republican men—to demonstrate the party's strength. A Republican newspaper in Dubuque took comfort in the presence of "hundreds of ladies" at a local campaign rally, seeing it as a sign of the party's broad-based support. Local Republicans no doubt gave hearty thanks to Ann Cotton and the other ladies of her Marietta church for organizing the festival in support of Ohio's Republican gubenatorial candidate in the fall of 1863.[23]

After the passage of the Emancipation Proclamation, African American women occupied a more prominent position at Republican rallies and activities. Black women had not ignored the Republicans prior to 1863, but with so many Northern states denying suffrage to black men, the party had paid scant attention to those outside its majority white constituency. And with black men excluded from the Union army early in the war, Republicans had given less consideration to arousing black supporters either male or female. As a result, the Republican Party had tended to overlook black women, and many felt little inclination to involve themselves in party activities. But with the coming of emancipation, and a new enthusiasm for blacks in military service, the political climate underwent a noteworthy change. Several Northern black women—including Mary Ann Shadd Cary, Harriet Jacobs, and Josephine St. Pierre Ruffin—began working as recruiters for African American Union regiments. Sojourner Truth, with the backing of a number of white abolitionist women, organized rallies throughout Indiana in an attempt to counteract the Copperheads' influence in that state's legislature. Dressed in a red, white, and blue uniform and escorted by armed soldiers, Truth sang "The Star-Spangled Banner" and defended the right of free speech. In November 1864, Truth declared her support for Lincoln's reelection. "I hope all will do all they can," she wrote to her friend Amy Post, "in putting him in President again." In the fall of 1862, Frances Harper addressed a public meeting in Columbus, Ohio, to champion "the President's Proclamation." The emancipation edict gave Harper renewed faith in the wisdom of the nation's leaders. "We may thank God that in the hour when the nation's life was convulsed," she wrote to a friend, ". . . the President reached out his hand through the darkness to break the chains on which the rust of centuries had gathered." Edmonia Highgate, a young black schoolteacher from New York State, also spoke publicly in support of Lincoln, at a meeting of the National Convention of Colored Men held in Syracuse in the fall of 1864. By choosing to speak out in such a highly charged political context, Highgate, in the eyes of one black newspaper reporter, apparently lost some of her feminine qualities. The young woman's vocal support for Lincoln in the 1864 election, he declared, demonstrated that she was "a strong Lincoln MAN."[24]

White women had political opportunities that black women did not, sometimes even to occupy a political office. One of the likeliest points of women's political infiltration was the post office. Far more than a place to buy stamps and mail letters, Civil War–era post offices served as essential focal points for local party politics. The ruling party earned the right to reward supporters with patronage spots, including the very lucrative and influential position of local postmaster. Postmasters, in turn, commanded a veritable patronage army, distributing numerous positions as clerks and letter carriers to other party loyalists. The local postmaster could also control the flow of political information in an area by waiving the postal fees on tracts and speeches favorable to the ruling party. Thus the post office not only represented political power but was itself a highly political place where political news and current events were often hotly debated.[25]

Throughout the war, Northern women frequently inserted themselves into partisan battles over post office control. "I hope the Post Master will be exchanged in Mount Joy for a better one if you are reelected," Mary Frazier wrote to Lincoln from Mount Joy, Pennsylvania, in 1864, "although he calls himself a Republican He is a poor specimen of a true one." Some women even joined the army of office seekers besieging Lincoln for post office appointments. Claiming to speak for the many "unrepresented tax paying women of America," Lydia Hasbrouck, the editor of the women's rights journal *The Sybil*, seized on the partisan possibilities that women might now pursue. "Thousands of Post and other offices," she wrote Lincoln in April 1861, "might be filled . . . by worthy women." She included herself among them. In April 1861, in Lincoln's hometown of Springfield, Illinois, his former law partner, John Stuart, advanced the claims of an in-law, Elizabeth Grimsley, for the position of Springfield's postmistress, although he acknowledged that "the appointment of a lady would be unusual." Grimsely, in the end, did not get the Springfield post, but in 1863 Lincoln declared himself in favor of appointing a female postmistress in Rockford, Illinois, particularly if she were a Union widow. No doubt the fact that fewer Republican men were available encouraged party leaders to turn to women to fill the political void, as did the Republican Party's emerging paternalist ethos toward the female relatives of Union men. In May 1863, Mrs. M. A. Meily became the postmistress of Ono, Pennsylvania, apparently having a double claim on that office: her husband was a Union soldier, and her father had been the original postmaster for the community. In 1866 Henry Ward Beecher could look back on the wartime experience and declare that a woman "makes as good a postmistress as a man does a postmaster."[26]

Postmistresses helped to give the world of politics a more feminine face. So did Anna Dickinson, a young abolitionist from Philadelphia who first began her speaking career in 1860. Initially a protégé of the abolitionist and women's rights movements, Dickinson began turning to war-related themes in the fall of the war's first year. A fiery public denunciation of General McClellan in September 1861 led to Dickinson's dismissal from her position with the U.S. Mint, compelling the nineteen-year-old Quaker orator to rely mainly on her lectures for financial support. In a time when women's rights leaders downplayed many aspects of their feminist agenda, Dickinson felt freer to pursue the broader political themes of the day. In the fall of 1862 she drew on her experiences in military hospitals to present lectures on "Hospital Life," using that subject as a springboard to demand a more aggressive military policy from the Lincoln administration.[27]

By the beginning of 1863, the Republican Party had begun to take notice of Anna Dickinson. Especially after Lincoln's Emancipation Proclamation, Republican leaders saw Dickinson as an ideal champion of their principles and their candidates. In February 1863, the chairman of the Republican Party in New Hampshire, Benjamin Prescott, arranged for Dickinson to deliver a series of lectures in that state on behalf of local candidates. He was particularly anxious to have Dickinson address the ladies of the Granite State. For New Hampshire Republicans, Dickinson's role was to help cement female support for the war, particularly when morale seemed to be declining. "The women in this state who have sons in the war," Prescott wrote to Dickinson in February 1863, "are considerably nervous and want the war closed (and you know the women are not always right) . . . Please encourage them in all possible ways, and in this way you can do much good." From New Hampshire, Dickinson moved on to Maine and Connecticut, where she endured a grueling lecture schedule while earning significant fees for her speeches. So successful were her talks that many New England Republicans credited her with swinging critical races in their favor.[28]

Although Dickinson's wartime lectures made little direct mention of women's rights, her appearances were a source of pride to female Yankees. Dickinson earned praise and admiration from women, many of whom commented on her ability to speak as well as, or better than, many male lecturers. "She was perfectly self-possessed and spoke equal to any man I ever saw," remarked Annie Dudley, who saw Dickinson in Washington in January 1864. When young Lizzie Corning of New Hampshire heard "Anna Dickerson" of Philadelphia speak in February 1863, she pronounced her "very eloquent, a splendid speaker." Lillie Chace, a friend and admirer of Dickinson, was hardly an impartial observer, but she understood the impression that the Philadelphia orator could make on young women who were newly politicized by the tumultuous events of the war. Chace applauded Dickinson on her success, she wrote, "because I am a woman, and as such I thank thee from the bottom of my heart for the great work thee is doing for us."[29]

Dickinson was clearly associated with a particular partisan perspective, but her political actions were also shaped by Republican attempts to create a bipartisan coalition. By the fall of 1861, in parts of the North where political feuding was particularly bitter, the Republicans had begun to rechristen themselves the "Union" party. In doing so, they hoped to build a broader political alliance that could stretch from their own antislavery ranks to even loyal and supportive Democrats. The times, they argued, demanded unusual affiliations. In addition, some Republicans clearly believed that the message of cross-party cooperation could best be articulated by a woman. Dickinson's appearances drove home the point that, just as the times demanded more women in politics, so they also demanded that men think differently about their traditional political loyalties. A local Republican organizer in Sandwich, New Hampshire, wrote that Dickinson must come speak for them "for it may be the means of saving us. Such men as we want to hear a lecture will not turn out to hear a man." In fact, he noted, "a few of our copperheads heard her" and perhaps had changed their views. Everett Clapp in Westchester County, New York, hoped Dickinson would have a similar effect in his community. "We believe you could do a great good here," he wrote in October 1863, "in not only convincing the weak of the justice of the union cause—but in converting the copperheads." Such thinking may have caused Republicans to arrange for Dickinson to speak, in the fall of 1863, to draft-resistant miners in Pennsylvania, and to use her in a Connecticut campaign that, as suffragist Elizabeth Cady Stanton noted, was aimed not at women but at Democratic men.[30]

At the end of 1863, Dickinson's prestige earned her a coveted prize: an invitation to speak before congressional representatives in the nation's capital in January 1864. The invitation indicated how highly Republicans had come to value women's participation, as well as how much partisanship now shaped Dickinson's political thinking. Like many abolitionists, Dickinson viewed Lincoln as a weak and conservative president, not force-

One of the most prominent speakers on the lecture circuit during the Civil War was the youthful Anna Dickinson, sometimes referred to as the Union's Joan of Arc. Credit: Library of Congress, Prints and Photographs Division [LC-DIG-cwpbh-02348]

ful enough on either reconstruction or emancipation. Yet when Lincoln and his wife entered the hall during Dickinson's speech, the fiery young orator reversed her previous stance on Lincoln's reconstruction proposals and came out in support of his candidacy on the "Union" ticket. Despite renewing her critiques of Lincoln later that year, Dickinson felt the pull of her party and financial obligations and agreed to hit the lecture trail again in support of the party's nominee.[31]

Anna Dickinson's career offers a clear indication of Northern women's increasing involvement in partisan politics. Because wartime circumstances placed a premium on women's political affiliations, women like Dickinson could play a forthright partisan role. The Republican Party, in particular, valued female participation because it recognized that women like Anna Dickinson could help attract and encourage female support for the Union military effort. Civil War Republicanism cast women in a variety of noteworthy political roles: as prominent speakers, as critical constituents, and as keen observers of the home-front scene.

Yet Dickinson's position on the political lecture circuit also highlights the significant political obstacles women faced in the mid-nineteenth century, and the political barriers that the war brought into sharper relief. Dickinson, in the end, won favor and approval so long as she presented herself as somehow above the partisan fray. Her appearance in the normally male-only world of partisan stump-speaking was admissible because she spoke out during a period of crisis and turmoil, when it seemed more acceptable to infuse politics with the voice of women's moral wrath. One Hartford Republican who usually opposed women's public speaking, applauded Dickinson as one who "seemed as if she were raised up for this present crisis, like Joan of Arc." Numerous Republicans repeated the Joan of Arc analogy, which put Dickinson in a unique political position. A friend of Benjamin

Prescott wrote that he believed Dickinson would "occupy a prominent place in the history of this nation . . . in a way like that of Joan of Arc to the French." Worried that this might imply an inappropriate degree of involvement in the conflict, however, Prescott added: "not perhaps in a military capacity."[32]

Likening Dickinson to France's female martyr offered Republicans a way to package Dickinson less as a partisan spokesperson of the Republican agenda and more as a moral beacon whose words could cut through tempestuous party politics. Joseph Allyn, who wanted Dickinson to speak to his naval division to help raise troop morale, believed she was an effective speaker because she occupied a "pure and unselfish" position, a plateau that stood above the more rancorous world of political wrangling. But as Dickinson sometimes discovered, an exalted pedestal was not always the ideal position from which to influence the political scene. When she strayed too close to the role of the traditional stump speaker, Dickinson risked reprimands and condemnation. Henry Homes, for example, who heard Dickinson lecture in Albany in 1863, warned her not to use the kinds of phrases "which however frequently employed by political orators addressing mass meetings, do not need to be used in halls where a lady addresses persons of both sexes." Likewise Dickinson's close associates, especially those linked to the abolition movement, continually urged her not to align herself too closely with the Republicans. Theodore Tilton hoped that Anna would continue her "mission" of "developing a higher sense of the value of our institutions." Rather than directly praising Lincoln in the 1864 campaign, Tilton preferred that she hold up "the grandeur of the cause . . . like a cloud over the people." Tilton spoke partly as an abolitionist who was, in the summer and fall of 1864, skeptical about Lincoln's candidacy. But he was also influenced by a traditional notion of women's political role, not as a direct player in partisan affairs but as an indirect and purifying influence on political activity.[33]

❧

Women who were drawn into the absorbing world of wartime politics often had trouble embracing the calculating and compromising nature of nineteenth-century partisanship. "Politics," confessed Lillie Chace in August 1864, "engross my thoughts much of the time now." She tried to stay focused on a higher moral purpose, to believe that even if McClellan won the November election, right would triumph, but the attempt to mix politics and morality left Chace in a quandary. "It is hard now," she admitted, "to tell what is right." Catharine Peirce also tried to reconcile politics and morality, and in the end she wasn't sure if God or the 1864 election would settle the nation's future. "It is my humble opinion," she wrote to her husband from their Des Moines home, "that [God] formed this earth for the good and breave and if this war do not exterminate all cowards and cop[perhead]s that he will send another flood or some thing else in its place." Still, she professed, "I have great faith in the Nov elections." In Minnesota, Rhoda Southworth felt a new political responsibility to express her views to Lincoln, especially because she had a son in the army. But the view she wished to express downplayed the political aspect of the war. "It is better to trust in God," she wrote to Lincoln, "than to put confidence in man."[34]

Perhaps in an attempt to reconcile these conflicting sentiments, some women tried to cast their new interest in politics in an apolitical light. They viewed Lincoln, for example, as not just another party politician but as a natural, even divinely sanctioned leader. Mrs. John Hodges excused her April 1863 letter to the president by presenting it not as a female intrusion into political matters but as a natural appeal to the country's "Father." Mrs. W. H. Planck likewise upheld the propriety of her decision to write directly to Lincoln in February 1864, to ask for her husband's military discharge, as something "an American loyal woman has a right to do with the Father of her country." And Ellie Reno explained that her decision to become a soldier in the army was bound up with her departure from her natural father's home and her adoption of Lincoln "in stead—the Noble Father of our Glorious Banner." Reno, like others among the several hundred women who served in the military, may well have disguised herself as a man to join the army, but still identified herself as "a Lady in every respect." Clearly women felt the need to express their own political views and even, as in the case of Ellie Reno, to cast themselves in dramatically new roles. But many also cloaked their political expressions in traditional garb, and defined themselves as the filial dependents of the national father.[35]

As the war encouraged women to take on new political identities, while simultaneously reminding them of long-standing barriers to their political work, many felt a growing sense of frustration with their inability to assert a stronger political presence. Northern women began to confront the limits of their political leverage, their need for political power and their lack of it. Mattie Blanchard, watching disloyal Democrats sweep into political office, wished soldiers' wives could use their husbands' votes to stop them. So did C. I. H. Nichols in Quindaro, Kansas, who gave her support to a new abolitionist women's group. "A hundred thousand loyal voters of Illinois," Nichols explained in 1863, "are grappling with the traitors of the South. If the hundred thousand loyal women left in their homes had been armed with ballots, copperhead treason would not have wrested the influence of that State to the aid and comfort of the rebellion." Perhaps more than other moments, the 1864 reelection campaign seemed to compound women's political frustrations, because what was at stake in the election—whether the war would be fought to the finish or settled by compromise—seemed so high. Ann Cotton believed that Lincoln's reelection would bring not just a close to the war but an immediate surrender from the Confederacy. "Oh I do hope & pray that Lincoln will be reelected," Cotton wrote to her husband in an Ohio regiment, "if he should be everyone thinks the rebels would give up." But Cotton could only watch the political events from a distance. "How can any one," she asked in frustration, "be so blind to the best interests of themselves & country as to vote for such a man" as McClellan?[36]

Certainly such sentiments do offer evidence of Northern women's developing suffragist sympathies. And they also point to the heightened sense of disappointment that many Northern women experienced now that the war had laid bare just how little influence they really did have in the affairs of the day. It was one thing to defy a local Copperhead, but wartime politics seemed to revolve increasingly around decisions made far away from the town councils and local legislatures, and many women felt helpless to effect any type of change. Elizabeth Livermore felt left out on November 8, 1864, as she watched the drama of Lincoln's reelection unfold from the sidelines. "It seems to me," she confided to her diary, "the men must think themselves monarchs . . . today—almost kings in their powers & prerogatives." Her anguished words would no doubt have resonated with many women who felt, on that election day, not like full-fledged citizens but like political peons awaiting the judgment of their all-powerful male sovereigns. Laura Beatty, a Minnesota soldier's wife, clearly felt like a lesser citizen when, in challenging her husband's wish that she act the part of a true female patriot, she declared that "all that a woman could say would not make a particle of difference in the fate of our country." As Beatty implied, the war placed political power, and the ability to influence the federal government, far beyond the reach of ordinary women.[37]

The tendency to feel alienated from the political process may have been particularly pervasive among women who experienced the war firsthand. To them, the war turned not on elections but on the men who were actually fighting in the field. If Elizabeth Livermore felt inconsequential watching the men in her town cast their ballots, Cornelia Hancock, a nurse with the Army of the Potomac, felt "more insignificant than words can express" when she saw soldiers "faithfully plodding through the dust protecting me." Such feelings, she observed, made politics seem particularly unimportant. "I have lost all interest in political affairs," she wrote in July 1864 from City Point Hospital, "have no eyes, ears, for anything but the sufferings of the soldiery." Katharine Wormeley, a nurse on a hospital transport ship, also became less interested in newspapers and political developments as she became more attuned to the specific needs of the soldiers she served.[38]

Directing and implementing the nation's military work overshadowed politics and just about any kind of work that women might do. Despite their new level of engagement in the national political scene, Northern women faced not only long-standing prejudices against women's rights but also a climate in which political work paled in comparison with military combat. Even the Republican Party, the object of many women's partisan sympathies, put extra effort into muting that partisanship in its attempt to build a "Union" movement that would replace party politics with national loyalty. With wartime politics determined less by traditional partisan practices and more by appeals to higher forces of unquestioning patriotism, women found it difficult to chart a course for political activism.

In May 1863 a number of prominent abolitionist women, including Elizabeth Cady Stanton, Susan B. Anthony, Ernestine Rose, and Lucy Stone, hoped to chart one forthright course for political action when they convened a gathering of women in New York City for the purpose of promoting the new Union cause of emancipation. The organizers proposed to build on a movement, already initiated in a number of regions, in which women formed associations—sometimes called Loyal Leagues—that mirrored the men-only Union Leagues. These associations were designed to build a broad coalition of support for the Republican administration and the war effort. The conveners of the New York meeting, however, hoped to give their work a more proactive agenda by urging the ladies to go beyond simply supporting the administration. "We have heard many complaints of the lack of enthusiasm among Northern women," Elizabeth Cady Stanton wrote in her appeal for the gathering. The problem, said Stanton, lay not with Northern women's quietude but with the failure of the Union administration to fully engage their sympathies. The cause of emancipation, organizers maintained, would now draw Northern women more fully into the struggle. Emancipation would mobilize women by providing a sharper political focus.[39]

As the proceedings suggest, however, the Woman's Loyal National League (WLNL) felt considerable pressure to keep its focus on national loyalty, and on the kind of nonpartisan message that "Union"-minded Republicans favored. Indeed some, in contrast to Stanton, may have found the Unionist mantle of nonpartisanship tailor-made for women. Mrs. Hoyt, a representative from the Ladies' Union League of Madison, Wisconsin, seemed willing to accept the antislavery agenda, particularly now that the Union cause had taken up emancipation. But she also spoke on behalf of a constituency that seemed more comfortable having women lend their unqualified loyalty to the government and the soldiers, and less comfortable with a political agenda that urged a particular course of action. In her part of the country, she explained, they kept their Ladies' Loyal Leagues "sacred from Anti-Slavery, Woman's Rights, Temperance, and everything else, good though they may be." Instead, they took a more traditional route, emphasizing unconditional support for the military effort. Most emphatically, Mrs. Hoyt objected to any injection of a feminist agenda. "We all know that Woman's Rights as an ism has not been received with entire favor by the women of the country," she declared, "and I know that there are thousands of earnest, loyal, and able women who will not go into any movement of this kind." In fact the only resolution at the National League meeting that failed to pass unanimously called for civil and political rights for "all citizens of African descent and all women."[40]

While downplaying women's rights, the WLNL firmly embraced an antislavery agenda. Members organized a massive petition campaign aimed at collecting one million signatures to demand the passage of a constitutional amendment outlawing slavery throughout the United States. But although the petition campaign made considerable headway, many doubted the effectiveness of such seemingly muted political tactics in the context of the war and national upheaval. At the second meeting of the organization, members observed that many who supported the principles behind the petition balked at signing. Arguing that the day for this type of appeal had passed, "that the bullet and bayonet are now working out the stern logic of events," women again confronted the problem of how the war had devalued their traditional political activities.[41]

The organization's leaders also faced another, perhaps more challenging, political obstacle. In 1864 several of the WLNL organizers wanted to play a more active role in party politics, particularly in that year's presidential contest. As strong backers of John Fremont's candidacy, which called for a tougher policy on reconstruction, both Stanton and Anthony hoped to make the Woman's Loyal National League a vehicle for the Fremont campaign. In their call for the WLNL's first-anniversary meeting, they said they hoped to see women "make themselves a power for freedom in the coming Presidential campaign," a phrase indicating their desire to see Fremont replace Lincoln on the Republican ticket. Yet their attempt to insinuate partisan politics in a movement dedicated to the causes of the Union and emancipation stirred up criticism, especially from fellow abolitionists, who once again urged a path of moral uplift and political restraint for Northern women.[42]

The most vociferous critic of the WLNL was the Boston abolitionist Caroline Dall, who publicized her dismay in a May 1864 letter to William Lloyd Garrison's newspaper, *The Liberator.* While encouraging women to involve themselves "in all national questions," Dall attacked the notion of turning the WLNL meeting "into an electioneering caucus, where all that disgusts us in political strategy shall be repeated, and where those who have no experience of the actual conflict, no long patience with the perplexities of the Executive chair, no far insight into the possibilities of this hour of retribution, shall hoist a party standard, proclaim a party purpose, and forfeit forever a moral stand-point which is fitly their own." Dall's warnings had a familiar ring, not only in urging women to make themselves a moral force in politics, but also in reminding women that the war had put a premium on a particular type of male expertise and executive-level experience that left women out in the cold. Echoing the concerns voiced by other Northern women, she even wondered if any political party or candidate mattered in the current crisis. "It seems to me," she concluded, "that it would be an unspeakable blessing if no vote needed to be cast during the war, that no diversion of interest should interfere with the one great question." Dall lamented the fact that women, now divided by partisan feelings and distracted by political developments, would be unable to muster their united moral power.[43]

Caroline Dall was no political innocent. Like Stanton, Anthony, and countless other Northern women, Dall found that the war had drawn her into a heightened state of political awareness. But like so many others, she masked her political sympathies in apolitical rhetoric. In fact her letter was a masterly partisan document, celebrating the moral righteousness of the current occupant of the "Presidential chair." "Through the uncertainties of statesmen," Dall intoned, "through the quarrels of demagogues, God safely led an honest and humble man to that seat—a man who had committed himself to nobody, who had pledged himself to nothing." Dall celebrated Abraham Lincoln as the ideal woman's candidate precisely because he was no mere candidate but an instrument of God's will. She marshaled the rhetoric of providence and purity in pursuit of her own political agenda, and the effort, it seems, was not lost on her candidate. Lincoln, Dall later pointed out, thanked her twice for her efforts on his behalf.[44]

Finally, there were some women who wondered if a full retreat from politics might not be the best course of action. By the spring of 1864, wealthy women of the North, who had experienced very little hardship during a war that for many was catastrophic, could no longer withstand the rebukes leveled against them for their apparent apathy. The previous winter, for example, Maria Daly, a strong supporter of the Democrats, had been appalled by displays of feminine elegance among New York socialites. "The women," she observed, "dress as extravagantly as ever, and the supper and dinner parties are far more numerous than they have been for several winters." Increasingly, wealthy women like Daly came to believe that the war effort called for a more traditional expression of feminine sacrifice. In May 1864 a group of women in Washington, including Mrs. Stephen A. Douglas, the editor Anne Stephens, and the wives of various politicians, called on ladies to boycott "imported articles of apparel, where American can possibly be substituted," for the remainder of the war. Under what they called "the ladies national covenant," women were asked to sustain the boycott in the interest of maintaining the nation's gold supply. Affiliated movements sprang up in other Northern cities. In New York, Maria Daly became president of the Board of Managers for the New York wing of this national movement.[45]

Referring to those who had led boycotts during the American Revolution, women were urged to find beauty in simple homespun apparel and to sacrifice their love of "extravagance." The movement consciously avoided partisan entanglements. Even so, while many newspapers and commentators praised the work and many women found satisfaction in making sacrifices for the Union, the movement floundered. The privileged-class outlook of the movement could not, despite some valiant efforts, be denied. "It must not be said of us that we have been willing to give up our husbands, sons, and brothers to fight or die for the Union," the covenant's organizers proclaimed, "and yet [we] refuse to renounce our laces, silks, velvets and diamonds." The movement's leaders tried to ally themselves with other Northern women, but the distinctions were too obvious to escape notice. The *New York Times* pointed out that while some women now proposed to give up silks, less wealthy women had already given up far more than that. Some found it ludicrous that the organizers of the movement wore "robed silk dresses" at the very meeting at which they proposed to start economizing. And Clara

Barton, who had neither the money nor the inclination to indulge in luxuries, found the whole movement irrelevant. "They must go beyond wearing apparel," she remarked, "before it will reach me, when they get down to bread and water, I will listen to them . . . I have no time to join in dress festival."[46]

In the end the movement was stymied by the very thing the organizers had hoped to avoid: politics. A number of Republican congressmen and commentators raised objections to the proposed boycott, arguing that it would only deprive the federal government of essential revenue from the tariffs on imported goods. When Mary Lincoln was asked to sign on to the pledge, she refused for the reasons cited by congressional Republicans. It was becoming impossible to build a movement, even a women's dress reform movement, without confronting the widening partisan divide.[47]

Perhaps the most ominous warnings against female political activity came from reports that circulated about the New York City draft riots. Although women constituted a relatively small minority of those involved in the uprising, many press reports highlighted the female component of the mobs and suggested that women played an unusually significant role. "A large number of workingmen's wives," explained a report in the *New York Herald*, "began also to assemble along the various avenues, and, if anything, were more excited than the men." Numerous reports portrayed women as inciters and supporters, if not actual deed-doers. Women, Maria Daly contended, "assisted and acted like furies by stimulating the men to greater ferocity." According to *Harper's Weekly*, while many men and boys got drunk on liquor, the women became "equally intoxicated with excitement," generally under the direction of an unscrupulous leader. And once "roused to fury," those women were identified with some of the most heinous crimes of the riots: the brutal attacks on the

Colored Orphan Asylum, the grisly murders of Union officers, the ransacking of abolitionists' homes. Here, in other words, were women whose political sympathies had been inflamed to the point of hysteria, women whose politics drove them to treason and disloyalty. From the vantage point of other women, the shocking reports indicated how deeply divided Northern women had become—and cast class and ethnic divisions in a political light as well. "The sight of an Irish man or woman," wrote Elizabeth Gay to a friend whose home had been ransacked during the riot, "became so odious to me, that I could not treat them with external decency." Probably no one thought Elizabeth Cady Stanton or Susan B. Anthony would commit such depredations in the name of their own party loyalties. But the draft riot served to some as an extreme example of the dangers that could result when women moved from the high ground of patriotism to the more emotional and aggressive ground of partisanship.[48]

During the Civil War, countless Northern women learned to live and breathe politics, sometimes intensely partisan politics, in ways they never had before. They observed and reported on the dramatic political developments on the home front; they grappled with their own newly aroused sympathies and looked for ways to exercise some political influence in the matters that profoundly affected their lives. They found, too, that the national parties, especially the Republican Party, showed a growing concern for their distinct political views. Although she may have thought about it more deeply and purposefully than many, Sarah Chamberlain, the mother of Joshua Lawrence Chamberlain, conveyed something of her own political enlightenment that resulted from the war. "Since the war," she wrote in 1866 to her son, now the Republican candidate for governor of Maine, "I have been quite a politician—even studying all the political speeches that fall in my way." Numerous Northern women who had also become attuned to politics during the sectional crisis were no doubt doing the same.[49]

Yet the heady atmosphere of wartime politics also highlighted long-standing obstacles that continued to impede Northern women's civic engagement. Many were influenced by traditional notions of women's political purity, and so expressed their views hesitantly and with considerable qualification. Others held back because they believed the sweeping events of the war could scarcely be affected by a group that exercised so little real influence. Battlefield decisions, presidential policy, and electoral contests seemed more removed than ever from the feminine sphere. Sarah Chamberlain, despite her political awakening and her defense of radical reconstruction policies, still deferred to her son when she contemplated the turbulent conflicts of the postwar South. "May be I don't understand all about it," she wrote, "but you do and I trust you are right." Even Chamberlain's wartime political education did not make her confident of her own ability to understand the political problems of the postwar world.[50]

Clara Barton emerged from the war more aware than ever of women's political weaknesses. In fact, she seemed to take from the war a sense of female vulnerability and the need for male protection. "In your hands," she told the men attending her postwar lectures, "rests the future well or ill of this dear noble land, to you comes the appeal of the lonely widowed mother in her desolate home . . . [and you must] see to it that the fatherless children she is raising in toil and penury shall not like their father fill the martyrs grave." Speaking in 1865, Barton emphasized the image of the soldier's vulnerable widow, not the emboldened and politicized soldier's wife. She believed women would have to rely on the goodwill and clear thinking of others. "The laws of the country tell her she is weak, and make her powerless," Barton explained. "To you comes her appeal and the cry of her orphan children, that you so preserve their rights and its liberties, that they may not only live, but live like citizens worthy [of] the great country which gave them birth."[51]

The war may have pushed women further into the realm of civic and political engagement, but it had also made them sharply aware of their inability to effect real and tangible change in the world of national politics. Some, no doubt, learned a lesson about the need for greater female activism, especially in pushing for the political tools—like the vote—that they obviously lacked. But it seems that the war also imparted a sobering lesson about just how wide was the gulf between women's voices and national power, and how many obstacles remained before it would be crossed.

Chapter Five

Aiding the Cause, Serving the State

🌿 🌿 🌿

Sewing circles, mother's groups, prayer meetings: all these activities established a rhythm in Mrs. Bardwell's small-town Vermont life in the 1850s. Like many middle-class women in antebellum America, Bardwell spent considerable time engaged in moral and religious work, as well as in her own often demanding domestic routine, which involved a perpetual cycle of sewing, knitting, and quilting for her elderly husband, a grown daughter who lived at home, and herself. In some respects the Civil War did not disrupt the finely tuned pattern of Bardwell's days, although it certainly gave her work a more intensely ideological context. Thankful that her own husband was at home, Bardwell thought often of the "poor soldiers" and their "many sufferings." She scrupulously observed the "National Fast" day declared by Lincoln on September 26, 1861, in order to dedicate herself to prayer for the cause of the soldiers. She was thankful, too, to have the strong guidance of her church pastor who could help direct her prayers in this time of national crisis.

By October 1861, when more young men in her vicinity were answering the recent call for another one million Union troops, Bardwell believed her support for the soldiers' cause had to move beyond prayer. That month, more than a hundred people crowded into Bardwell's Walpole, Vermont, home, for a gathering where "much was said about making comforts for soldiers." Bardwell's guests listened to a report from the recently formed United States Sanitary Commission (USSC), an organization that aimed to centralize relief efforts and provide aid for soldiers that "they could not get anywhere else." With Bardwell herself serving as president, the new Walpole soldiers' aid society began meeting regularly, working to make bed quilts, stockings, and other items that the enlisted men could use.[1]

The scenario in Walpole was repeated in thousands of towns and cities across the Northern states in the spring, summer, and fall of 1861. Identified as "soldiers' aid societies" or "ladies' aid societies," these organizations comprised an extensive network of women, both old and young, whose efforts sustained the largest military operation on American soil. They prepared clothing, hospital paraphernalia, bedding, foodstuffs, and countless other items that Union soldiers required, in sickness and in health. They packed and shipped, and sometimes personally delivered, their boxes of supplies. Many sponsored fund-raising events to secure cash support for their work. Some recruited and evaluated women who wished to serve as nurses. And some extended their soldier support work to the families that were left behind, bringing aid and relief to impoverished wives and children of enlisted men. Meeting in informal sewing circles as well as more formally constituted societies, hundreds of thousands of Northern women reached out to the Union's fighting men and their families to offer help in time of war.[2]

Far from being busywork, the relief efforts had significant ideological and practical ramifications for Northern women in the Civil War period. It is one of the few aspects of Northern women's Civil War experience that has received focused scholarly attention, and we have learned much in recent years about how the women involved learned to value their economic contributions, forge bonds of sisterly cooperation, and challenge male officialdom. Some historians have seen evidence of an emerging political consciousness taking shape among aid society women that ultimately helped to invigorate the postwar women's movement and suffragism. Perhaps of greater interest, though, is the new relationship the soldiers' aid work signaled between women and the national polity, and what the implications of that relationship were. Unlike earlier reform efforts that had engaged middle-class women's energies, the soldiers' aid work had an obvious civic dimension: it drew women into the work of preserving the nation and directly called on them to serve the government. In this regard, the relief efforts taught lessons of civic responsibility and civic obedience, with women learning to follow the demands of government agencies and personnel. And while some may have chafed at the relatively limited and restricted nature of the relief work when compared with more active endeavors such as soldiering or nursing, the soldiers' aid arena drew Northern women squarely into the war and many of its critical issues. As the Union struggle intensified, and as pressure increased for women to show their support for the war effort, women engaged in relief work had to consider the nature and degree of their patriotic sacrifice and decide how to focus and direct their feelings of loyalty.[3]

❦

The Walpole aid society to which Mrs. Bardwell contributed so much time and effort came late to a scene already crowded with relief societies, which had been cropping up since that spring. Ladies from Haverhill and Bradford, Massachusetts, met on April 22, 1861, to organize a joint soldiers' relief society and voted to send invitations asking "all the Ladies in Town and in Bradford" to participate. Hundreds of other societies had also formed in the wake of the Fort Sumter attack, with the women of Bridgeport, Connecticut—who organized themselves on April 15—forming the first recorded society in the North. Like most Northerners, as well as Southerners for that matter, many women doubted the war would last long and so held back from extensive organizing and relief work. With a relatively small number of men enlisting at first, women felt little pressure to provide direct aid and support. The Union defeat at Bull Run in late July, however, underscored the need for serious and sustained efforts to defeat the Confederacy, and a new burst of organizing took place late in the summer and in the fall of 1861. Women throughout the North showed a new patriotic determination to help the war effort and to assist men in their communities who were responding to Lincoln's call for one million enlisted men. Bardwell's group met on October 1, 1861, and soon after that Bardwell herself was busy knitting soldiers' socks. Other ladies throughout the North began meeting that fall. A society formed in Richmond, Pennsylvania, in September 1861; in October it met with the men who had joined a local company and presented them with a flag.[4]

The spontaneous emergence of women's societies was reflected in their diverse organizational structures and directions. Some had formal ties to national relief associations—like the United States Sanitary Commission or the United States Christian Commission—while others did not. In some societies, such as the one in Richmond, home-front men served as the titular heads of the organizations while women occupied all the practical, decision-making offices. Elsewhere—in Detroit, for example—all the officers were women. In May 1861 in Weymouth, Massachusetts, Mary Baker's sewing circle agreed to "form a society to work for the soldiers," a decision that apparently prompted a change of venue from a female member's home to the offices of a male supporter, perhaps because more space would be required. In some societies nearly all the sewing and knitting was performed by women volunteers, who obtained materials and patterns from a central distribution point and then worked either in groups or on their own. In other societies, at least some of the work was done by poorer women who were employed by well-off members to work as seamstresses. By January 1862, Mrs. Huntington Wood of Boston was keeping "thirty poor women in sewing" as part of her war-related efforts. In Canandaigua, New York, work was divided between a younger ladies' aid society that formed in May 1861 and an older women's group. The older women cut the materials and the younger women did the sewing. The younger ladies also planned "to write notes and enclose them in the garments to cheer up the soldier boys."[5]

The work drew mainly on the energy of the North's middle and upper classes. Middle-class women often had some organizational experience, such as with missionary and moral reform societies, and they could draw from that experience—and those societies—in their soldiers' relief activity. Middle-class women were also more likely to have some free time when they could use their domestic housekeeping skills to make comforts for the soldiers. Even wealthy women prided themselves on certain domestic and organizing abilities that they now put to use for the soldiers' benefit. They also availed themselves of contacts with men who could provide them with meeting spaces and funding. Less priveleged women did not go unrepresented in soldiers' aid work, although they generally participated in less noticeable, and less consistent, ways. Some joined local societies themselves while others, like those employed by Mrs. Huntington Wood, worked as hired seamstresses for wealthy aid society members.[6]

In addition to being predominantly middle-class, members of the aid societies, at least in the early phase of the war, were almost exclusively white. Northern black women were organized into relief societies, but prior to 1863 they focused their attention on sending aid and support to former slaves in the South. Just as black men were largely excluded from the Union military effort until the beginning of 1863, black women were excluded from the mobilization and support work that energized white women in 1861 and 1862. But by 1863 some African American women, especially middle-class women in urban areas, had embarked on the soldiers' aid crusade, in many cases forming separate, blacks-only organizations. In Philadelphia, black women formed the Colored Women's Sanitary Commission, which had male and female officers. In the same city, the most elite women in the African American community organized themselves as the Ladies' Sanitary Association of St. Thomas's African Episcopal Church. More than simply aiding specific soldiers, black women tended to see their work as a way of advancing the cause of emancipation and the standing of the race. While many white women's groups kept their focus on local soldiers, black women's groups generally adopted a broader perspective in support of freedom and racial justice throughout the Union. The goal, claimed the ladies in the Sanitary Association of St. Thomas's Church, was to see "that justice and right towards every man shall henceforth be the motto adopted by this Nation." Toward that end, black women's aid societies readily embraced the two causes of soldier relief and freedmen's aid, seeing them as joint projects in the same struggle. They also more readily shifted their focus from local enlisted men to the national level.[7]

White women, in contrast, devoted considerably more attention to soldiers' relief work, and were less inclined to link the endeavors of soldier relief and slave emancipation. The precise extent of their aid work, however, is difficult to determine because significant numbers of women chose not to affiliate with any society and preferred to work on their own. Jane Thompson told her husband that she would "work for the soldiers cheerfully but I will do it at home for I do not believe in these societies for they always end in a fuss and I do not want to be in." Women with young children at home often found they could contribute only an occasional shirt or pair of stockings and could not commit to the ongoing work of a society. Some women participated sporadically, when there seemed to be a particularly pressing demand. In August 1862, news of the Second Battle at Bull Run prompted Elizabeth Rogers Cabot to pull lint and roll bandages, a task she worked at consistently through the first two weeks of September. Close on the heels of the bloody battle of Chickamauga, on September 23, 1863, all the ladies in Marietta, Ohio, were, by Ann Cotton's report, "busy sewing for the sick & wounded soldiers." Ann herself, who could not leave her two-year-old son to attend the gathering, managed to send some jelly with her older daughter. In New York, Caroline Dunstan sat occasionally with friends and worked at preparing hospital supplies. Other times, she met with larger groups of women, such as those with whom she prepared a quilt to be sold at a fund-raising fair for "the hospital sick and wounded soldiers at Washington." Like many women, Dunstan directed her support efforts to very specific soldiers: men who came from her own circle of friends and relatives. In May 1861 she purchased a knife and fork to give to an acquaintance going into the army, and the following month she sent some pills to an acquaintance stationed on the "Eastern bank of [the] Potomac." In this way, her aid constituted personal gestures among family and friends.[8]

Those who did meet collectively with other women clearly derived certain pleasures and comforts from the social aspect of soldiers' aid work. The meetings provided a forum for women, where they could gather, communicate, socialize, take comfort from each other's companionship, and provide support to those in distress. As the war seemed to spin out of control, the aid societies offered a familiar and stable venue where women might piece together bits of news, learn to distinguish truth from rumor, or simply escape the anxieties of daily life. And given that most gatherings were exclusively female, societies allowed participants to share the particular worries and concerns they experienced as women in wartime. When Elizabeth Livermore attended her aid society meetings in Milford, New Hampshire, she would often read from letters she had received, particularly from acquaintances who lived closer to the seat of war. Sharing news with her fellow seamstresses allowed Livermore to assimilate the news and make the war more comprehensible. By July 1862, with the military effort in the South escalating, Livermore's news encouraged several women to share their fears about the conflict's effect on their own families. For Caroline White, a visit with other women doing work for the soldiers provided a refuge from the sense of crisis that engulfed her when the war first began. Toward the end of April 1861 she stopped at an acquaintance's home in Brookline, Massachusetts, to get some advice on her sewing and, finding several other ladies gathered there, "had a good laugh & a pleasant chat."[9]

Younger women, especially, may have been more inclined to participate in the relief work because of the socializing the work afforded. Twenty-year-old Anna Ridgely attended soldiers' aid meetings in Springfield, Illinois, in the winter of 1863. At one gathering, when she and some other girls were unable to find a place around the quilt, they retired to a backroom where, along with some boys, they "sang together and acted charades and made a noise generally." Gathering to help the nation did not preclude pleasurable socializing. Caroline Richards's society in upstate New York catered to some of the romantic impulses of its youthful membership. Aside from sending notes to soldiers with their supplies, they also agreed, Richards explained, "that if any of the members do send a soldier to the war they shall have a flag bed quilt, made by the society, and have the girls' names on the stars." Upon her engagement to a Union lieutenant, Richards herself became eligible for a quilt.[10]

Such diversions aside, relief society work offered its members more than companionship and pleasant conversation. Many women invested their aid work with a seriousness that, at least in the language used, implied that participants had little time to chat. In private reflections and in public reports, women spoke of the work as a welcome and significant expression of their patriotism, a vehicle that demonstrated their support for and interest in the war. Lacking the military and political outlets that men had, many women derived satisfaction from being able to make a contribution to soldiers in the field. And in a period when a premium was placed on "doing," aid work was one of the few pastimes that could actively engage women's energies for the war. Although she confessed to her soldier brother that at times she really wanted to be a man and "seize a gun," Fanny Pierce of Weymouth, Massachusetts, apparently made do with knitting needles instead. When she sent her sibling a night cap she explained that it was "very pleasing to me to have an opportunity to make or do something for you." As the most readily available alternative to soldiering, aid work was endowed by many women with a patriotic force akin to men's military efforts. To the women of the Worcester Soldiers' Relief Society in Massachusetts, their first year of service stood as a testament "to the untiring energy and self-sacrificing interest of the women of the county."[11]

Sustaining a nation at war, women stressed, required far more than moral compassion or an occasional jar of jam. Women spoke of their new responsibilities as daunting and demanding, and implied the need for a new level of commitment and seriousness not previously displayed in women's benevolent activities. Members must realize, explained the ladies of the Rochester Soldiers' Aid Society, "that the service required is something more than the result of occasional spasms of patriotism; that it is work, undisguised, continuous work, that we must render." And as several noted, continuous work demanded a businesslike plan of organization: aid workers had to learn how to juggle their societies' finances, keep careful accounts of goods and cash, and maximize productivity. The Haverhill and Bradford Soldiers' Relief Society, for example, moved quickly toward a plan of increased efficiency. Noting that, at the beginning of the war, they lacked a sense of the soldiers' "real wants," members of the Massachusetts group soon brought the work under "judicious management" and had their efforts "systematized." In this case, systematizing entailed a careful accounting procedure by which the articles produced were identified, along with the name of the producer and an assigned monetary value. Women around the country discovered that working for the soldiers required financial calculations and market negotiations. The women of Melrose, Wisconsin, "solicited donations of wheat from the farmers" and then "sent it eighteen miles to market, sold it, and bought materials." The ladies of the Richmond Soldiers' Aid Society called on women in the surrounding towns to knit stockings and take advantage of their Pennsylvania government's offer to pay them 25 cents a pair. They planned to deposit the money in a fund that could be used for hospital supplies "or for such other purposes for the aid & comfort of our troops." The Worcester Soldiers' Relief Society, like other groups, tried holding fairs and teas to raise money but found this work to be "laborious and wasteful." In August 1864 members devised a new scheme: they arranged with 500 operatives in the local machine shops "to give the proceeds of half an hour's labor to our Committee." Framed as a demanding responsibility that required organization and efficiency, aid work compelled middle-class women who previously had minimal contact with the commercial sphere to become increasingly savvy about the marketplace.[12]

The seriousness of the relief enterprise required more than businesslike efficiency. As many saw it, relief endeavors demanded a thorough commitment of body and soul. An Ohio woman thus hoped "to give myself to the cause of a time," while a Boston woman observed how an acquaintance had been thoroughly transformed by the relief effort and now "fairly slaves for the cause." In Milford, New Hampshire, in the early stages of the war, Elizabeth Livermore steeled herself for the demands to come; her goal, she explained, was "to work like a martyr all the time for soldiers." The descriptions were telling: as "slaves" and "martyrs," women submerged themselves in the task at hand. But such phrases did more than accentuate women's energy: they spoke, too, to Northerners' new-found appreciation for loyalty and patriotic devotion. No longer derided, as it had been by some intellectuals, as a purely personal tribute shown to monarchs, "loyalty" increasingly became an acceptable quality that connected men and women to their native land and institutions. Indeed, during the war a number of observers believed that, as loyal Americans, Northerners must learn to commit themselves to their government without conditions or qualifications. For women, who had always demonstrated loyalty to children and family members, this meant learning to direct their loyalty to the soldiers and the Union cause, and to subordinate themselves—even to "give" and "martyr" themselves—to such endeavors.[13]

Loyalty and obedience became important objectives for ladies' aid work as women embraced the significance of national fidelity. "We must be willing to contribute what we can now to serve our country," remarked aid worker Ellen Harris, who added, "[I] myself am willing 'to be spent' in her service." Devotion to country likewise refocused the energies of the Philadelphia Ladies' Aid Society. The attack on Fort Sumter, the group observed, generated "a spirit of loyalty which yearned to find expression in *appropriate* action," the emphasis perhaps signifying the struggle women faced in learning to channel their energy in new directions. Some used the language of the military to express their new-found devotion to a higher cause. The Philadelphia women explained that they had "enlisted in the service of our soldiers for the war." The Haverhill and Bradford aid society echoed that sentiment. "Though not beside you in the hour of danger," the women wrote to one of their soldier correspondents in the field, "our hands shall not be idle . . . The Soldiers Relief Society has enlisted for the war."[14]

Soldiers' aid work, then, offered women an avenue to the "higher claims" of the war, a cause that went beyond the concerns of home and family and drew them into an imagined national community. Many women who had no soldier kin—Mrs. Bardwell, for example—participated in the relief efforts and identified with the broader network of families that did. And all aid workers, whether they had soldier relatives or not, were encouraged to see themselves as part of a nationwide enterprise that cut across class, ethnic, and religious lines. The very act of working for the soldiers, who came from all parts of the Union to defend a common country, suggested that women themselves participated in a similar network of national consolidation. "The North," wrote Elizabeth Cabot in May 1861, "continues splendidly united and there is something beautiful in the way everybody is at work in the same cause. I had twelve pair of flannel drawers all finished last Saturday and if I had strength should take more work tomorrow and it is the same in every household." However, even in May 1861 Northern unity was not quite as splendid as Cabot imagined: poor women felt little inclination to join in relief work when they needed assistance themselves after their men had left for war. Yet news of the battlefield gave Union women an impression of interclass solidarity. "The terrible certainty of those suffering thousands of our noble martyrs," observed Caroline White after Second Bull Run, ". . . has made the day one of untiring industry in all this vicinity among all classes to relieve as far as possible that suffering." Although middle-class women predominated in the relief work, Mary Livermore recalled the wartime support efforts in the warm glow of romantic nationalism, as work that linked "patrician and plebeian, Protestant and Catholic," all of whom "scraped lint, and rolled bandages, or made garments for the poorly clad soldiery." Just as the military had, in its own way, created a national community of soldiers, so had the ladies' aid movement, at least as Livermore and others imagined it, created a nationwide community of female supporters.[15]

But in inspiring such nationalistic and thoroughgoing devotion, the aid work could serve to mute political differences. While women's political engagements gave their patriotism a partisan face, soldier's aid work offered a return to a seemingly purer form of patriotic commitment. With many groups counting both Democrats and Republicans in their ranks, political talk, no doubt, had to be silenced. Members, after all, were urged to work for the soldiers, not for a particular political objective. Although it was closely allied with Republicans, the U.S. Sanitary Commission emphasized its nonpartisan features. The newspaper at the commission's New York fair, for example, was advertised as "an unpolitical sheet" that would be devoid of "party spirit." Some women, in fact, may have welcomed the relief work precisely because it offered a refuge from troubling wartime politics. "Do not fold your hands and discuss the question whether you think the North is right," urged the president of the Soldiers' Aid Society of Detroit. Work for country, she advised, or for the sake of humanity. Moreover, if ladies' aid work was equivalent to soldiering, many believed it should have the same apolitical cast. "The great uprising among men," recalled relief worker Mary Livermore, "who ignored party and politics . . . in the fervor of their quickened love of country, was paralleled by a similar uprising among women." In upstate New York in the winter of 1863, Caroline Richards's aid group demonstrated its desire to ignore party and politics. Despite counting staunch Republicans among its members, the society expressed its interest in wartime developments by writing a letter of support to General George McClellan, an avowed Democrat. Wishing to counter the criticisms hurled against the Union commander, Richards's society claimed a broader patriotism that rose above partisan differences. "So long as our country remains to us a sacred name," the members wrote, "and our flag a holy emblem, so long shall we cherish your memory as the defender and protector of both."[16]

Relief work, in short, placed a premium on loyalty and obedience to the Union cause, with considerably less focus on political engagement. Women, relief organizer Mary Livermore recalled, accepted "the policy of the government uncomplainingly," and despite mounting defeats "continued to give the government their faith." Henrietta Colt, a relief worker from Wisconsin who distributed supplies to wounded soldiers in Tennessee, reflected the truth of Livermore's observation. "I know now," she remarked after visiting a Memphis army hospital, "that love of country is the strongest love, next to love of God, given to man." Still, not all home-front women agreed on where, precisely, they should direct their fidelity. Should they obey soldiers' wishes directly, or heed soldiers' demands through an intermediary form? Mary Livermore thought that women's ultimate allegiance must be to the government, although, like other organizers of the U.S. Sanitary Commission, she believed that the commission represented the ideal vehicle through which allegiance to government could be expressed.[17]

First organized in June 1861, the Sanitary Commission aimed to fill some of the gaps in the Union's relatively weak federal apparatus, especially its lack of preparation for a large-scale military mobilization. Functioning as a volunteer, civilian review board, the commission conferred with and made recommendations to the War Department and other branches of government regarding the public health conditions for Union soldiers. They focused especially on bringing more up-to-date methods of health care to the Union effort, promoting the introduction of open-air hospitals and a modern ambulance service. They also worked to centralize and coordinate local relief efforts, encouraging women throughout the Union to follow USSC recommendations as to what the soldiers needed and to channel their offerings through the commission's network. Eventually they established ten "branch" commissions—in Boston, Philadelphia, New York, Chicago, and elsewhere—where subdepots received the goods and contributions from local societies within that region. But beyond its organizational objectives, the leaders of the Sanitary Commission hoped to instill in Americans a sense of national obligation and duty, to redirect men's and women's humanitarian impulses away from individual and local claims and toward the nation-state. The project, explained USSC president Henry Bellows, entailed "a great scheme of practical service, which united men and women, cities and villages, distant States and Territories, in one protracted, systematic, laborious, and costly work—a work of an impersonal character—animated by love for the national cause, the national soldier, and not merely by personal affection or solicitude for their own particular flesh and blood." In articulating this message, Bellows emerged as one of several prominent men who, during the war, began to redefine notions of patriotism and loyalty as divine and sacred principles, not subject to conditions and qualifications. Bellows clearly hoped to extend his doctrine of "unconditional loyalty" to the women who would support the Sanitary Commission, calling on them to abandon personal and sentimental impulses and subordinate themselves to a national and even "impersonal" agenda.[18]

Male organizers of the USSC were not the only ones championing a centralized system of relief and unquestioning loyalty. In April 1861 the female organizers of the Woman's Central Relief Association (WCRA)—led by physician Elizabeth Blackwell and including a number of socially prominent New Yorkers—had pinpointed the problem of uncoordinated benevolence less than two weeks after the start of the war. As they explained in their call for the WCRA, the outpouring of feminine sympathy would make women "liable to waste their enthusiasm, to overlook some claims and overdo others." The WCRA proposed to bring the various volunteer societies together and to channel their contributions through a centralized apparatus. From the outset a number of women insisted on the need to serve more than local constituencies, and to act in a broader civic capacity that addressed the wider demands of the Union war effort. Yet female reformers, even socially prominent ones, ultimately could not challenge the primacy of men who wished to use relief work as a stepping-stone to greater political power. By the summer of 1861 the USSC had received the blessing of the Lincoln administration and was in the process of absorbing the WCRA, attempting to bring into its orbit the thousands of ladies' aid societies that had already formed, and the thousands more that had not yet been organized. For the remainder of the war, the Sanitary Commission and the WCRA coexisted in an at times uneasy working alliance.[19]

While the relationship was not always harmonious, many of the women who became actively involved in the WCRA and other auxiliary bodies of the USSC strongly embraced the commission's ideological ethos of centralization and national loyalty. Abigail May, the director of the New England auxiliary of the USSC, believed that the commission's message to the local societies should be that what government "cannot do it has officially given to the San'y Commission to do, and has also given it facilities for reaching the men in their" hour of greatest need "as no other agency can." The USSC's government affiliation, May believed, could be advertised as a source of efficiency and thoroughness, a means by which home-front women would know what soldiers needed most at any particular time. Yet she acknowledged that the system required women to subordinate their local and individual interests to the USSC's agenda, and channel their patriotism through obedience to the commission itself. Women in New England, May explained, must do whatever was in "the best interest of the U.S. Sanitary Commission," avoiding any consideration for "individual views, or specialties."[20]

❦

Many women, though, hesitated to give up their "individual views" and "specialties." After all, how could they follow the Sanitary Commission's directive to raise money for surgical instruments if their own friends and family members were writing home with requests for socks? Indeed, as women felt a weakened sense of domestic authority and worried that they no longer exercised the same moral influence on men who had chosen to put country ahead of home, they may have hoped to reinforce that "home" influence through their personal relief efforts. In countless letters, soldiers' wives and mothers and sisters insisted that their menfolk tell them what they needed. They sent boxes of goods that would remind their men of home and family, not in a generic sense but with focused specificity. Rebecca Lincoln, in fact, did not want to simply send clothes to her husband, Frank, but wished she herself "could run down and bring . . . a shirt or two." Emeline Ritner hoped her homemade tomato pickles would conjure up her presence for her husband, Jake, a soldier with the Twenty-fifth Iowa Infantry. "You must think of me when you eat them," she wrote. Women felt a strong desire to reestablish a domestic connection with their loved ones and had a hard time envisioning their menfolk in a large, impersonal pool of soldiers, where their needs might or might not be met. When Fanny Pierce in Weymouth, Massachusetts, wrote to her brother in the Thirteenth Massachusetts Regiment, she conveyed this wish to do something personal amid the vast relief network that had apparently engulfed them all. "Aunt Susan has been knitting a pair of 'soldier's stockings,'" she wrote with reference to a new and seemingly anonymous part of the soldier's wardrobe, "which she wishes were for you." Aunt Susan would have preferred to have her "soldier's stockings" go to a soldier she knew, rather than to a vast and depersonalized supply network. [21]

Home-front women resisted the kind of mentality, pervasive in the Sanitary Commission leadership, that wished to efface local pecularities and attachments. Many found it difficult to disentangle themselves from their own immediate circle of neighbors and kin from whom local regiments had formed. Soldiers' aid societies often formed in conjunction with the departure of local men, and women felt bound to honor their obligations to those regiments for the duration of the war. Many aid societies undertook their first efforts to benefit local soldiers, perhaps providing a farewell banquet, or sewing and presenting a regimental flag, or simply visiting the men in camps before they left for the South. Severing such grassroots links proved difficult for women around the country. In 1862 the governor of Wisconsin urged the state's women to move beyond their small communities and consider the needs of Wisconsin boys more generally. The newly appointed president of an aid society in Detroit also tried to counter local women's tendency to give only to those they knew. "God," she explained, "does not designate who is to be the recipient when he said, 'It is more blessed to give than to receive.'" The Worcester Soldiers' Relief Society in Massachusetts made a point of designating boxes for specific regiments, including one box sent on December 25, 1861, to Richmond, Virginia, for members of the Fifteenth Massachusetts Volunteer Regiment who were held there as prisoners. Throughout the war, the Worcester society kept its attention fixed on Massachusetts soldiers: in May 1864 members declined a request for aid from an Iowa soldiers' relief society.[22]

This is not to say that the women in local aid societies were incapable of embracing the idea of a wider network of wartime relief. But for many, whether in Wisconsin or Massachusetts or Iowa, it was difficult to believe that their loved ones—without focused attention from home—would not go wanting in the vast machinery of war. In this regard, women objected not so much to the national agenda of the Sanitary Commission, nor to its emphasis on patriotic loyalty, but to the depersonalized and bureaucratized approach that commission leaders advocated. Many women were more than willing to send aid to soldiers from outside their own immediate vicinity, but they wished to make the connections themselves, rather than have commissioners and relief agents do it for them. In the fall of 1861, Hannah Lamb, a new Englander who had a brother serving as a military doctor in St. Louis, found that many of her female neighbors were anxious to have their comforts go "for our western soldiers." Lamb's friends began sending Lamb countless soldiers' socks, which she then forwarded to Missouri. In New Hampshire, Elizabeth Livermore, who had no immediate kin in the military, felt a connection to soldiers serving in the west. With many meetings she attended given over to reports on the progress of the war, Livermore was continually reminded of the needs and the suffering that afflicted a wide array of soldiers, beyond those who came from New Hampshire or even New England. When there was hard fighting in Tennessee and Mississippi early in 1862, she came to sympathize in particular with "the brave glorious western soldiers" whose acts made her "feel ashamed of us doing so little." Ladies in Pennington, New Jersey, likewise felt a growing sympathy for western soldiers and hoped to do more to alleviate their suffering. The aid society there sent $5 to Ellen Harris, a Philadelphia relief agent who was traveling to a military hospital in Nashville. "I have often felt," Harris's New Jersey correspondent explained, "that our armies in the West were suffering for the want of just those attentions which the Ladies Aid of Philadelphia were showering upon the Army of the Potomac." Like Elizabeth Livermore and the women of Pennington, countless other Northern women were acutely conscious of the Union-wide struggle against the South and, in sympathizing with the soldiers' sacrifices, were able to link the trials of their own enlisted men with the trials of those from other parts of the Union.[23]

Yet, if they balked at the Sanitary Commission's bureaucracy, local aid society women accepted the notion that efficiency in relief efforts often required following the decisions of male superiors. The Philadelphia Ladies' Aid Society, acting on advice received from the War Department, told its affiliated societies that the choice of what to send to soldiers must be "subject to the direction of the surgeon in the supply and administration of food or medicine." Clara Barton, who worked as a distributor of supplies to New England soldiers before she became well known as a Civil War nurse, likewise believed women had to act with the sanction of male officials. "Ladies," she wrote in a letter to the Ladies' Relief Committee of Worcester, Massachusetts, "remember that the call for your organized efforts in behalf of our army was not from any commission or committee, but from Abraham Lincoln and [Secretary of War] Simon Cameron." Women, Barton maintained, owed their allegiance to their elected leaders, not the U.S. Sanitary Commission.[24]

To Barton and increasing numbers of other women, the Sanitary Commission could never truly become the conduit to the soldiers because it lacked a direct and personal link to the enlisted men. In the overwhelming, depersonalized climate of military mobilization, destruction, and death, home-front women felt driven to keep the personal needs and concerns of the soldiers directly in their field of vision. Clara Barton, for example, believed the sufferers in hospitals had "become mere machines in the hands of the Government," deprived of the "many luxuries which the country at large endeavors to supply them with." Others less familiar with specific hospital problems also became convinced that soldiers suffered from a lack of personalized attention. "Many impositions are practiced on the Volunteers," remarked Elizabeth Cooper in Pleasantville, Pennsylvania, "that have left good homes to serve this our once glorious union." Unable to pinpoint a responsible party, Cooper worried about what seemed to be a wholesale neglect of the enlisted men. As she and other women realized, all soldiers throughout the country endured hardships, but they learned more quickly, and in greater detail, about the hardships suffered by their own local boys. In February 1862, Elizabeth Livermore received the kind of troubling account that relief society women everywhere in the North were beginning to hear. The Eighth New Hampshire Regiment, to which her society had been sending supplies, was reported to be "poorly provided with hospital comforts" and "the cotton quilts we make are not used but are left decaying." The Eighth New Hampshire had somehow been lost in the Union's extensive military machinery, and the soldiers thus deprived of the personal care to which Livermore and her sisters had devoted themselves.[25]

As the war continued, Northerners became even more unsettled by the impersonal nature of the Union military operation and the escalating destruction of property and human life. Relief workers became convinced that big bureaucracies and anonymous third-party agencies, which lacked any personal investment in the soldiers, were thwarting their efforts and contributions, sometimes unintentionally but often to fill their own pocketbooks. Because home-front women provided goods and services that had an economic value, many worried that their products would be misappropriated. Indeed, like the soldiers' wives who felt besieged by dishonest debt collectors and unscrupulous merchants, aid society women felt increasingly vulnerable to those who would reap enormous wartime profits at their expense. And when boxes were sent but soldiers remained in need, the women's fears seemed well founded. Relief workers repeatedly registered complaints about the uncertain and sometimes troubling fate of the goods that they had so painstakingly produced. A box sent by Brattleboro ladies to the Fourth Vermont Regiment, so they were informed, "was opened by the carrier between Washington and the camp—and such articles as could be eaten as they were were taken out." William Hadley, a commission agent, reported being inundated with accusations against the USSC, including charges that "the Surgeons drink up all the wine and eat up all the delicacies." Mary Livermore came upon a box of cookies in her USSC office to which the sender had attached the following note: "These cookies are expressly for the sick soldiers, and if anybody else eats them, I hope they will choke him!" Women frequently accused USSC distributors themselves of corruption, of "selling our supplies to the soldiers." To other women, specific scoundrels could not be identified but the general problem was clear: "that the articles in being distributed more or less, fall into hands of speculators."[26]

Outraged by such corruption, some women withdrew from soldiers' aid work altogether. As the war dragged on, support for many relief societies' efforts waned, in part because women felt an economic pinch after trying to support both their families and the soldiers in the wartime economy, and also because some no longer wished to contribute to an enterprise that had questionable results. The problem of possible misappropriation prompted some women, midway in the war, to shift their contributions from Sanitary Commission agents to the U.S. Christian Commission. Because it was promoted by local ministers, many women saw the Christian Commission, a charitable organization formed in November 1861, as preferable to the USSC. To them, "Christian" trumped "Sanitary" not only because the Christian Commission brought religious inspiration to the soldiers but also, no doubt, because its supposedly more upright distributors would be less inclined to try to turn a profit from a box of soldiers' blankets or bed linens. Of course many other women believed that the scandals confirmed their initial impulse to make their relief work as direct and personal as possible. They chose to forgo affiliation with any nationwide network, either Christian or Sanitary, and intensified their local efforts, sending boxes and supplies directly to the soldiers they knew.[27]

At the war's midpoint, the conflict between the Sanitary Commission's national relief effort and the approach of home-front women sharpened over a movement at the local level to redirect relief efforts into fund-raising fairs. By the fall of 1863, middle- and upper-class women (and sometimes men) in hundreds of small towns and communities throughout the North, as well as in large metropolitan areas, had been seized by what some called "fair mania" and were planning and organizing fund-raising fairs to raise cash to fund such work as that of the U.S. Sanitary Commission. Drawing on a decades-old tradition of women's fund-raising activities that included antislavery fairs before the war, Northern women revived and expanded the tradition and put it at the service of the Union military. Coming after two years of military stagnation, the fairs also helped to counter allegations of waning Northern patriotism. Anxious to jump-start flagging energies, relief society women hoped that the excitement and novelty of the fairs would renew Northerners' spirit and prompt a new outpouring of patriotism, not to mention money and clothing. Many fair organizers were no doubt stung by the public commentary that began to circulate suggesting that women's sacrifices, even in their relief efforts, had been insufficient. With the fair movement, it became harder to berate Northern women's patriotism. Unlike the private, needle-driven work of the aid societies, the fund-raising fairs put women's patriotic work on public display in dramatic, large-scale venues. It also gave their work a more obvious economic value, transforming tens of thousands of homemade pin cushions and pot holders and pencil cases into millions of dollars. One postwar history of Civil War women trumpeted Northern women's "liberality"—as demonstrated through the efforts of the fund-raising fairs—noting that women's efforts even began to outstrip the work of men who, by the middle of the war, were enlisting in fewer numbers. The Chicago fair held in October 1863 far exceeded organizers' expectations, ultimately drawing thousands of visitors and raising more than $100,000. Subsequent fairs yielded even more: $146,000 in Boston and $280,000 in Cincinatti in December 1863; $320,000 in Pittsburgh in June 1864. The largest intake came from New York City's enormously successful Metropolitan Fair in April 1864, which brought in, according to some estimates, about $2 million.[28]

Despite the public enthusiasm for the fair movement, leaders of the Sanitary Commission initially objected to this burst of fund-raising activity. To some female leaders, the fairs minimized the importance of doing steady, ongoing work for the commission and reflected a "spontaneous combustion" style of benevolence. Abigail May of the New England Women's Auxiliary Association told her "country correspondents" that she believed that fair work should be a "secondary thing" because it seemed to diminish the Sanitary Commission's need for hospital supplies. Indeed many Northerners did get the mistaken impression that clothing and medical supplies were no longer required because the fairs were taking in so much cash. But perhaps even more worrisome for USSC and WCRA leaders was the possibility that women would focus their attention on amusements and entertainments, not the serious business of war and saving the Union. WCRA leader Louisa Schuyler believed the fairs should not be allowed to overshadow the need for soldiers' supplies, "which can be only obtained through the constant industry of the women of the land."[29]

Gradually, however, and reluctantly, USSC leaders came to accept the fair phenomenon. Alfred Bloor, the USSC's corresponding secretary, offered a friendly reprimand to Abigail May for her pessimistic response to the New England women's fair enthusiasm. Bloor agreed that the fairs were a distraction, but he suggested that May tolerate the fair hysteria as a mother might withstand her children's antics or, more significantly, as a more cultured people might endure the amusements of the masses. Likening the fairs to religious revivals, Bloor explained that "pretty well-cultured people" had little interest in such things but that "the multitude," who had a need for "periodical incitements," would be revived by the fair activity.[30]

Ultimately even USSC leaders found it best to support the fair phenomenon, despite initial tensions in the early stages of the movement. In Chicago, Mary Livermore and Jane Hoge, both affiliated with the commission but less influenced by commission philosophy than Abby May, first proposed a Chicago fair to the "gentlemen of the Commission, who languidly approved our plan, but laughed incredulously at our proposition to raise twenty-five thousand dollars for its treasury." Livermore and Hoge had a vision of a national enterprise that could tap into home-front energies in ways that previous relief efforts had not. Under Livermore's direction, the Chicago fair came to embody women's idea of a national community—not the bureaucratic and impersonal community promoted by the USSC hierarchy, but a more personalized and localized community that stood united with soldiers and other loyal supporters across the North. Over time, other fund-raising fairs, including those with more explicit USSC support, drew on a similar vision of a national community that celebrated individual and local distinctions.[31]

Fair organizers frequently touted local particularities and promoted friendly competitions among themselves. New York organizers gloated that they had managed to "eclipse the efforts of [their] sister cities with a sun-like blaze of magnificence." Brooklynites, long "overshadowed by [their] mighty neighbor" in Manhattan, felt compelled to respond to the great success of the New York fair and "show a proud record." Philadelphia fair organizers likewise proclaimed that their city "has never been behind any of her sisters in devotion to the soldier," while residents in Watertown, New York, publicly debated whether to join the fair in Albany or hold an event of their own. While such civic competition certainly enhanced women's sense of localism, it also boosted the nationalist thrust of the fairs. The competition, after all, required each locality to demonstrate its patriotism and its commitment to national unity. Thus while New York organizers relished their specific urban achievements, they also identified themselves as part of a larger American movement. "Nothing," they claimed, "could be more characteristic of America than these fairs."[32]

The fairs also sought to project an image of cross-class, multiethnic cooperation. Whereas USSC leaders sought to minimize such distinctions in their efforts to create an "impersonal" network of loyal supporters, fair organizers emphasized the distinct contributions of city and country folk, rich and poor, Catholic and Protestant, native born and immigrant. The Chicago fair women, for example, paid particular attention to soliciting German contributions to their event, with the wife of the Wisconsin governor taking specific responsibility for those donations. "The German ladies of the Northwest," the organizers explained, were invited "to cooperate with Mrs. Salomon in her undertaking, with the assurance that every facility will be granted them for the display and sale of the beautiful handiwork and fancy wares in which they so greatly excel." Because the fairs put a premium on individualized creations—whether in the form of local produce or ethnic handiwork—organizers stressed the array of contributions from different social groups. "Every profession, every trade, every business," declared writers in the New York fair's newspaper, "is represented in the Fair." Perhaps most important, though, especially in light of class tensions exacerbated by the war, was the ability of the fairs to project an amicable cross-class environment by allowing Northerners of all income levels to offer donations. "No contribution, however humble, was denied," explained New York's fair organizers.[33]

Yet, when all was said and done, the fund-raising fairs of 1863 to 1865 were prime showcases for middle- and upper-class patriotism. Unlike other patriotic ventures, the fairs offered women of the most priveleged classes the opportunity to be patriotic without calling undue attention to their wealth and elite status. Because buying and contributing were essential components of the fairs, upper-class women clearly could, and often did, play prominent roles in the events. In this context, spending wads of money marked one not as idle and indulgent but as loyal and patriotic. Maria Daly, for example, judged herself a worthy patriot even though she had not been an active organizer of the New York fair. "I have taken no active part in it," she observed, "though I have expended a good deal of money upon it." The fairs allowed wealthy women to do more than showcase their spending, though; they could also play more humble roles—sitting at sales tables or serving meals—that disguised their class status. "The wives of congressmen, professional men, clergymen, editors," observed Mary Livermore, waited on tables in fair restaurants. "None were above serving at the Soldiers' Fair dinners," she remarked.[34]

Getting their start as they did in the midst of the heated debate about Northern women's patriotism, the fairs may well have represented their most successful response to the charge of lackluster loyalty. Like the Ladies' National Covenant, the dress reform movement organized in 1864 by upper-class women who agreed to stop buying imported fabrics for the duration of the war, the fair drew on significant upper-class participation. But unlike the National Covenant, the fairs more successfully masked their upper-class bias and created an image of national

THE KNICKERBOCKER KITCHEN, UNION SQUARE.

SKETCHES OF THE METROPOL-
ITAN FAIR—Continued.

In the Union Square Buildings the KNICKERBOCKER KITCHEN

—illustrated on this page—attracts a large share of the attention of visitors. Meals are served up in the old Knickerbocker style to all who wish them; and old Knickerbocker gentlemen visit the place nightly to smoke their pipes and chat pleasantly together in the corners. Several of the ladies having this department in charge appear in the apparel of the old times, made of the most costly and elegant materials. Some of the visitors to the Kitchen, according to the reports of the daily papers, carry extensive appetites. One day "one youthful gormandizer boasted that he had 'put away upward of fifteen Dutch cheeses' in the course of a tolerably long meal. An old gentleman from Ulster County appeared early in the day and called for breakfast. Soon after he returned and inquired for a little lunch."

That having disappeared, he retired apparently satisfied. Not many hours elapsed, however, before he again turned up craving for dinner. At 5 o'clock he was enjoying a little something some more before retiring for the night."

THE MUSICAL DEPARTMENT

is a most delightful resort, in which lady visitors find especial pleasure. The instruments are all of the first class, and have been sold at large prices. There is also a select assortment of sheet music,

musical books, etc., and at all hours of the day some performance discourses sweet sounds for those present. Another point of great interest in the Union Square Buildings (illustrated on page 203) is the

INTERNATIONAL DEPARTMENT,

which is crowded with rare selections of Science and Art contributed from different countries. One of the principal ornaments of the department is a fountain in full play, surrounded by vases of flowers. The sales here have been very large.

unity. Unlike the dress reform movement, which focused largely on a boycott of expensive European textiles, the fairs provided room for less privileged women to participate. All were invited to contribute, and most fairs kept the price of admission relatively low, so people of all classes could attend. Perhaps most notably, the fairs combined patriotism with commercialism to convey an image of a broad, democratic marketplace. Value at the fairs was judged not so much in purely economic terms, but in a patriotic context. Nothing demonstrated this more clearly than the story circulated at the New York fair of a simple dollar bill, offered by a poor woman to the fair, that generated a $100 contribution. The bill, reported the New York fair's newspaper, came from "a woman who depends upon her daily work for her own support and that of her children." The woman's pastor, the initial recipient of the bill, saw that it was torn and shredded and offered to replace it with an unmutilated piece of currency. He discovered, however, that the original bill "was in brother Sam's pocket when he was wounded. He's dead now, and we have his torn pocketbook; and mother said (the mother is a widow and he was her only son), we will give that dollar to the Sanitary Commission; we cannot spend it." Thus a single dollar came to embody a poor woman's patriotic sacrifice and, as such, achieved a value far in excess of its monetary worth. By the time the fair concluded, the original dollar bill had been sold to a wealthy New York woman for $100. The fairs in effect turned patriotism into money and, in turn, drew Northerners from a variety of ethnic, social, occupa-

Among the most spectacular and lavish of the wartime fund-raising fairs was the New York Metropolitan Fair, held in April 1864. Prominent among the fair's displays were the Knickerbocker Kitchen (top) and the Music Hall (bottom). Credit: *Harper's Weekly,* April 23, 1864

tional, and geographic groups into a nationwide community of loyal donors and consumers.[35]

Fair organizers were committed to the notion that the USSC should act as the legitimate representative of soldiers' needs, and that those wishing to serve the soldiers could best do so by serving the commission. Yet the fairs also reduced some of the tensions between local societies and national officials by making it possible to demonstrate obedience to the commission and its objectives in a more individualized way: by donating handicrafts, or dressing up in costume for an exhibit, or simply buying an admission ticket. Instead of simply following commission directives to make, collect, and send off specific supplies, through the fairs women could use their own creative impulses and reflect the kinds of "individual views" and "specialties" that commission leaders had previously disdained. In this way, the fairs managed to mute political divisions between home-front women and relief organizers.

The soldiers' relief efforts of the Civil War era did, in the end, impress a new civic identity on many Yankee women. The work, whether directed through the U.S. Sanitary Commission or not, encouraged women to view themselves as the government's dedicated supporters and collaborators in the military effort. Despite the differences that emerged between Sanitary Commission leaders and home-front women, there were noteworthy similarities in how all aid-society women saw their responsibilities and obligations. Although women disagreed about the importance of an intermediary bureaucracy, they ultimately agreed on the need for unwavering and unquestioning devotion to the soldiers. Such devotion ultimately meant that Northern women learned to accept their subordinate position to the men who engaged in, and directed, the fighting. Relief worker Marjorie Rogers articulated this lesson with stunning clarity. While traveling by train, late in

the war, Rogers encountered a group of injured soldiers, now re-
cuperated, on their way back to the field. "My experience all
these years of the war with those that were afflicted and suffering
mentally," she observed, "had been with women, not men who
had experienced all the horrors of a battlefield . . . and now re-
covering were ready to return out of pure love for country and
good government to fight again for the Flag." The experience
made Rogers wonder if she could ever successfully emulate the
men's patriotism. "I could not comprehend such loyalty, it was almost divine; I felt like bowing my knee to them as superior beings. I had no words to express my admiration, so said nothing." The encounter left Rogers speechless, but the lesson of
loyalty and civic responsibility was firmly impressed on her mind.
Through their aid-society work, Northern women came to view
loyalty and obedience from a new and more expansive perspective that drew them more fully into the civic arena; in entering
that arena, they also learned to place a premium on obeying
those men who, whether in positions of government or military
authority, embodied the Union cause.[36]

Chapter Six

Saving the Sick, Healing the Nation

❦ ❦ ❦

"I tore home through the December slush as if the rebels were after me," wrote one New Englander in the middle of the Civil War, "and like many another recruit, burst in upon my family with the announcement—'I've enlisted!'" The writer was not a man but the fledgling Massachusetts author Louisa May Alcott, and the speaker was not a young soldier who had just joined the army but the character Tribulation Periwinkle, who had decided to become an army nurse. Through the voice of Periwinkle, Alcott sought to capture the sense of urgency that she and many Northern women felt on the outbreak of the war, a desire to "do something" for the military effort. In fact Alcott herself responded to the need to act when, in December 1862, she spent one month serving as a Union nurse in the Union Hotel Hospital in Washington. Her stint was brief: she nearly died after contracting typhoid fever and returned home to Concord to recuperate. But soon thereafter she recounted her experiences in her 1863 publication, *Hospital Sketches*. The book introduced Alcott's voice into the literary world, where she would remain a fixture for the next twenty-five years.

Although her own nursing career was abbreviated, Alcott managed to convey many of the sentiments that motivated Northern nurses during the Civil War, as well as the conflicts and tensions they encountered in their work. Periwinkle, Alcott's fictional stand-in, felt a strong desire to be actively engaged in aiding the Union cause and turned to nursing as a reasonably acceptable outlet for her energies. Like other nurses, she was at first overwhelmed by the horrors of the work—by "the sight of several stretchers, each with its legless, armless, or desperately wounded occupant, entering my ward." In time she learned to steel herself to some of the atrocities and to develop a motherly relationship with her suffering patients, attending carefully to her motley contingent of "boys." After accepting her appointment to a hospital in the nation's capital, Periwinkle promised "not to desert, but stand ready to march on Washington at an hour's notice." While still at home, she "called my dinner my rations, saluted all new comers, and ordered a dress parade that very afternoon." Using military metaphors, Alcott highlighted the parallels between nursing and soldiering, and thus drew on an analogy that shaped the thinking of Northern nurses in many different and seemingly contradictory ways.[1]

Perhaps more than any other wartime activity undertaken by women, nursing placed them in an active and immediate relationship with government and Union officials, gave them a way to identify with rank-and-file soldiers and the "higher claims" of the nation, and encouraged them to commit themselves to a hard and grueling task—one that many officials and observers, at least at the beginning of the war, found unsuitable for women. At the same time, their new involvement with affairs of state and the military had restrictive consequences as well: it served to remind the nurses that they were part of a larger hierarchy that privileged male authority and leadership and reinforced cultural lessons about subservience to men, the limits of feminine influence, and the awesome power of male military might.

❦

Almost from the war's inception, Northern women began considering, and pursuing, the possibility of joining the Union struggle as nurses. Two weeks after the attack on Fort Sumter, the *New*

York Herald reported that it had received numerous "communications from ladies" proclaiming their desire to aid the suffering soldiers. By the fall of 1861, with casualties mounting and the war showing no sign of abating, thousands more began to consider the path of nursing. "There is several Females through this section of the Country," reported Mrs. Hummel of Shiloh, New Jersey, "that is desirous of rendering their services if they could first gain information." Still, the prospect of women working as nurses, at least at the outset of the conflict, did not win universal support and approval among Northerners. The field was neither well established as a profession nor deemed suitable for most women. Quite a few believed that wartime nursing was a dangerous and dirty business in which women had no place. The contact with men and unclean male bodies, would, many believed, be morally compromising. Maria Daly, at least in the first year of the war, had nothing but suspicion for young women, especially unmarried ones, who wanted to be nurses. "If I were [one of] the boys," Daly reflected, "I should not want a lady about my sickbed unless she were some motherly person with a snowy-white cap and ample shape."[2]

In light of such prejudices, many women who were interested in nursing, even if they lacked the ample shape, tried to project an image of motherliness and propriety. Many drew on the model established by Florence Nightingale in her work for British soldiers during the 1850s Crimean War and framed their nursing in terms of offering feminine care and attention. Worried about the possible unseemliness of having women leave home to work at caring for dirty and diseased strangers, men and women who encouraged female nursing often emphasized the propriety and respectability of the enterprise. "I propose," wrote one *New York Herald* correspondent, "that we form a company of ladies of respectability to accompany some regiment, in a dress suitable for the occasion, and let our hands be those to cheer and minister to the sick and wounded who need our care."[3]

This language of "respectability," employed at the very outset of the war, has mystified our understanding of those who served as Union army nurses. Because nursing was not a professional classification in the 1860s, many different kinds of tasks, as well as many different kinds of personnel, were part of the mix that made up women's hospital work in the Civil War era. Nursing could encompass food preparation, letter writing for convalescing soldiers, laundering, and house cleaning, as well as the more standard medical practices that we associate with the nursing profession today. In this regard, thousands of women served in a nursing capacity, in hospitals, with army regiments, and in the more informal settings of homes and churches. Many of the women, though, especially if they were black or poorer white women, were designated as laundresses or cooks. Many black women, moreover, came from the ranks of freed slaves, and once behind Union lines they often were pressed into various types of government service, including hospital work, in exchange for minimal wages. Thus while lower-class women, white and black, attended to sick and dying patients early in the war, they were seldom defined as "nurses." Instead that title was reserved for soldiers, usually convalescent ones, who attended to their sick comrades and, over time, for more privileged white women, some of whom received salaries and some of whom were volunteers. These women, too, might do laundry or scrub floors, but they increasingly differentiated themselves as a class of female hospital workers who occupied a more privileged relationship within the medical hierarchy and had a more direct connection with the soldiers. They were also the ones most likely to receive federal pensions after they were granted to U.S. Army nurses in 1892. Based on pension accounts, about 9,000 women can be counted in the officially designated, and more elite, category of Union "nurse."[4]

Women who aspired to these positions could travel different paths to get there. By June 1861 Dorothea Dix, a one-time crusader for mental health and prison reform, had met with War Department officials, who accepted Dix's offer to recruit a corps of female nurses for military hospitals around Washington. Eventually Dix's field of operations widened to include other military and field facilities. Anxious to demonstrate women's moral suitability for nursing, Dix established strict standards, at least in terms of appearance and deportment: recruits had to be between the ages of thirty-five and fifty, "matronly" in appearance and with "habits of neatness, order, sobriety and industry." With no professional standards on which to draw, Dix gave scant attention to medical training or ability. She did, though, offer wages of twelve dollars per month. Soon after her appointment as superintendent of women nurses, Dix's office was flooded with applications from women across the North. In the end, about 3,000 women served under Dix's oversight.[5]

The Woman's Central Relief Association, formed in New York in April 1861, also participated in the recruitment of female nurses. Founded as a clearinghouse for women's relief efforts, the WCRA initially placed Dr. Elizabeth Blackwell, the nation's first officially degreed female doctor, in charge of the nursing drive. Blackwell wished to legitimize and professionalize medical training for women, and thus placed considerably more emphasis on technical abilities in selecting her recruits. But when the WCRA was quickly absorbed into the male-run U.S. Sanitary Commission, Blackwell's mission found little support among commission leaders. Instead, the USSC began to accept untrained middle- and even upper-class ladies for nursing jobs, at first sending its recruits to Dix but later, after expressing some frustration with Dix's methods, placing their nurses only in Sanitary Commission facilities. Many of these women offered their services voluntarily, although some received small stipends. Finally, numbers of women from less elite backgrounds became nurses by attaching themselves to specific army regiments, often those companies with which their husbands or other male kin served.[6]

Depending on the path they pursued, numerous women who became nurses did receive monetary remuneration; few, however, identified financial gain as a significant motivation in their decision to take up nursing. Influenced by a domestic ideology that disdained wages for women, elite and middle-class nurses preferred to place their services in a very different context and to emphasize the nonremunerative component of their contribution. Volunteer nurses saw their wage-free status as a sign of their moral and humanitarian dedication to the work and their supreme commitment to the suffering soldiers. They worked, in other words, in the spirit of self-sacrifice that many believed epitomized woman's nature. And even those who received money often belittled their wages as a trifling concern, suggesting that the meager pay surely paled in comparison with the lofty motives that had prompted them to serve. "I learned," wrote one of Dix's recruits, "to appreciate the noble-heartedness of the untiring nurse whose duties were for humanity's sake, not surely for the 12 dollars a month, and soldier's rations." Whether they received wages or not, disdain for pay was an important aspect of the nurses' perspective that allowed them to elevate their work to a higher moral plane.[7]

By deemphasizing their wages, nurses could highlight their patriotism. Their work was not simply a manifestation of female self-sacrifice on behalf of others, but self-sacrifice for the health and well-being of the nation. "To think that I, poor Amy Bradley, would come out here to work for money," Bradley wrote from her position aboard a Sanitary Commission boat, "and that, the paltry sum of twelve dollars per month and Rations! . . . Thank God I had a higher motive than a high living & big salary." In March 1862 Clara Barton applied to work as a nurse with the Twenty-fifth Massachusetts Volunteer Infantry, emphasizing her willingness to serve without pay. Her eagerness for the job, she wrote to the regiment's Captain Denney, stemmed from her up-bringing as a soldier's daughter, when she "learned that next to Heaven our highest duty was to love and serve our country and learn to support its laws." Surgeons, politicians, and even army officers, or so some women suggested, could not be placed above the suspicion that their true motivations were financial. But nursing women, because they made nothing or made so little, could hardly be thought of as money-grubbers. "You see," explained Hannah Ropes, a nurse at the Union Hotel Hospital in Washington, "I have given myself to this work, not as the strutting officers on the avenue have, for a salary, and laziness, but for love of country." Such thinking did little to advance some nurses' calls for better compensation, but it did allow women to transform their distance from the commercial arena into a badge of patriotic honor and untarnished loyalty.[8]

Sophronia Bucklin, a Dix-appointed nurse who was very much dependent on her wages, argued that women felt the "same patriotism" as the scores of men who responded to Lincoln's call for troops after the attack on Fort Sumter. So motivated, Bucklin set forth to "do and dare for those whose strong arms were to retrieve the honor of our insulted flag." Because they served men from across the Union, not just one particular state or region, nurses felt more strongly the war's national objectives than did many women on the home front. Jane Woolsey, who nursed in a Washington hospital, deplored the benevolent lady who visited her facility asking if "any Alaska soldiers" were there; Woolsey took comfort when the surgeon responded that they were all "United States soldiers" and should be treated "all alike as nearly as possible." Indeed, the nature of the nurses' sacrifice, far from home and close to the battles, convinced many that their contribution was akin to that of the soldiers. Sally Gibbons, a New Englander who traveled with her mother to the South to assist in military camps and hospitals there, paid tribute to a young female friend and nurse who had died while attending to a sick enlisted man. "Who can say," Gibbons remarked, "her life was not given to her country as truly as that of any one of the band of heroes who have fallen in battle?" For nurses, the analogy between soldiering and nursing served to underscore their patriotism and their commitment to something beyond home and family.[9]

The soldier analogy no doubt performed a psychological function as well as an ideological one. By becoming "soldiers," Yankee women crossed a formidable divide, from a relatively safe and secure world to one of unknown horrors and difficulties, from a world of feminine comforts to one of masculine endurance. When she made her decision to leave home, for example, Tribulation Periwinkle "turned military at once." Others made the transformation from domesticated ladies into tough wartime nurses more gradually. "No soldier," wrote Clara Barton at the end of the war, "has eaten harder 'tack' or slept on barer ground, or under more malarious damps than I have within these four years." Emily Parsons dismissed her parents' pleas that she leave nursing and return home, insisting that her contribution was just as important as that of her brother Chauncey, a soldier. "I am in the army just as Chauncey is," she explained, "and I must be held to work just as he is." Soon after she became a nurse with the Army of the Potomac, Cornelia Hancock began to adopt a similar way of thinking—or at least she found it a useful means for ex-plaining to her family the drastic changes she had experienced. "A soldier's life is very hardening," she observed, "you do not care where you are so you can eat and sleep." After two months of ser-vice, Hancock already felt like a war-weary veteran.[10]

As much as female nurses identified with the soldiers, many also described their specific role with metaphors that were more traditionally feminine. Nurses by necessity had to learn to iden-tify with a broad community of men who were not their own immediate relatives or acquaintances, nor even, in many cases, from their own social class. To more easily embrace such a di-verse population, they spoke of their obligation in familial terms. "If war was right," claimed a nurse with the Ninth New York Regiment, "it was right for women to go with brothers, and hus-bands, and sons." As she and others knew, women would be called on to care for men who were not their family members. Still, they could comfort themselves with the thought that they were caring for other women's relatives. "Oh, how I long to stay and go to work" for the soldiers, wrote Julia Freeman in her diary before she dedicated herself to hospital work. "Perhaps I might be the means of saving somebody's husband or brother." Alcott's Tribulation Periwinkle found that she might play the part of any female relation, that she was "the poor substitute for mother, wife, or sister" to the suffering soldier. This perspective allowed women to render the work—much of which involved close, inti-mate contact with unknown men—an acceptable feminine pur-suit. More important, it allowed women to envision a national community that was more like a broad, extended family than a socially stratified and ethnically divided society. Hannah Ropes thought of herself as a mother substitute for her soldier patients, and this allowed her to act on their behalf and to give herself a central role in serving the nation. "I am a mother," Ropes explained, "and I have only to remember that each of these sick ones [has] a mother somewhere, and for the time I act for them."[11]

Quite a few women, especially those over thirty, gravitated toward the kind of maternal role taken on by Ropes and, like her, saw their poor, suffering "sick ones" as their "boys." One of the most famous Civil War nurses, Mary Ann Bickerdyke, became known to nearly all around her as "Mother Bickerdyke." Mary Livermore recalled attending to sick and wounded men on a Mississippi River steamer and falling "into maternal relations with them, as women instinctively do when brought into juxtaposition with weakness." Women who played the part of mother saw themselves occupying a pivotal position in the national family, bringing comfort and restored health to a community of menfolk who struggled and sacrificed for the Union. "Your past life," Jane Swisshelm remarked to a suffering patient in one of her wards, "is sufficient certificate of your manhood; and now has come your time to be a baby, while I am mother."[12]

The descriptions of nursing, and the place of womanly influence in that endeavor, suggested that women not only identified with the broad national agenda but also gave themselves a central part in unifying the fractured national community. The softening and refining influences that nurses exerted—whether as "mothers" or simply as ladies of elevated character—could, in effect, smooth the rough edges on hard-bitten men and erase obvious manifestations of social class. When soldiers became their nurse-mother's "boys," they also became members of the same family and shared in the same moral values demonstrated by their female parent. Georganna Woolsey believed that the most effective nurses were the most refined. "It is astonishing, or rather it is not," she remarked, "to see how instinctively the 'common soldier' recognizes and respects the *lady* in his nurse." Julia Freeman agreed. "The experience of this day," she wrote of her initial foray in a Washington hospital, "teaches me that no one—especially a lady—who is in sympathy with our cause can visit these hospitals without doing good." Katharine Wormeley likewise found that ladylike qualities were essential to the smooth functioning of operations on her hospital transport boat: "It is not too much to say that delicacy and refinement and the fact of being a gentlewoman could never *tell* more than they do here." Such assertions were more than simple justifications offered by elite women for their place in military hospitals. They reflected the desire on the part of nurses to carve out a central place in the national struggle. In bringing a woman's touch to army life, nurses suggested, they also brought a leveling influence to the soldier population, making them all the recipients of refined womanly care.[13]

Clara Barton took great pride in her ability to forge a patriotic community of men out of a gang of scruffy, cantankerous workers. In one of her postwar lectures, Barton told the story of her ambulance drivers, "rough" men who "were not soldiers, but civilians, in Government employ . . . [who] had driven thro the whole peninsular campaign." It was likely that none, Barton speculated, "had ever passed an hour in what could be termed ladies' society in his life." On their first outing, Barton explained, the men expressed considerable reluctance about their jobs, and were especially loathe to come close to scenes of battle. Nonetheless they pushed on, eventually reaching a stopping point where Barton prepared them dinner. Before long, she recounted, her influence turned this group of rough and ornery toughs into a compassionate collective of patriots. They apologized for their poor behavior, while Barton, in turn, reminded them that "as men, it was their duty to go where their country had need of them." In the end, they stayed with her for six months, helped her care for the wounded, "and if possible grew kinder and gentler every day." These tough, reluctant patriots, thanks to Barton's influence, not only lost their lower-class "roughness" but also did their part admirably for the national cause.[14]

Projecting an air of refinement and respectability could transform even relatively weak and inexperienced women into significant figures of authority, and notions of feminine self-sacrifice and moral purity convinced many that Northern women nurses naturally had the best interests of soldiers, and the broader Union cause, at heart. In hospital settings the women often summoned that power of maternal authority to establish their own systems and methods of organization, or to challenge what they believed were inefficient or immoral practices in the Union medical facilities. Hannah Ropes, for one, became the embattled and crusading mother of the Union Hotel Hospital when she realized the iniquities being practiced on the patients. On discovering that a hospital steward had been imprisoning some of the patients, Ropes proceeded to bring this case before the hospital authorities, and eventually the government. "Certainly one would suppose," she wrote after her first attempt to convince the head surgeon of her allegations, "the opening up of any iniquity like this would be looked upon and hailed by all as the best possible good a motherly woman could do." When the surgeon failed to respond, Ropes took her case to the secretary of war, who arranged for the arrest of both the offending steward and the collaborating surgeon. Mary Ann Bickerdyke, it seems, created a similarly maternal, although perhaps less confrontational, atmosphere in her Memphis institution. In reviewing her own postwar experiences, Mary Livermore found that she never knew any of the surgeons or stewards, not even the surgeon in charge, at "Mother Bickerdyke's Hospital." "They were really overshadowed by the matron" she recalled. And Livermore herself, determined to seek aid and comfort for her "helpless boys" who wished to be discharged from the army, personally pleaded their cases before their commanding officer, General Ulysses S. Grant. The general agreed to Livermore's request, apparently willing to acknowledge her maternal expertise. Livermore was often told, she said, that her only hope of success "lay in the fact that I was a woman, and that 'women could do anything they desired with army officers.'"[15]

Here, in Livermore's startling phrase, rests an idea with considerable feminist appeal: that the wartime crisis had created a significantly empowered female nursing corps, or at least a body of women who, in highlighting their moral and maternal qualities, managed to pursue a path of heightened independence and authority. More than a few historians have pointed to this new level of self-assertion and have seen its repercussions after the war in the heightened political activism of the suffrage movement and the efforts of women to establish themselves in medicine. Many nurses no doubt gained a new and welcome sense of independence from the experience of asserting themselves and speaking up for their soldiers. "All who know me," explained Cornelia Hancock, "say it is easier to grant my request [for a soldier's furlough] than to undertake to deny me because I am so persevering." Yet such signs of assertiveness cannot be read in a vacuum but must be placed in the context of women nurses' new relationship with a whole array of military, government, and medical professionals. The evidence suggests that many—even women like Bickerdyke and Hannah Ropes—discovered not the power of their maternal authority but noteworthy limitations on their influence. Certainly many found ways to bend rules and maneuver around powerful men, but they also discovered just how dependent they were on male power and control in the first

Several thousand women served as nurses for the Union army, including these women stationed in Fredricksburg, Virginia, pictured with officers of the United States Sanitary Commission. Credit: Library of Congress, Prints and Photographs Division [LC-DIG-cwpb-01195]

place. Before she took her case to Secretary of War Stanton, for example, Hannah Ropes got a lesson on her lowly position in the hospital chain of command. She wrote to Surgeon General Hammond, detailing the charges against the offending steward, only to be told by Hammond that she would have to "prove the grave charges made against the steward" before he would do anything. Ropes was shocked to find how little credibility her own word carried. When the steward's misdeeds against patients continued, Ropes desperately sought the help of powerful male acquaintances to see that something was done. She first called on General Banks, and when that failed, she sought the help of a friend's husband. "I was ready to catch at any hand of the stronger sex who would help me over this unpleasant piece of duty," Ropes confided to her diary.[16]

Other nurses felt downtrodden by the power of the hospital hierarchy. A nursing friend of Jane Woolsey's explained that the surgeons in most army hospitals made it difficult for nurses to reform hospital dietary practices. "All that we women can do," Woolsey's acquaintance observed, "is to keep up a steady glare with the 'eye of justice' and that, I assure you, we do." Clara Barton, too, although certain that improved victuals would be enormously beneficial to the patients, believed she could effect little change in the hospital kitchens. She would be stymied, she said, by the established line of command. "First," she noted in her diary, "it is not my province, I should be out of place there, next Miss Dix is supreme, and her appointed nurse is Matron, next the surgeons will not brook any interference, and will, in my opinion resent and resist the smallest effort to break over their own arrangements." Georganna Woolsey encountered obstinate surgeons who reprimanded nurses for bestowing small kindnesses on the soldiers. Such men, Woolsey concluded, are "a fixed fact" in the hospital and, rather than challenge them directly, nurses had to learn to accommodate them in "the right way."[17]

If some nurses, like Barton, felt discouraged by their inability to confront the hospital and military hierarchy, others were more than willing to acknowledge their relatively weak position in a world they believed was rightly dominated by male surgeons and military officers. Georganna Woolsey, in fact, was not so sure that the power of the hospital surgeon was a bad thing. Most of the time surgeons, and other male officials, Woolsey implied, were to be respected for their sound scientific judgments, their professionalism, and their no-nonsense organizational skills, especially in controlling ladies who might feel overly benevolent. Even Jane Swisshelm, not one to shy away from assertiveness, freely acknowledged the wisdom of her supervising surgeon, Dr. Baxter, regarding his decision to limit the presence of nurses in his establishment. "From the manner in which he cares for his patients," Swisshelm observed during her brief stint as a nurse in Washington, "and the reasons he gives for his decision, I have no disposition to quarrel with it." Katharine Wormeley likewise tipped her hat to her male superiors. As a Sanitary Commission nurse stationed on a hospital transport boat during the spring 1862 campaign on the Virginia Peninsula, Wormeley often stood in awe of the capabilities of the military, hospital, and USSC officials with whom she worked. She was especially impressed with the power of Sanitary Commission men like Frederick Olmsted and Frederick Knapp. "We women," she observed, "are but a drop in the bucket of relief, every one on board, except us, being worked to his very utmost." Wormeley, in fact, worked pretty hard preparing the boat to receive patients and getting the wounded men settled, but she gave the lion's share of the credit to the men. She resigned herself to the fact that her work as a nurse would pale in comparison to the work of the male commissioners. "As for us women," she remarked, "all we could do was to give drink, stimulants, and food to the poor fellows." Regarding the men, she concluded, "The lives saved are theirs."[18]

Cornelia Hancock apparently absorbed a similar lesson about the power of male officialdom. A young New Jersey woman deemed too young for Dix's brigade, Hancock became a nurse in the summer of 1863 by accompanying her brother-in-law, a

Philadelphia doctor who served with the Army of the Potomac. Thrust into the horrific aftermath of the Battle of Gettysburg, Hancock received her baptism by fire. "I feel assured," she wrote her sister, "I shall never feel horrified at anything that may happen to me hereafter." Like other young women, she could be both sister to her patients and a fellow soldier, although Hancock seemed most comfortable in the latter position, as one who served her government and her country. "I have torn almost all my clothes off of me," Hancock wrote soon after her arrival, "and Uncle Sam has given me a new suit." Thus inducted into government service, she often wrote of her commitment to "Uncle Sam," even when she decided to step back from the work temporarily. When the Gettysburg hospitals became overrun with nurses she determined that "the most patriotic one was she who took her board off of Uncle Sam until there was greater need of services." Yet, even after her exit Hancock continued to think of herself as one of the army's enlistees.[19]

Cornelia Hancock learned to use her place as a woman in the army as a springboard for assertiveness. Looked on by many as "the shiftiest woman on the ground," she said, she figured out how to get her Gettysburg men some steak during their arduous recuperation. And in the fall of 1864 she was the one chosen to appeal to General Grant for a furlough for a soldier whose wife had recently died. "No military man could go," she explained, "because it was informal and would not be granted." The surgeons, though, "all had faith" in Hancock's abilities, and "in two hours time a furlough was in the soldier's hands for 20 days." Hancock exulted in her accomplishment. "My fame," she wrote to her mother, "has spread the length and breadth of this camp. Such a miracle accomplished in so short a time."[20]

Although it was precisely Hancock's separation from the established formalities of the military world that made the interview with Grant even possible, she continued to see herself as a soldier. She reminded her family that she had chosen a "soldier-ing" life, that she knew the same hardships and triumphs as those who fought with guns and sabres, though her weapons were washcloths and quinine. Upon learning in March 1864 that a package had arrived for her from the provost marshal's office, Hancock felt momentarily alarmed, thinking she had done some-thing to distress the authorities. She concluded, though, that she should have no fear, because "no woman has served the Army of the Potomac with any more self denial or faithfulness than I have." She had become a good soldier who performed her duty and followed her orders. Indeed, the military metaphor con-ferred on Hancock a second-class status in a hierarchical world. This meant obeying not only "Uncle Sam" but hospital officials as well, and surgeons frequently praised her services "very highly." To Hancock's thinking, not enough women accepted this need to bow to authority, and they became meddlesome and irritat-ing. And Hancock had little patience for female authority figures in army medical facilities, believing that the women lacked the knowledge and experience of men. "Mrs. Swisshelm," she wrote to her sister in the summer of 1864, "nor no other person ought to have the direction of nurses. Not one woman in ten thousand is fit to have one might of authority." The real power, Hancock believed, must emanate from men.[21]

Mother Bickerdyke, whose presence weighed so heavily in the Memphis hospital where she toiled, also acknowledged the need for obedience and subservience. At least this was the lesson that Mary Livermore drew from observing Bickerdyke's work. Bickerdyke had her share of clashes with hospital authorities, in-cluding one confrontation with a surgeon in Cairo, Illinois, whom she discovered was stealing supplies meant for wounded men. When the surgeon ordered her to remove herself from his hospital, Bickerdyke refused. But while she could become assertive in the face of impropriety, she also understood her position as a subordinate in a strictly ordered chain of command. A volunteer surgeon who worked with Bickerdyke was so impressed with the hospital matron's deferential style he was convinced she had received an official military appointment. "We all had an impression," he recalled, "that she held a commission from the Secretary of War, or at least from the Governor of Illinois. To every surgeon who was superior, she held herself subordinate, and was as good at obeying as at commanding." Mary Ann Bickerdyke epitomized the lesson that war imparted to the ranks of female nurses: the virtue of proper obedience.[22]

Judging by the way medical regulations evolved over the course of the war, obedience on the part of nurses came to be a very highly regarded trait. Even at the outset of the war, the Woman's Central Relief Association placed a premium on subordination for those interested in military hospital work. "The nurses," the WCRA explained in response to an inquiry from the Michigan Soldiers' Aid Society, "must of course be amenable to military discipline and subject to the surgeons in charge." Not all nurses proved themselves so amenable. Many surgeons found Protestant women particularly resistant to their authority and so came to prefer Catholic nuns, 600 of whom served as nurses during the course of the war, precisely because they wanted a more compliant hospital staff. Mary Livermore, soon after the Battle of Shiloh, "found everywhere . . . the greatest prejudice against Protestant women nurses," as "medical directors, surgeons, and even wardmasters" urged "that only the 'Sisters' of the Catholic Church" receive appointments. When she asked why this was so, Livermore was told that the nuns were properly subordinate: they "never see anything they ought not to see, nor hear anything they ought not to hear, and they never write for the papers."

Catholic nuns, so many doctors believed, showed a greater willingness than Protestant women to accept male authority.[23]

Perhaps the main hindrance to efficient nursing, from the physicians' perspective, came from Dorothea Dix. Many doctors disliked the control Dix exercised over her nursing corps and the kind of nurse—usually older and less easily intimidated—that Dix appointed. Increasingly, army surgeons wished to make their own decisions about which nurses were, or were not, acceptable in military hospitals. In the middle of the war, with support from the U.S. Sanitary Commission, army physicians banded together to promote their own candidate for U.S. surgeon general, one who would be more sympathetic to their concerns and less tolerant of Dix's authority over nurses. The new surgeon general, William Hammond, issued directives in 1863 that allowed his office to bypass Dix in appointing and dismissing nurses. Cornelia Hancock, for one, fully understood the import of Hammond's order. The surgeon general, Hancock explained, "both could and would appoint ladies at the request of a surgeon *irrespective of age, size or looks*, merely at the *request* of a Surgeon-in-Charge. He said that was particularly inserted to allow surgeons to choose their *own* nurses, as many objected to Miss Dix's." One imagines that Hancock herself was precisely the type of nurse the surgeons preferred: young, cheerful, and ultimately deferential to all hospital authorities.[24]

Toward the end of the war, "submission" and "obedience" seemed to be the official watchwords for nursing. A Sanitary Commission bulletin in March 1864 conveyed to prospective applicants the USSC's view on the qualities that made ideal nurses. Successful recruits, they explained, "have owed their usefulness to their strict obedience and conformity to army regulations, and only those docile enough and wise enough to respect the superior knowledge and authority of the surgeons have been for any considerable time able to keep their places, or to make themselves generally serviceable." Jane Woolsey found these qualities codified by her hospital in the spring of 1864, when officials there issued new regulations regarding the deportment of female nurses. One order, Woolsey noted, prohibited them from having "deliberations, discussions, and remarks having the object of expressing comparative praise or censure of the medical officers of this Hospital." Fully aware that most "deliberations" had tended toward censure, Woolsey found the inclusion of the word "praise" decidedly ironic.[25]

But if some nurses, like Woolsey, bristled at the iron grip of male officialdom, others willingly accepted the need for obedience and subordination. Quite a few came to appreciate the importance of submission in their efforts to get lower-level hospital employees, especially black workers, to be properly deferential and obedient. "The hardest piece of work I have done yet," Katharine Wormeley observed two weeks into her stint on the hospital transport boat, "was to keep two colored ladies steady to the work of the lower deck." Cornelia Hancock mentioned having trouble with an apparently difficult black woman, although the woman may not have done much more than assert her own opinion. "The only thorn in my flesh," Hancock wrote from a facility for former slaves in Washington, "is the colored matron, who was here before me. She is acting up some but I am in hopes of getting things straightened out with her."[26]

Hancock had a relatively unusual experience in encountering a black woman in a position of authority. In most Union hospitals, lines of privilege were strictly drawn on the basis of race and gender, with black women generally occupying the lowest ranks in the medical establishment. Except when they worked in all-black hospitals, or for all-black regiments, black women were almost always classified as cooks and laundresses, not as nurses, and they were paid two to six dollars per month less than white nurses were paid. When white women became nurses, they entered a fiercely hierarchical environment that made them subordinate to white men; black women were subordinate to everyone who was white. White nurses learned to work within the parameters of the hospital hierarchy not only by submitting to the authority of white male officials but also by exercising their own authority over black women. Indeed, their role in overseeing black hospital workers may have offered white middle-class nurses a means by which they could legitimize their own place in the chain of command. When black laundresses defied her authority, Mary Phinney von Olnhausen struck one of the women and later remarked, "If I'd been big enough and strong enough I would have slapped them all." Other nurses reproduced slave-like relations even more explicitly. "We have one very nice nigger gal that I shall try and send home to you if possible," Amy Bradley wrote to her sister from Virginia. "Do you want her?" Such language of ownership reflected the nurses' ability to assert their own degree of power in a world that demanded their strict obedience to white male authority.[27]

What these new relationships meant for the black women involved is hard to gauge. Many were ex-slaves who had fled to the Union side seeking a haven from slavery and the means to begin a new life outside of bondage. The experience instilled in some a sense of gratitude and obligation to Union soldiers. But the fact that black women hospital workers continued to be victims of various forms of abuse, and often failed to receive the promised pay, no doubt made many feel marginalized by the federal government. "I gave my services willingly for four years and three months," recalled former slave and wartime medical worker Susie King Taylor, "without receiving a dollar." Although she rejoiced at receiving freedom, Taylor's experience encouraged her to view the government's relationship with black men and women, especially after the war, with a skeptical eye.[28]

It does not seem likely that African American women happily accepted the domineering authority, or sense of entitlement, that was displayed by white nurses. Interestingly, the nurses' language of control rarely extended to black soldiers. For the most part, white nurses expressed respect and admiration for African American fighting men. Clara Barton, for example, could comment on her attempts to teach "my Contraband to wash" and at the same time praise the "negroes" who "fought well and did not lose a man." Such seemingly conflicting views may have reflected the ambivalent racial views of the white nurses, but they also revealed their reverence for the soldiery, both white and black. For most Yankee nurses, the soldiers were the objects of their devotion, the ones for whom they toiled and sacrificed and, occasionally, even bent rules. While many women learned to adopt a maternal approach to their suffering patients, the experience of treating hundreds of men wounded in horrific battles also instilled in the nurses a sense of reverence and awe for the Union troops. "If you could see the sight," Bell Robison remarked to her family in describing the thousands of wounded men who poured into the hospital after one battle, "you couldn't avoid shedding tears and to hear them say when their wounds are being dressed, 'never mind, I'm a soldier.' Sure enough they are soldiers. Oh the bravery, it is the success makes them feel so."[29]

Ultimately, the nurses knew, it was the soldiers who did the real and dangerous work of saving the nation. The women played their part, but they could do no more than improve the health and well-being of the men who would then go back and fight again. When Tribulation Periwinkle, in Alcott's *Hospital Sketches,* encountered her first batch of wounded soldiers, she was reminded of just how brave the boys were: "Cowards could hardly have been so riddled with shot and shell, so torn and shattered, nor have borne suffering for which we have no name." In the face of such manly suffering, Alcott implied, no woman could really play the part of mother, a figure of authority who demanded some level of obedience from her "boys"; women could do no more than "cherish each [soldier] like a brother." Jane Swisshelm was similarly overcome by the sight of the wounded men. "I knelt reverently by the mangled limbs of these heroes," she explained in June 1863, "and thank God and man for the privilege of washing them." Cornelia Hancock had to rethink her own relationship to the soldiery when she realized the depth of their sacrifice and suffering. Even though she frequently referred to herself as a soldier, she ultimately acknowledged how inadequate the analogy was. In the end, she thought the real soldiers should be judged as the true heroes. "God bless them, I say, when I see a soldier faithfully plodding through the dust protecting me," she observed. "I feel more insignificant than words can express."[30]

In a world that put a premium on male military might, Hancock felt as if she had lost her voice. She, like so many other nurses, came to revere the soldiers and military officials. She could not return to her old situation of domestic comfort and so found herself embracing a new way of thinking about the world. She had to become disciplined and tough like the soldiers, even if she did not do the same work they did. She became increasingly contemptuous of philanthropic women, whom she found useless and inconsequential to the all-important military agenda. The war, Hancock believed, would be settled by brave men and daring generals. Talk of politics and world affairs now seemed to mean little. Her experience as a nurse did not excite an interest in politics or even in the broader coverage of the war but made her dismissive of any news that did not have a direct connection to her immediate circumstances. Time after time Cornelia Hancock told her family members that she had completely lost interest in following the war news. "I look at it in this way," she explained, "that I am doing all a woman can do to help the war along, and therefore, I feel no responsibility." Katharine Wormeley expressed these same sentiments on numerous occasions. She stopped following the war news and could provide her family, she said, with "little public information." Her mind was completely focused on the circumstances of her own hospital steamer. Significantly, when she did make a rare political comment, she revealed how much weight sh⁻ gave to military officials, even a man like McClellan, for whom she subsequently had little sympathy. "When will the nation learn," she insisted, "that it is in the hands of its greatest man, and wait calmly for his results, only taking care in the mean time to strengthen his hands?" Everyone, Wormeley believed, must learn to put their trust in the hands of the nation's military leaders.[31]

Casting their lot with the soldiery, nurses came to discount their own political observations. If they likened themselves to soldiers, they argued, they must learn to accept others' pronouncements and not formulate their own opinions. And if they saw the soldiers' work as the foremost work of the war, nonmilitary activities, especially those carried out by women, became strikingly insignificant. Clara Barton came to believe her job had very little to do with politics. "I am a U.S. soldier you know and therefore not supposed to be susceptable to *fear*," she explained to one solicitor who had asked for her support in promoting

Katharine Wormeley, shown here in her nurse's garb, served as a U.S. Sanitary Commission nurse aboard a hospital transport ship during the 1862 Virginia Peninsula campaign. Credit: Photo Archives, U.S. Army Military History Institute

peace efforts, "and, as I am merely a soldier, and not a statesman, I shall make no attempt at discussing *political* points with you." The whole subject of politics, she remarked, was one of which "I am supposed to be profoundly ignorant." Perhaps the most striking comment along these lines came from a nurse who wrote of her experience in treating wounded men near Pittsburg Landing in April 1862. "The log-cabin," she explained, "was speedily filled with bleeding, suffering humanity, and Mrs. Turner and myself soon realized, though not for the first time, that women have a more serious mission than haranguing public assemblies." Women had to get their priorities straight: their place was not on a political podium, documenting social injustice, but in the army medical corps where they had the "right" to serve the wounded and suffering men of the battlefield.[32]

In the postwar years, some women who had served as Union nurses did take to "haranguing public assemblies" on behalf of women's political rights. Mary Livermore and Jane Swisshelm, for example, both spoke on behalf of female suffrage in their postbellum careers, and Clara Barton, too, eventually expressed support for giving women the right to vote. But both Livermore and Swisshelm had planted themselves on the path to political activism before the Civil War, and Barton's message, immediately after the war, was an appeal to the men who had fought the good fight, "the strength of the land" as she called them, to use their votes wisely in the service of widows and orphans. Wartime nursing did not necessarily propel women into suffrage politics, although the experience did encourage some limited forms of activism. Some championed better professional training for nurses in the postwar years; others went on to advocate municipal and public health reforms. Many of these women no doubt were inspired by the sense of camaraderie they felt with other nurses in working for reforms that would enhance the status of women in the medical profession. But these women showed less interest in women's politics than in carving out a small niche in the growing bureaucracy of reform. In fact, more nurses probably participated in Civil War veterans' societies and gatherings, where they could rejuvenate memories of their service on behalf of Union soldiers and rekindle their bonds with one another, than in other postwar social or political organizations. Certainly for many younger nurses—the ones who became mature women in the Gilded Age—the wartime experience stressed respect for male authority and the strength and fortitude of soldiering men. Union nurses learned significant lessons in civic engagement and patriotic expression, but those lessons placed considerably less emphasis on expressing independent opinions than on respecting the established hierarchy and following the orders of male superiors.

Chapter Seven

Wartime Emancipation

❧ ❧ ❧

One month after the Confederate assault on Fort Sumter, there were already tentative signs that the Civil War would bring an end to the system of human bondage that had been the foundation of Southern society for nearly two hundred years. In May 1861, three slaves made it to the Union outpost at Fort Monroe in tidewater Virginia, having run away from a Confederate fortification where they had been forced to labor. The slaves hoped for freedom; the slaves' owner, a Confederate colonel in angry pursuit, hoped for their speedy return. The Union commander at Fort Monroe, a former Democrat and no supporter of abolition, faced a dilemma. Although no friend of the slaves, General Benjamin Butler found the Confederate slaveholder's demand somewhat illogical in the context of the war. Claiming that the fugitive slave law did not apply when slave owners had seceded from the Union, Butler refused to return the runaways and, in language that would be repeated throughout the land, identified the escapees as "contraband" of war. A few months later, nearly a thousand "contrabands" had found their way to Benjamin Butler's "Freedom Fort." These black men and women represented the opening wedge of the thrust toward emancipation in the Civil War, foreshadowing the transformation of the sectional conflict from a struggle to keep the Union whole into a war that would sound the death knell for Southern slavery. That transformation would be felt most profoundly, of course, by the men and women who would move from bondage to freedom within a re-

markably short period of time. But the transformation would res-
onate throughout the nation, among men and women, white and
black, North and South, all of whom would confront the implications of its expansion of freedom and citizenship.

Among those viewing the arrival of "contraband" slaves at
Fort Monroe was Laura Hildreth, Benjamin Butler's sister-in-
law. Like many white Northerners, Hildreth saw not the "new
birth of freedom" but the emergence of a social problem. "Negroes," she wrote to her sister Harriet Heard in June of 1861,
"come in every day from outside, and one day as many as forty
came into the backyard; of all ages, from babies up to old men
and women. It was a ludicrous and at the same time a sad sight to
see the poor creatures, homeless, not knowing when or where
they were to get their next meal." Over time, as the emancipation
process gathered steam, growing numbers of Northern women
echoed Hildreth's concerns about the problem of black freedom,
especially the problem of how men and women once so dependent on others would now become self-sufficient. Over time,
they came to imagine solutions in terms of new relations of dependency and subservience. And as the ex-slaves were drawn
into a new relationship with the federal government, and questions were raised regarding African Americans' responsibilities to
that government, Northern women had occasion, once again, to
reflect on issues of loyalty, obedience, and civic obligation.[1]

In June 1861, when General Butler was presiding over a contraband fort, emancipation was hardly a pressing concern for
most Northern women. With the conflict barely under way,
Northern white women spent little, if any, time imagining slave
emancipation at all. Even after Butler's contraband policy took
effect, most women in the North, like their male counterparts,
continued to believe the war should be fought to preserve the
Union, and that the question of abolition was merely inciden-

tal to that larger struggle. Before long, however, the issue of emancipation would occupy a central position in the Union agenda, and the problem would compel Northern women from all walks of life—abolitionist and nonabolitionist, black and white—to confront the question of black freedom. As the war increasingly brought Union forces into contact with former slaves, and Union soldiers participated in the destruction of slavery, Northern women found themselves contemplating the significance of emancipation.

Most did not have Laura Hildreth's firsthand perspective and so considered the question from the vantage point of the home front, reacting to news of their loved ones' encounters with slaves and former slaves. Some, Northern black women especially, played prominent parts in organizing relief efforts on behalf of freedmen and women. A few Yankee ladies, black and white, viewed emancipation from even closer quarters, as nurses who encountered African Americans in hospitals and freedmen's camps, or as teachers who traveled to the South to instruct this newly liberated band of students. And while Northern black women frequently mingled sympathy with pride in their views of the freedpeople, Northern white women more often voiced the uncertain sentiments conveyed by General Butler's sister-in-law in the early months of the conflict. Most found it difficult to fully imagine and reckon with the possibility of a completely free and independent population of former slaves. Many, in fact, took away from the emancipation experience yet another lesson in civic subordination, a lesson that had implications for themselves as well as for the former slaves.

Even before the war began, a small band of women had recognized the centrality of slavery in the increasingly volatile sectional struggle. Abolitionist women had spent years criticizing the Southern system of bondage, urging the federal government, even at the risk of losing the Southern states altogether, to take steps to curtail the peculiar institution. During the 1840s and 1850s, with most national politicians coddling their slave-owning constituents, there was little hope that government action would spawn abolition. But when the first committed antislavery president took office in 1860, many sensed a crisis was at hand. In Manhattan, Kansas, in January 1861, Maria Patec had an premonition of strife and bloodshed, rooted in her abolitionist sensibility. Now that Lincoln had been elected and secession was under way, Patec believed a showdown was imminent, and that the struggle to defeat Southern bondage would occupy center stage. "The time has come I think," she wrote to a New England cousin just before the Republican president's inauguration, "when the battle of Armageddon is to be fought, the day of preparation is at hand, the irrepressible conflict has begun as in the days of the Israelites in Egypt." Viewing the crisis from the blood-soaked fields of Kansas, where pro- and antislavery combatants had already fought over the question of abolition, Patec saw biblical precedents for the deeply moral conflict looming on the horizon. "God," she explained in January 1861, "will no sooner look [favorably] upon bondage in America than he did in Egypt."[2]

Like other abolitionists, Patec welcomed a final judgment on the sins of slavery, even if it came as the result of war and tumultuous destruction. By the spring of 1861, other antislavery women, including those who had favored disunionism and the peaceful departure of slave-owning Confederates, promoted warfare as the best possible means of expurgating slavery from the nation. As it began to appear that the Lincoln administration would have to pursue a more determined course against the South, female abolitionists found themselves not only cheering on the war but lauding the federal government as well. To many, this was an unfamiliar stance to take. Lillie Chace, for example, was surprised to find herself supporting the "stars and stripes." "One year ago," she admitted in June 1861, "I could not have been made to believe that I should do even that, or in the slightest degree render aid to our government, but—times have changed." Swept up in the patriotic enthusiasm, Mary Livermore underwent a similar conversion. "Never before," she confessed, "had the national flag signified anything to me." Now, though, she saw it as the "representative of government" and "nationality" that had been insulted by the South, "and all in the interest of human slavery." The politics of war forced abolitionist women to express their politics, and their patriotism, in new and unanticipated ways.[3]

Initial enthusiasms, however, quickly gave way to censures, and many abolitionist women found themselves honing their critiques of Republican policy. The Lincoln administration's hesitancy about emancipation involved abolitionist women, especially in the first two years of the war, in an occasionally heated political dialogue with the federal government. Antislavery women assumed the right to criticize government policy, and further complicated their patriotism by linking loyalty with abolitionism. Thus when Lincoln removed General John Fremont from command in Missouri in the fall of 1861, largely in anger over Fremont's emancipation edict, Northern abolitionist women jumped into the debate. "Perhaps it is all right, that he should be removed, just on the eve of battle, too," Fanny Pierce wrote with considerable skepticism to her soldier brother, "but it don't seem so to me, and it makes me feel sad." Other women dispatched their complaints directly to the commander in chief. "Havent we sent our Fathers; our Brothers; our *dear Husbands* to support you?" Mrs. L. C. Howard asked Lincoln. Women had made their sacrifice, but what support was Lincoln giving them, she asked, and "with what kind of courage do you suppose [the men] will obey your future orders to their Generals?" In other words, how could women remain loyal supporters of the war effort if Lincoln weakened the war's moral foundation? For Mrs. E. A. Spaulding in Connecticut, Lincoln's posture toward Fremont was the final push she needed to go from silent observer to politically engaged woman. "When it becomes necessary for a female," she wrote to Lincoln in September 1861, "a weak insignificant female in view of the times to lift up her voice in defence of right, it most conclusively proves that there is an existing wrong."[4]

Even after the Lincoln administration moved more decisively in an antislavery direction, some abolitionist women cast themselves as political watchdogs and sought to apply pressure in various ways to keep the government on its emancipation course. Before ultimately endorsing Abraham Lincoln for reelection in 1864, Anna Dickinson frequently made caustic public remarks about the president's reluctance to confront the sins of slavery. The organizers of the Woman's National Loyal League likewise maintained their right to support the government when it advanced the cause of racial justice, and withhold their support when it did not. Without the certainty of fighting for "justice and humanity," explained league organizer Ernestine Rose, "I am not unconditionally loyal to the Administration." Indeed, Rose explained, there was no need for women to maintain unconditional loyalty to the government, "for the law has never yet recognized us." Antislavery principles compelled abolitionists like Rose to complicate the picture of steadfast female patriotism by giving their patriotic sentiments a political orientation.[5]

Still, among many abolitionist and even nonabolitionist women, the emancipation agenda pursued by the Lincoln administration in the second half of the war generated a more enthusiastic embracing of the Union cause. That agenda gathered steam toward the end of 1861 with Congress's approval of the first Confiscation Act, which declared that property used "in aid of the rebellion," including slave property, could be confiscated by the Union army. A second Confiscation Act, passed in July 1862, aimed to bring freedom to the slaves of all rebel slave owners. Finally, the Emancipation Proclamation, issued in September 1862, declared that all slaves residing in states that, as of January 1, 1863, remained in rebellion were "then, thenceforward, and forever free." Although the proclamation freed only slaves in the still-embattled Confederacy, it opened the door for increasing numbers of African Americans to seek and eventually realize freedom as the Union army moved South.

This steady antislavery course cheered abolitionist women. Even more, the government's antislavery agenda encouraged those with male relatives in the army to support the "higher claims" of the war effort over the immediate demands of home and family. "I am willing to make sacrifices for our beloved country," Rhoda Southworth explained to her soldier son one week after Lincoln issued the preliminary Emancipation Proclamation, "and now since we are taking steps in the right direction I feel more anxious to do what I can to advance the cause of freedom." Sophia Buchanan, whose husband, John Claude, served with a Michigan regiment, balanced her remorse over her husband's absence with her concern for the country and her desire to see the "accursed sin of slavery" destroyed. The South's proslavery path incited Buchanan's wrath, and she felt her determination for war renewed on January 1, 1863, the day the Emancipation Proclamation took effect. Elizabeth Boynton felt justified in sacrificing her fiancé for the higher objective of emancipation after reading a powerful antislavery novel in March 1864. As she "closed the book," she said, and "thought of all the evils attendant upon slavery I thanked God that I had been called on to give him who is dearer to me than all else, to a war that will eventually produce its overthrow." Such women felt less torment over the competing claims of home and country as the "country" grew increasingly entwined with the ultimate moral and political objective of emancipation.[6]

The emancipation agenda could even inspire those who had not previously embraced abolitionist principles. Eliza Otis felt reconciled to her husband's continued military work in light of the final goals of the conflict. "While his Country needed him," she observed in April 1863, "in this great strife for Freedom, and National existence I would not say one word to keep him from the field." Other women likewise felt energized as the Union's antislavery program took shape, although some seemed reluctant to pass judgment on an issue that smacked of political controversy. Referring to the Emancipation Proclamation's decree freeing the slaves in rebel states as of January 1, 1863, Mattie Blanchard wondered what her husband thought the results would be. "Please write and tell me," she wrote. "I am thinking there will be a great change in what way I am not able to say but I hope for the better." In Iowa, Catharine Peirce hesitated to express her opinion on a matter that had such complicated consequences, although in the end she agreed that emancipation represented a step forward. "Father Abraham is all right on the Nigger as well as all other national affairs," she wrote in a December 1863 letter to her husband, in reference to Lincoln's pronouncements on wartime reconstruction. But, like Blanchard, she worried that she had waded into a controversial quagmire and added this qualifier: "if I be aloud to have an opinion on the subject which I suppose I can take this far from the seat of government and privately to thee if it will not amount to much to any one."[7]

Confusion and controversy abounded in the minds of Mattie

Blanchard and Catharine Peirce, no doubt because abolition had ceased to be an abstract consideration and was becoming a social and political reality. Emancipation raised countless questions for Northern women, most of whom had little sympathy for the abolitionists' goals and considerable uncertainty about the status of the newly freed. Distraught over the continued bloodshed of the war, Rebecca Lincoln pondered the decision to enlist freedmen in the army. "What think you," she asked her husband, "of the slaves as to their serving? Are there intelligent ones enough to do anything?" Ann Cotton hoped her husband's proximity to the former slaves might give her insight into the course freedom might take. "Do you see many contrabands?" she asked Josiah, who was serving as a surgeon with an Ohio regiment. "I do not like to see their black ugly faces—& wish they might all be kept away from our free states." Clara Wood, too, expressed concern about the newly freed men and women, especially their ability to care and provide for themselves. "I should think it would be amusing to see those Darkies," Wood wrote to her husband, "you say they have got a lot of Babies. I do hope they will not *increase* any faster now the *Government provides* for them then they did when they lived with there *masters.*" Here, as voiced by these three women, were some of the central worries that Northern women, including abolitionists, would have in the aftermath of emancipation: Were the freedpeople capable of self-support and independence? Who would take ultimate responsibility for the former slaves? As Clara Wood's comment implied, Northern white women were reluctant to imagine the former slaves as fully independent beings and assumed that their liberation did not completely release them from the shackles of dependency. And while most urged a program that would place the freedmen and women on a path to economic self-sufficiency, Yankee women nonetheless seemed hesitant to fully embrace the consequences

of that self-support. Most believed that obedience and subordination must remain part of the ex-slaves' identity, perhaps because without that submissiveness black men and women might
stray from restraint and discipline toward anarchy. More than
anything, Northern women hoped the freedpeople would retain
a sense of allegiance and obligation, if no longer directed toward
plantation masters then perhaps toward some other higher authority.[8]

Sometimes Northern women imagined themselves as the new
recipients of that allegiance. "I brought a capital contraband that
I have had since last May," explained one Northern nurse stationed at Fort Monroe, "I am going to carry her home when
I go." While nursing in North Carolina, Mary Phinney von
Olnhausen confessed to a relative, "I am sometimes tempted to
send you a nigger." Home-front women, too, frequently used the
language of possession in discussing the former slaves. Anticipating her husband's final return from the postwar South, Libby
Bowler expressed her desire for a souvenir from her husband's
wartime experience. "When you come home," she wrote in April
1865, "try to get a nice little negrow boy to bring with you." Na-
poleon Bartlett's mother expressed a similar desire. "I would like
to get a good black girl to work for me," Mrs. Bartlett wrote to
her son, "one that understood cooking & washing & ironing.
There must be some good girls down there; send one along by
some of the boys." Anxious to find occupations for former slaves,
the Pennsylvania Abolition Society in fact solicited requests from
Northern white women who seemed ready to play the part of the
Southern mistress. "I would like to have a coulored Girl," wrote
one woman, "from 12 to 14 years of age of rather dark coulor of
sprightly appearance, one that would be well calculated for general housework in the country." Another asked for a "Black boy
. . . who can milk," specifying that she did not "want a yellow boy,

but as black as he can be." Apparently some Northern white women believed that the most direct solution to the problem of black emancipation would be to transfer the ex-slaves' dependency from their former plantation masters and mistresses to themselves.[9]

Still, much as Northern white women indulged in this fantasy of black ownership, most recognized that the process of helping former slaves make the transition from bondage to freedom would require more complicated responses. More than a few Northern women understood that emancipation had, to a great extent, generated a humanitarian crisis that required an outpouring of charity and assistance. As former slaves crossed Union lines, Northerners learned of their suffering, especially their need for food and clothing. In many Northern cities, black women organized relief societies, such as the Chicago Colored Ladies' Freedmen's Aid Society and the Contraband Relief Association in Washington. Elizabeth Keckley, a former slave who worked in the Lincoln White House, helped to organize a branch society of the Contraband Relief Association in Boston. The Boston group managed to send "eighty large boxes of goods, contributed exclusively by the colored people of Boston." A number of Northern black women—including ex-slaves like Keckley, Harriet Jacobs, and Sojourner Truth—also worked directly in refugee camps and "freedmen's villages," providing care and relief to recently escaped slaves who had made their way to the Union side.[10]

White women, especially those associated with antislavery work, also came to the aid of the former slaves, raising funds and preparing packages to send to the contraband communities. Some women who had initially focused on soldiers' aid efforts came to believe, as the conflict progressed, that their work should encompass all—soldiers and freedpeople—who experi-

enced wartime suffering. In April 1865 Mrs. Bardwell in Walpole, Vermont, made the change from sewing for soldiers to
sewing for freedpeople, with apparently little difficulty, perhaps
because she viewed the new work as an extension of missionary activities that she had previously supported. Others, even if
they were not directly engaged in freedmen's relief work, supported the cause and undertook joint activities. In 1862 Elizabeth Dwight Cabot found her mind "dreadfully tacked between
the San. Com. & the Negroes as they both seem to need every
cent we can raise." The Worcester Soldiers' Relief Society, in July
1863, unanimously agreed to hold a joint "County fair and Tea
Party" with the local freedmen's aid group. As black men filled
the ranks of the Union army, moreover, it became difficult to
distinguish the cause of the soldier from the cause of the freedman. In February 1864 Boston industrialist Edward Atkinson appealed to Abigail May, leader of the New England Sanitary Commission, to mobilize sanitary workers to provide supplies for a
smallpox hospital for freed slaves in Newbern, North Carolina,
arguing that it was only fitting for the commission to help supply the "wants of the wives, children and relatives of United
States soldiers." The black man, Atkinson argued, demanded relief workers' attention, if not as a freed slave then as an enlisted
man.[11]

Yet most Northern whites, especially those on the home front,
saw black Southerners first and foremost as contraband and only
secondarily as Union soldiers and their families. In this respect,
freedmen's relief work did not readily engage the sympathies of
all reform-minded Northern white women, and clearly spoke to a
smaller constituency than that focused on aiding the soldiers. After receiving Atkinson's plea, Abby May consulted with J. Foster
Jenkins, the USSC's general secretary, who indicated how the
commission would define and prioritize its work. Although he

encouraged May to give her assistance to Atkinson for "this req-
uisition," Jenkins said he believed the commission would not
be "justified in assuming general care of civil hospitals for the
contrabands." Soon after the war ended, Ellen Collins, a prominent leader in the soldiers' aid work, encouraged women to turn
their attention toward the former slaves. Yet she acknowledged
that many might be unwilling to shift their focus, as "this new object has not the same hold upon the popular sympathies" as the
work on behalf of the "poor soldier." Certainly many women
found that aiding the soldiers carried patriotic connotations that
freedmen's aid did not. Moreover, soldiers' relief work was a focused task that had relatively immediate consequences: a victory
for the Union in the presumably not-too-distant future. Aiding
former slaves, in contrast, was harder to quantify and evaluate in
terms of direct results. How much aid, many wondered, was
needed?[12]

Emeline Ritner felt moved to give to the suffering contraband, but with certain qualifications attached. Her church, she
explained in an 1863 letter to her husband, had raised $117 for
the "Freedmen's Relief Association," with the money to be used
for "clothing the Negroes that are freed by the war." The clothing, she explained, would not go to just any "Negroes" but specifically "those that are away down where they can't get work to
do." Like Ritner, many Northern white women placed a premium on moving black Southerners rapidly down the road to
self-sufficiency.[13]

Black women placed far fewer conditions and qualifications
on their support efforts, stressing instead the importance of racial solidarity. When African American women in New York City
sponsored a Grand Calico Dress Ball in February 1862, they sent
the proceeds directly "to the contrabands, who must know that
they have friends of their own race at the North, who are proud

to aid them." In a similar vein, Northern black women who went South, often to work as teachers among the former slaves, also believed that in aiding the freedpeople they furthered the advancement of black people everywhere. "I think it is our duty as a people to spend our lives in trying to elevate our own race," explained a Rhode Island black woman in her application to work as a teacher with the American Missionary Association. "Who can feel for us if we do not feel for ourselves? And who can feel the sympathy that we can who are identified with them?"[14]

Many Northern white women had sympathy for the freedpeoples' plight, but they expressed considerable wariness about the nature of the freedom experiment and about what, ultimately, freedom would mean for the former slaves. The women worried that freedom would open an uncharted void in which black men and women would live without direction or industry. When Ellen Mills visited Washington in March 1865 to attend Lincoln's second inauguration, she and her party made a point of visiting the contraband village in Arlington, Virginia. The refugee camps, she found, did not always provide uplifting images. "They swarm with darkies," Mills remarked, "who seemed not to have much occupation." White women who undertook sustained work with the former slaves likewise worried about the need for constraints and regulation in the emancipation process. Lucy Chase, a teacher in occupied Virginia, insisted that the ex-slaves "ought to enter freedom through the path of moral restraint." Harriet Ware, a Northern missionary in the South Carolina Sea Islands in 1862, worried about the absence of restraints, and feared that the former slaves might believe this to be characteristic of their new condition. Former slaves, argued Ware, "should have the care and oversight of white people in this transition state." While Northern white women favored self-support for freedmen and women, they did not believe freedom should mean complete self-ownership and self-management. Emancipation, or so many believed, required a new regulation of and obedience from Southern blacks. And as Northern white women tried to impart lessons about black obedience, they also learned new lessons about their own submission and subordination.[15]

❧

Those lessons framed the work of thousands of Northerners, both men and women, white as well as black, who went south in wartime and in the postwar years to work—in a variety of capacities—among the former slaves. Although generally referred to as teachers, that description paints a somewhat misleading picture of what they actually did. With many undertaking such varied tasks as plantation management and medical care, as well as school-based instruction, "missionary" might be a more appropriate term for their occupation. The work became available to women toward the end of 1861, with efforts to teach and assist the contraband population at Fort Monroe. The most sustained projects, though, got started after November 1861, when the Union army took possession of the South Carolina Sea Islands and made itself responsible for thousands of slaves who had been left in the wake of their owners' desertion. Dozens of Northern men and women signed on for what became known as the Port Royal experiment, which entailed the initiation of a free labor system and schooling among the Sea Island blacks. Thereafter, with each advance of the Union army into the Confederacy, more of the region's slaves came under federal oversight, thus entering the pool of freedpeople who might receive Northern assistance and instruction. Sponsored by religious and secular societies in the North, and with various degrees of government assistance, 900 teachers went South in the wartime period. Three-fourths of them were women.[16]

Northern women who enlisted as teachers during the war had

much in common with their Yankee sisters who undertook other forms of wartime service. They desired to do more than just wait and pray—or even ply their needles—at home; like men, they wanted to act. Most of the women who became teachers also embraced the principles of those abolitionists and sympathetic Republicans who believed the time had come to do more than just criticize slavery, that it was time to hasten the demise of the "peculiar institution." As the advance of the Northern army drew more slaves into the Union, a group of abolitionists, along with members and supporters of the Lincoln administration, pushed for a program that called for Northerners to guide black men and women across the threshold of emancipation, to teach them, in their own way, what freedom meant. Although a number of abolitionists objected to this work as meddling paternalism, as indeed it often was, the men and women who participated in the various freedmen's aid commissions and missionary societies saw this as an important humanitarian and educational opportunity.[17]

Aside from abolitionist sympathies, other factors shaped the pool of those who undertook this wartime missionary work. More than half of those going south hailed from New England, and most of the female recruits were unmarried. In addition, most teachers were white, but a few black women served as well, including some who had been recently freed from bondage. In general, the black female teachers came from less privileged economic circumstances and so were more dependent on the meager salaries (between $20 and $30 per month) that were provided. Black teachers also tended to persist longer in the work than their white counterparts.[18]

Like black soldiers' relief workers, African American teachers often stressed lessons of racial pride. Charlotte Forten, a young black Philadelphian, made a point of teaching her Sea Island charges about "the noble Toussaint," the leader of the Haitian slave uprising some sixty years earlier. Forten believed that the freed people "sh'ld know what one of their own color c'ld do for his race. I long to inspire them with courage and ambition (of a noble sort), and high purposes." Not surprisingly, such objectives carried considerably less weight for most white teachers. In general, white women showed more concern to teach restraint, control, and obedience—to indicate, as Lucy Chase put it, the "path of moral restraint" that would pave the way to freedom. Lucy's sister Sarah, also a teacher in the South, advanced a similar perspective. Sarah asked one man if freedom meant that he was now free "to run and do just as you please." His response was clearly to her liking. No, he replied, "I'm free to hold myself, to learne, to show my best behavior to everybody, to serve my country, and to be always a gentleman." This, as many white teachers saw it, was one of the most important lessons to be inculcated.[19]

The emphasis on teaching freedom with a strong dose of obedience and allegiance resulted, in part, from the ambivalent status that the "contraband" slaves occupied, especially in the early phases of the war when Republican officials hesitated to make any sweeping moves toward emancipation. As Butler's policy stated, escaped slaves of rebel owners would no longer be the property of those masters. Yet Butler asked the Lincoln administration soon after implementing his "contraband" strategy, had "all proprietary relation ceased"? Prior to the Emancipation Proclamation, the answer remained unclear, at least in terms of just how free the freedpeople were.

Salmon Chase, Lincoln's secretary of the treasury and the man who oversaw the Port Royal experiment, believed enslavement ultimately had to be replaced with self-support. "The persons who have been abandoned by their masters," he explained to his Port Royal agent, "and who are received into the services of the country can never, without great inhumanity on the part of the government be reduced again to slavery. You will, therefore . . . have reference to fitting them for self-support by their own industry." But even Chase acknowledged that some degree of obedience and obligation, perhaps even servitude, was owed to "the country" and the federal government in the transition from slavery. If the freedmen now obeyed some power, surely that power must be the government. Austa French, a participant in the Port Royal experiment, suspected a considerable, perhaps even overbearing, degree of government authority in the matter of the contrabands' status. "As slaveholders have not now power over these people," she wondered, "who has? Government? Who will say that government holds them, except to protect them as citizens, to require of them, as of all citizens, subjection to law, and to military law, when necessary for their and the general weal." French disliked the idea of government ownership of ex-slaves, but many teachers recognized that, with emancipation yet to be clearly defined, federal authorities by necessity assumed significant control in overseeing the conditions and occupations of the former slaves. Teachers, white women in particular, increasingly understood their task as one of communicating this new sense of obedience and obligation to their black charges.[20]

Government power quickly became a defining force in the lives of many former slaves. In the occupied Confederacy, many black men were forced into military and other forms of government service, while many freedmen and women were directed to grow cotton for U.S. Treasury Department agents who were assigned to manage the former slave plantations. To address the fears and anxieties of the contraband regarding these new arrangements, Northern women often found themselves pressed into service as the government's spokespersons, explaining the requirements and restrictions incumbent on the newly freed. "We ladies," explained Sea Island teacher Laura Towne in April

1862, "are borrowed, to go talk to the negroes, from one plantation to another." What they talked about, for the most part, was
the restricted nature of their freedom, and the requirements that
the military and the government now imposed. The teachers explained the new dependence on government and the service the
freedpeople should provide that government by growing cotton
or undertaking military service. When one ex-slave approached
Sea Island missionary Susan Walker about getting paid for the
work he had done, she enlightened him as to whom he now
served. "We have paid part in clothes, you know, Uncle Robert,
and the Government will take care you have the rest some day,"
she remarked. After the war ended, Northern women continued
to teach the same lesson. Cornelia Hancock, who had shifted
her attention from nursing to distributing clothes to the former slaves, tried "to impress . . . upon [the freedpeoples'] minds
that it is the government gives them these articles." Even after
the war had concluded, the lesson of fidelity to government remained an important facet of the teachers' agenda.[21]

Nonetheless, Yankee women at times expressed dismay with
the government's heavy-handed employment and impressment
policies, recognizing that such actions could spread fear and distress among the contraband population, and might ultimately
alienate the freedpeople from their new Yankee superiors. Susan
Walker felt particularly distraught when she was asked to select
black men from her Sea Island plantation who would be drafted
into the army. This assignment, Walker observed, was "the saddest duty I ever performed." It was not that Northern women
objected to the imposition of government and military authority; they mainly disliked the manner in which it was enforced.
The female teachers hoped to give a softer and friendlier face to
government authority. When a Union captain arrived at Susan
Walker's plantation to compel the men there to enlist, Walker

intervened. Finding the "negroes" distraught at this flagrant display of military power, Walker assured them that General Hunter, the departmental commander, was "their friend" and that she would "take good care of [the men's] families in their absence." Laura Towne likewise tried using friendly persuasion, as opposed to military bravado, to convince her charges of the need for military service. Towne, however, had no objection to seeing black men in the army and believed the experience would "teach them order and systematic obedience." She displayed the flag near her Sea Island schoolhouse and held mock military drills with her students and field hands.[22]

Other women also gave voice to the military agenda. Frances Gage, an experienced abolitionist and women's rights crusader who had come to the Sea Islands in October 1862, delivered a rousing Thanksgiving Day speech to convince black women to send their sons to war. It was, reported Charlotte Forten, "a beautiful appeal to the mothers, urging them not to keep back their sons from the war . . . but to send them forth willingly and gladly as she had done hers, to fight for liberty." Anna Gardner, who was teaching in New Berne, North Carolina, in January 1865, lent a feminine face to the new military imperatives when she organized a farewell ceremony for a local black regiment. Gardner arranged for her students to purchase a flag for the troops and to have "an interesting young lady of color" present the banner to the men of the First North Carolina Heavy Artillery. In their own way, Gardner, Gage, and Towne taught black men and women the lesson of obedience and subordination in a manner they hoped would be more personal and persuasive.[23]

One of the chief messages stressed by teachers was the abiding power of government in the former slaves' lives. Sea Island agent Edward Pierce recognized the need to inform the South Carolina contraband about federal authority, although he preferred using "the name of Mr. Lincoln . . . in addressing them, as more likely to impress them than the abstract idea of government." Other teachers followed Pierce's suggestions. A teacher in Norfolk, Virginia, on the eve of Abraham Lincoln's reelection, asked a student "if she didn't hope Mr. Lincoln would live four years longer." Even lessons about marriage, something female teachers especially encouraged as a benefit to black couples, offered civic instruction. Former slaves learned that their marriages constituted state-sanctioned relationships. After participating in the marriage ceremony, couples "were furnished with marriage certificates, neatly printed, bearing a picture of the 'old flag.'"[24]

Not only did Northern women impart these lessons to others, but many also learned them for themselves. Participation in the wartime emancipation experiment drew female teachers more forcefully into a world of government authority and military discipline in which they, as women, had almost as much to learn about obedience and national allegiance as their students. Elizabeth Botume, who went south to instruct former slaves in Hilton Head, South Carolina, in 1864, quickly grasped her new civic responsibilities upon arrival in her Southern home. After swearing an oath of loyalty "to the best government in the world," Botume said she felt that she "now belonged entirely to my country, to labor for that country's good." That sense of civic duty was reinforced in the recruiting policies of the missionary societies that supported women like Botume. These organizations understood that teachers were needed not simply to "do good" among the freedpeople, but to advance the Union cause by helping to secure a federal foothold in the occupied South. The New England Freedmen's Aid Society proclaimed that it would employ only "persons of undoubted loyalty to the Federal Government, who shall not permit their work to interfere with the proper discipline

Anna Gardner, a Northern teacher sponsored by the New England Freedmen's Aid Society who taught in different locations around the South, appears in this photograph from the 1860s with her students from Charlottesville, Virginia. Credit: Courtesy of the Boston Public Library/ Rare Books Department

and regulations" in the contraband communities. As the associations realized, female teachers would in effect become the government's faithful agents and practitioners in the emancipation experiment. Dispatched to the old plantations on the Sea Islands to explain the new labor arrangements, Susan Walker had clearly learned the two-pronged lesson of civic obedience. "Women gathered around me," Walker recounted, "and I tried to explain to them as simply as I could what government is; the power that I and they must obey."[25]

In numerous ways, in fact, Yankee teachers taught lessons of obedience and subordination to male power more generally.

Called on to teach not just letters and numbers but also the value of home life, teachers instructed contraband women, in particular, about domestic economy and household care. Implicitly, and sometimes explicitly, they tried to promulgate the Victorian image of male breadwinners who brought in all, or most, of the family income while women and children were maintained in orderly and carefully cleaned domestic spaces. Lincoln administration officials and Republican lawmakers often invoked the notion that former slave men, on becoming free, had acquired a certain proprietary relation with respect to their homes and families. "Remember, my friends," explained Congressman William Kelly to a group of freedwomen, "that you are to be mothers and wives in the homes of free men. You must try to make those homes respectable and happy." Abolitionist Lydia Maria Child found this advice sage enough to include in the textbook she authored for recently freed slaves. The assistant commissioner for the Freedmen's Bureau in Texas argued that freedom had brought black men the right of ownership and control over their womenfolk. "Freedmen could purchase and own any kind of property that a white man could," explained Edgar Gregory in January 1866 "— his wife, his children, a horse, a cow or lands." Female teachers may not have stated the new relationship so baldly, although they conveyed a similar message. As Lucy Chase saw it, black men enhanced their gender and their prestige by working for wages, although black women, apparently, did not. Paid employment, remarked Chase, "would be a crown of manliness" for the former slave. By encouraging the freedman's wage-earning "manhood" and the freedwoman's attachment to home life, even these Yankee teachers, professional women in their own right, reinforced prevailing notions of gender hierarchy.[26]

However, while they may have upheld traditional gender

roles, the teachers did not dissuade black women from paid employment. If anything, they vociferously championed wage work for former slave women, urging them to continue to labor in the fields or to learn new and marketable skills, like sewing. They did this not so much out of a recognition of black impoverishment and the need for women's income, but to end black women's economic dependency on the state. The teachers taught black women, and men, that one of their principle obligations to the government was to be self-supporting. Women, just as much as men, were told they had an obligation to avoid vagrancy and dependency. Writing from the South Carolina Sea Islands, U.S. Treasury agent Edward Pierce insisted on the suitability of paid field work for emancipated black women. "Field-work," explained Pierce, ". . . may not be consistent with the finest feminine culture or the most complete womanliness . . . [but] better a woman with a hoe than without it, when she is not yet fitted for the needle or the book." Female teachers showed every indication that they agreed with Pierce's sentiments, encouraging their female students to work in the fields or in missionary households, especially when men were called away for military service. The teachers also helped get black women "fitted for the needle." They taught the basics of sewing, opened numerous sewing schools, and encouraged black women to sew for wages.[27]

In the end, of course, the Civil War destroyed the institution of chattel slavery in the United States, and it did so in a way that extended the reach and power of the federal government in the lives of ordinary citizens. For the former slaves, the government became the new recipient of their obligation and obedience. Government agents oversaw the work of freedmen and women in the occupied Confederacy, while Union officials recruited and drafted ex-slaves for military service. To advance the government's agenda, female teachers consistently taught black men, women, and children lessons of civic allegiance and obligation. And along the way, the teachers learned their own lessons of obedience and loyalty to the nation. Increasingly, and sometimes simultaneously, the war served to impress the government's power on both former slaves and Northern women.

Chapter Eight

American Women and
the Enduring Power of the State

❦ ❦ ❦

On a hot July day in the nation's capital, shortly after the end of
the Civil War, Mary Surrat walked with three other prisoners to a
scaffold in Washington's Old Arsenal Penitentiary. Clad in a black
dress and veil, Surrat climbed the steps to the gallows platform,
where her arms and legs were restrained and a hood was slipped
over her head. A strong noose was placed around her neck, although the hangman tied only five knots instead of the usual
seven, in anticipation of a possible last-minute pardon for the
condemned woman. No reprieve came. Shortly before 2 p.m. on
July 7, 1865, more than a thousand spectators watched as the gallows platform fell away and Mary Surrat, David E. Herold, Lewis
Powell, and George Atzerodt were hung. Tried and convicted for
her participation in the assassination of Abraham Lincoln, Surrat
was the first woman to receive the death penalty from the United
States government. Certainly there could have been no more
visible manifestation of state power over American women than
this execution of the widowed boardinghouse keeper from Mary-
land.[1]

The Surrat case does more than suggest women's subjection to
the awesome power of the state. It reveals, too, the other side
of women's newly transformed status: that women increasingly
stood before the state as independent political actors, no longer
fully hidden within their male kin's political identity. It is true

that, as a widow, Surrat may have been especially vulnerable in this regard. But the willingness of the federal government to prosecute and execute Mary Surrat for her participation in the president's killing suggests a new awareness had surfaced with respect to women's ability to assert their own civic identity.

Most women, of course, would never feel the power of the state in quite the way that Mary Surrat did. Nonetheless, women living in post–Civil War America found themselves grappling with a more powerful federal government that demanded new levels of obedience and allegiance, and engagement, from all its citizens. Women found themselves drawn into a more intense civic role than they had previously experienced, yet it was a relationship that tended to stifle their expressions of civic authority and critical political engagement. The Civil War had encouraged women to locate themselves more firmly within the civic sphere but it had also made that civic sphere less subject to their critical interaction. As the federal government expanded its power over American citizens, especially over women, it accentuated women's subordinate and dependent status. Women became the objects of the government's paternalistic oversight in employment policies and the federal pension program. In fact, for many women the ability to manage households and families became wholly dependent on federal disbursements. Even their private lives came under scrutiny, as the pension office requirements compelled female recipients to live within the state's moral parameters. Women who had played direct roles in the war effort— especially those who served as nurses or as teachers of former slaves—emerged from the war with a keen appreciation of the need for government control and for women's subordination to federal authority. Only Mary Surrat experienced the state's authority in the form of the hangman's noose, but all American women would live with a Civil War legacy that both propelled

them into the civic arena and made them feel increasingly es-
tranged from political affairs.

Some of that political estrangement was evident on April 15,
1865, the day when Mary Surrat's alleged evildoing became
known to most Northerners. On that day, with the North rejoicing over Lee's final surrender to Grant, and with many already
anticipating the soldiers' return home, news came of the assassination of Abraham Lincoln. Emotionally distraught, many Yankee women seemed overwhelmed by these final events that concluded the Civil War. "What crushing news!" remarked New
Yorker Helen Grinnell. "Our joy and laughter turned to sorrow
. . . the nation is paralyzed by this awful blow." Because of Lincoln's magnified presence throughout the war period, his murder
left Northern women feeling especially bereft. "O dear beloved
President," observed Elizabeth Livermore in New Hampshire,
"no kinder heart will beat for suffering human nature for years to
come." Ruth Whittemore, ever the astute political observer in
upper New York State and a sworn enemy of all Confederates,
greatly bemoaned the loss of "Father Abraham" and his spirit
of generosity. "His merciful hand," she wrote to her brother
Charles, "is unable to write [the traitors'] pardon, as many believe he would have done had he lived."[2]

The assassination elevated Lincoln to near-divine status in the
eyes of many Northern women, thereby furthering a process of
sacralization that had already begun for the nation's sixteenth
president. Caroline White was one among many who deeply felt
the loss of this precious "Christian Ruler." "As long as Lincoln
was at the helm," White maintained, "I felt safe & sure . . . that
whatever he did, would be done in humble trust—in an Almighty
Direction." Caroline Richards was less certain that Lincoln himself embodied the wishes of the Almighty, although she believed
that the assassination should be read in a spiritual context. It

served, she asserted, as a warning that Americans had been "'putting our trust too much in princes,' forgetting the Great Ruler, who alone can create or destroy." The merging of politics and religion at this moment of national disaster revealed much about the way Northern women had learned to think about wartime developments. If nothing else, the assassination of Abraham Lincoln at the end of the war offered them a potent reminder that Civil War politics was the politics of crisis and national catastrophe and, as such, occurred on a plane far removed from the one on which ordinary women resided.[3]

Meanwhile, the plane on which women did reside—in their own homes and villages and domestic spaces—was troubling and unsettled in its own way. Even with their men returning, or about to return, there were few signs that Northern women would regain a reassuring sense of control over their domestic lives. Many, in fact, felt anxious or disappointed about the resumption of their disrupted domestic routine. Catharine Peirce, for example, expressed concern about her husband's hesitance to choose a permanent home. "There is one thing," she wrote to her husband, Taylor, in May 1865, in anticipation of his homecoming. "We will have more children and I am less able to knock about than I ever was so that we will be obliged to settle down someplace and stay if it suits or not." With soldiers having spent prolonged periods living in relative independence, with little feminine guidance or attention, their female kin often felt insecure and uncertain about the renewed domestic arrangements. Charles Ingersoll's mother worried about her son's new "roving disposition" and feared he would not even want to return home now that the war had ended. In New Hampshire, Harriet Pierce recounted her disappointment when her husband's return did not bring the hoped-for reigniting of marital bliss. "Frank don't love me to day," she noted soon after her spouse's release from the army. "I always feel unhappy when my dear Frank is distant." For Rachel Cormany, Samuel's return actually brought her "the saddest week of" her life. News of her husband's immoral indulgences left Rachel Cormany grief stricken. "My heart," she wrote in her diary in September 1865, "is almost broken."[4]

More than just personal estrangements, though, altered domestic relations. When husbands had been killed, or returned home too ill to support themselves, women looked to the Pension Bureau as their new breadwinner, or to government agencies that showed a willingness to employ soldiers' female kin. Northern women had to learn to apportion their commitments, to demonstrate loyalty not just to husbands and fathers but to the state as well.

The new imposition of federal authority may have been even more dramatic for Southern women than it was for their Yankee counterparts, especially as Confederate power was gradually replaced by Union authority. Indeed, as the Union army advanced and occupied greater expanses of Confederate territory, Southern women learned what were often unpleasant lessons about the power of federal officialdom. The Union government, pushing for new powers under the crisis of war, notably extended its authority over Southern women. One visible sign of Union rule in the Confederacy, with so many Southern men absent, was the control that government and military officials exercised over Southern white women, especially in restricting their actions and their movements, and even in defining their loyalty. The women's compliance represented a crucial step toward stability and legitimacy for the Union government in the South. This policy of control, which frequently took the form of demanding overt demonstrations of women's allegiance, strengthened expectations for expressions of civic loyalty and obligation on the part of Northern women as well.

Once again Union General Benjamin Butler, the initiator of the "contraband" policy of the early war years, gestured toward the new agenda. After bringing New Orleans under Union control in the spring of 1862, Butler found himself besieged by female supporters of the Confederacy, who routinely insulted his troops and inflamed other Confederate champions in the Crescent City. The insolence of the New Orleans ladies ultimately compelled Butler to issue, in May 1862, his infamous "Woman Order," which declared that "any female" who demonstrated "contempt for any officer or soldier of the U.S. . . . shall be regarded and held liable to be treated as a woman of the town plying her avocation." The order prompted anger and outrage from Confederates, and even some Northerners, who found Butler's directive to treat Southern ladies as common prostitutes highly offensive and dishonorable. For the remainder of the war, countless Confederates would disdainfully refer to Benjamin Butler as "the Beast."[5]

Yet, while the Woman Order was undoubtedly harsh, it actually represented a relatively minor imposition of military authority on female Southerners. The order did not so much require women to behave in a certain way or uphold specific beliefs as warn them away from obvious displays of insubordination. As Butler himself explained, the Woman Order was designed to be self-executing in its effect on the "ladies of New Orleans," to shame them into policing themselves. It was also meant to direct his own soldiers, perhaps more than the women, as to how to behave. "How do you 'regard and treat' a low woman and her remarks as she passes you in the street?" Butler asked a Northern acquaintance. "Pass her by, do you not? You are not bound to notice her acts or remarks . . . After that order, every man of my command was bound in honor not to notice any of the acts of these women." As former Secretary of War Simon Cameron explained, the order did not demand any political accountability from Southern women; it just required that they "not imitate bawds and strumpets, [but] act like ladies."[6]

But as the war progressed, self-executing acts of behavior modification proved insufficient to establish Union control. To truly begin the process of reestablishing federal power in the Confederacy, the administration found it necessary to impose greater control over Confederate women, demanding not just proper decorum but also loyalty and explicit obedience. Just as the stepped-up campaign for emancipation signaled the Union's pursuit of a "total war" against the South, so the military crackdown on Southern womanhood indicated that a remaking of Southern society was under way. To this end, the instrument that best allowed Union authorities to gain Confederate women's compliance was the loyalty oath.

The oath began its career in the North in the early years of the war, when loyalty became a strenuously pursued attribute among Unionists, highly prized among aid-society women and teachers of the former slaves, as well as members of the Lincoln administration. Northern intellectuals urged Union supporters to abandon the American heritage of respecting revolutionary upheaval and replace it with obedience to the nation-state. In a more practical vein, the federal government used charges of disloyalty in its pursuit of suspected Confederates in the North and the border states. Lincoln administration officials arrested and detained hundreds of suspected Confederate supporters, denying the detainees the writ of habeas corpus and assuming the power to hold them for an indefinite period of time. In February 1862, when Edwin Stanton became secretary of war and the Union began pursuing a more insistent campaign against Southern civilians, the loyalty campaign moved southward, fully incorporated into the Union army's strategy for war and reconstruction.[7]

By late 1862, many Union commanders had made the loyalty oath a critical weapon in their arsenals. They required civilians in newly occupied areas to take the "ironclad" oath, swearing both past and future loyalty to the U.S. government, as a means of making a region more secure and less hospitable to rebel supporters. Those who refused to take the oath could be banished beyond Union lines or sent to prison. When the Union army gained a more stable hold over an area, federal commanders continued to rely on loyalty oaths to help reestablish civil society. Those wishing to take part in certain common activities—traveling, selling property, marrying, schoolteaching—were compelled to swear an oath of loyalty. And while the oath-taking policies varied among Union commanders, many, especially as the war progressed, believed that women should also be required to swear their allegiance. Southern white women often lent aid and support to rebel combatants, and military officials recognized that the loyalty oath could be an important vehicle for establishing some semblance of Union control. "You should . . . at once drive out of your lines all persons, without reference to sex," urged a military directive of June 1862 to a Union commander in St. Augustine, Florida, "who have not taken and shall refuse to take the oath of allegiance." Union commanders throughout the South began requiring women who wished to travel, do business, or receive the Union army's protection to swear an oath of loyalty. The commander in charge of the area around Fairfax Court House in Virginia was particularly insistent that his underlings, who may have been hesitant to enforce military directives on women, not exclude the ladies from oath taking. "It is absolutely essential," explained Brigadier General Stoughton in March 1863, "to the entire security of the commands in this vicinity that the women and other irresponsible persons in this neighborhood be compelled to take the oath, or [be] placed outside the lines." In the highly contested region of Wheeling, Virginia, in August 1862, the local provost believed that ladies who "refuse[d] to take the oath" gave obvious evidence of their disloyalty and should therefore be imprisoned.[8]

Still, the administering of loyalty oaths was not, in any way, a guarantee of obedience and loyalty to the federal government. More than a few Southern women claimed to have taken the oath simply to be able to sell their wares or buy provisions. Nonetheless officials wanted some mechanism to bind women to the powers of the federal government and compel them to recognize the authorities on whom they were now dependent for the basic privileges and practices of everyday life. A woman in the occupied Confederacy would not be able to reclaim her property, or receive a pass to travel, simply because she was a woman and was therefore assumed to be inconsequential to the struggle. As the oath-taking policy implied, she would be allowed those benefits as a consequence of her civic commitment to the Union military government.[9]

This constituted a radical rethinking of women's civic status. It was a policy that insisted on women's individual obedience to the state, not an allegiance filtered through husbands and male kin. General William Sherman preferred to see the wife of a Confederate soldier take an oath as a condition for being allowed to remain within Union lines. "I venture to risk the opinion," Sherman suggested in August 1862, "that in war the parole of a woman citizen is not good, from them an oath should always be exacted, for the parole is a word of honor which according to the old feudal code, a soldier alone could make." Defining a parole as a pledge to remain neutral, Sherman opined that women had to be made more fully aware of their civic obligations and allegiance through a more binding and restrictive procedure of oath taking.[10]

Neither Sherman nor his Union cohorts had been the first to impose loyalty oaths on American women. During the American Revolution, various states required women to take oaths of allegiance, and the state of Massachusetts, in its "solemn League and Covenant as evidence of commitment," explicity included women in its oath-taking provisions. Tory females who refused risked having their property confiscated. Nonetheless, early nineteenth-century law was inconsistent on the question of whether married women could be expected to demonstrate their own allegiance to the state or if they made their civic commitments through their husbands. In a landmark Massachusetts case, the court ultimately upheld the view that "a feme-covert was never holden to take an oath of allegiance." Thus the Civil War loyalty oaths, as exacted by Union military authorities from Southern white women, represented a significant alteration of public policy. The federal government—in the form of the Union army—now expected women, regardless of the political views of their husbands and male kin, to stand before the nation as politically accountable individuals.[11]

The anger that oath-taking aroused among Confederate women indicates just how far the Union administration had pushed government control beyond its usual limits. One Virginia woman, for example, told the local provost that she would not take the required oath, as "it could not be a matter of importance what women thought or wished." Mary Lee, a vocal supporter of the Confederacy living in Winchester, Virginia, was outraged when she learned that women, at the end of the war, would be required to formally swear their allegiance. "Is it not absurd," she remarked, "that we should be made of so much importance, treating us as if we were men?" Clearly, from the perspective of these Virginia women, the imposition of the oath implied that

Union officials viewed women as significant civic actors, an idea that seemed both disturbing and strange.[12]

Southern women were not really treated "as if [they] were men." Union policy, especially toward the end of the war, did make distinctions in what the oath meant for the two sexes. As Union officials initiated the process of political reconstruction in the occupied South, they used the oath as a precondition for suffrage, and obviously the link from oath to suffrage applied only to men. In Arkansas near the very end of the war, officials seemed most anxious to secure allegiance from male heads of households, who were assumed to control most of the region's property. "Where the head of the family (male) is permitted to take the oath of allegiance," explained a memo from the Arkansas Department in January 1865, "it is not necessary, except in extreme cases, to extend the privilege to the females of the household." As the war reached its conclusion and greater degrees of military order and stability were achieved, Union officials looked toward the rebuilding of an economically and politically active civil society and increasingly directed their oath-taking policies toward men. In this context, the oath became less a weapon of compliance and more a "privilege" used to foster civic engagement.[13]

Nonetheless, Union policy made clear—both during and after the war—that Southern white women would be required to display their civic obedience in new and more explicit ways. Anyone wishing to teach in postwar Missouri, for example, had to sign a loyalty oath. In September 1865, the provost marshal of Savannah, Georgia, advertised separate hours when men and women could apply to take the oath. And women throughout the South who wished to reclaim confiscated property after the war found themselves obliged to swear their allegiance. In most cases they were no longer required to take the ironclad oath of past and future loyalty to the Union but could swear the far more lenient amnesty oath, as stipulated by Abraham Lincoln's midwar reconstruction program, that required only a pledge of future allegiance. Still, the wartime and postwar policies signaled the federal government's expectation that women would demonstrate a level of civic obedience and political accountability, not just through their families but on their own terms.[14]

The administration's insistence on Confederate women's obedience won considerable support from Northerners, including women. Many took the view that Dixie women had played a particularly prominent role in maintaining the war spirit in the South and thus must share in the blame of bringing on the rebellion. When General Butler first announced his Woman Order in May 1862, his wife, Sarah, heartily concurred with the seemingly harsh directive. "Never," Sarah Butler remarked, "has anything been more deserved. [The New Orleans women's] insolence is beyond endurance, and must be checked." By the time the war had ended, ever more responsibility was attributed to the ladies of the Confederacy for stimulating and prolonging the war. "O these guilty, guilty women," remarked Michigan journalist Lois Adams soon after the war had ended. "They have a fearful responsibility for the aid they have given in plotting, planning and pushing on the rebellion." Those who had debated the question of Northern women's patriotism in the midwar period often contrasted Northern women's allegedly lackluster performance with the virulent displays of Confederate womenfolk. Although commentators disagreed on the propriety of Confederate women's behavior, they nonetheless concurred that Southern white women had, in their own right, become political actors with whom Union forces had to reckon. Years after the war had ended, one Northern relief worker still retained bitter memories of the women's almost demonic demonstrations of Confederate patriotism. The ladies of Nashville, recalled Annie Witten-myer, were "more intense in war spirit and partisan feeling than the men."[15]

Quite a few Yankee ladies thought more should be done to curb Southern women's displays of treason. Michigan journalist Lois Adams found anti-Union sentiments rampant among women in wartime Washington, especially among those whose husbands worked for the federal government. Adams was outraged that such women could enjoy the government's support while simultaneously professing their hatred of "Yankees." Minnesota journalist Jane Swisshelm fumed about the wives and daughters of Southern sympathizers whom she believed to be in the employ of the United States government. While the men had taken an oath to secure their positions, "their wives and families are open and avowed secessionists and champions of the Rebellion, yet dependent for their daily bread on the salary of the father and husband or brother." Adams and Swisshelm were appalled that disloyal women could benefit from the government's coffers, and could hide behind their male kin's professions of patriotism and escape demands for their own loyalty. While living in Jacksonville, Florida, soon after the war's conclusion, Northern physician and relief worker Esther Hill Hawks found the political leeway offered to Southern women disturbing. One bitterly secessionist woman, she observed, had been advanced provisions by a Union official so she could open a boardinghouse for Union officers. Although the woman was required to take the oath, Hawks learned that she "only did it because she was obliged to" and was now making "quite a fortune" in her business enterprise. Oaths notwithstanding, the problem of Confederate women's wartime disloyalty pushed Northern women to call for closer monitoring of women's patriotic allegiance.[16]

As many Yankee ladies saw it, few Southern women more

clearly demonstrated the need for strict political oversight and control than Mary Surrat, arguably the most obviously disloyal woman of the Civil War era. Many welcomed Surrat's hanging in July 1865, when she was executed for her participation in the Lincoln assassination plot. While the state failed to present indisputable proof of Mary Surrat's guilt, the trial did provide significant evidence of her Southern sympathies and her links to Confederate conspirators. Even though the court proceedings raised doubts about Surrat's own involvement in the plot, many in the North lost little time in identifying Surrat as "the arch criminal among those" arraigned for the crime and loudly proclaimed their support for her execution. Few believed Surrat's gender should in any way shield her against such an extreme punishment. Womanhood in this case did not pose an obstacle to political accountability.[17]

It is possible, in fact, that Mary Surrat's sex increased her chances of getting the death penalty. The war had already established a precedent for holding Confederate women accountable for their actions and for exacting harsh punishments, including imprisonment, when they failed to demonstrate their loyalty. In addition, Northerners had begun to view Southern white women as particularly extreme and vicious in their Confederate sympathies, and some worried that the penalties against them had not been harsh enough. To many Yankee women, the case against Mary Surrat offered final proof of Southern white women's despicable treason and the need to hold them personally accountable for their crimes. Annie Dudley, who attended the trial of the Lincoln conspirators, believed that Mary Surrat played a more direct role than the others in the assassination plot. Dudley claimed she "was more convinced than ever that all except Mrs. Surratt, were mere tools in the hands of others." Surrat, she believed, "[knew] the whole plot, from beginning to end." Michigan journalist Lois Adams, for her part, saw Surrat as a stand-in for all of the guilty and disloyal women of the Confederacy. "While we acknowledge," she wrote in her column of July 18, 1865, "that it is an awful thing to hang a woman, we must remember that it is a still more awful thing for a woman to be so wicked as to deserve hanging. But no executions of this sort, though multiplied by thousands, can atone for the wrongs these Southern women are guilty of in connection with the rebellion." Adams believed that Confederate women had been especially defiant precisely because, as women, they had not been made to feel the full force of the law and military policy. The Surrat execution took a small step toward correcting that failure—and a significant step toward demonstrating the power of the federal government to hold women, as individuals, accountable for their own political beliefs.[18]

Loyalty oaths, imprisonments, and executions were clear indications that the federal government had raised the bar in terms of expecting obedience and allegiance from its female citizens. Women now had to be accountable as individuals before the state. This, of course, could and did open the door for women to express their political and partisan sentiments. Yet the government, and the wartime climate of national crisis, did little to encourage women's active political engagement. Women were expected to be loyal and obedient citizens, but wartime developments frequently had the effect of discouraging their active involvement in the political life of the nation. Indeed the war had, in many respects, made it more difficult for women to pursue a political agenda. The crisis of the war, for example, dampened the little support that did exist for woman's suffrage. In the spring of 1861 the feminist Martha Wright urged Susan B. Anthony to refrain from women's rights work "when the nation's whole heart and soul are engrossed with this momentous crisis and . . . when nobody will listen." Likewise, the *New York Herald* welcomed the quiet that descended on female political activism during the war, finding that few had "time for such nonsense and tomfoolery." The silence lifted in the postwar years, but disdain for woman's suffrage persisted and was clearly in evidence during the Reconstruction suffrage debates and in the final passage of the Fourteenth and Fifteenth Amendments to the U.S. Constitution. Among other points, these amendments established the idea that American-born women were citizens of the nation-state, and thus—in various ways—obligated to that state. Yet they also effectively barred women from participating directly in electoral politics. As the Fourteenth Amendment made clear, the government committed itself to protecting the suffrage rights not of all its citizens but of only its "male inhabitants."[19]

❧

With the Civil War bringing an end to slavery, the war's conclusion opened up a renewed and intensified discussion of suffrage, citizenship, and political equality. Female activists seized the moment to widen the debate to include women's rights. Feminists believed that the war's transformative spirit made full freedom and political equality available and accessible to all individuals, with no barriers imposed on account of race or sex. Thus they raised the demand for "universal suffrage," for extending voting rights to women and African Americans, not on the basis of their "special needs" as oppressed groups but on account of their citizenship. The opportunity opened up by emancipation and the expansion of suffrage, claimed one feminist, made it possible to "bury the black man and the woman in the citizen." Following this logic, longtime activists like Elizabeth Cady Stanton and Susan B. Anthony gathered and submitted petitions, asking congressmen who were now debating the question of suffrage for the freed slaves to extend the franchise to women as well. They were met, for the most part, with empty promises and stinging rebukes.[20]

The suffragists did win some backers in the immediate postwar era. Some radical members of the Republican Party expressed support, usually hesitant, for women's suffrage, and a few Democratic politicians, too, spoke up for the cause (although generally with the objective of making the calls for black voting seem all the more odious and unacceptable). The overwhelming majority of politicians, however, including most of the radical Republicans, opposed giving women the right to vote, with many arguing that women, who remained largely dependent on men, achieved political representation through the votes of male family members. A number of radical politicians claimed to support the idea of women's suffrage in theory but maintained that, given the historical imperatives surrounding Reconstruction and the need to arm Southern black men with the vote to counter the political power of ex-Confederates, black suffrage had to take precedence over women's enfranchisement. In this way, the congressional debate reaffirmed women's status as political dependents.

Moreover, much of the debate paid homage to men's military authority, as demonstrated in the war, and explicitly linked men's power as soldiers with their right to exercise the franchise. Women, pointed out New Jersey senator Frelinghuysen during the 1866 discussions of suffrage requirements for the District of Columbia, "do not bear the bayonet" and "have a higher and holier mission . . . to make the character of coming men." Senator Morrill of Maine concurred, arguing during the debate over the Fourteenth Amendment that "the ballot is the inseparable concomitant of the bayonet. Those who practice the one must be prepared to exercise the other." In the District of Columbia suffrage debate, Senator Williams of Oregon presented a similar line of argument. "When the women of this country come to be sailors and soldiers . . . when they love the dissoluteness of the camp and the smoke and the thunder and the blood of battle better than they love the affections and enjoyments of home and family," then the time might come to consider their enfranchisement. The arguments of these three Reconstruction legislators confirmed the wartime view of power: that soldiering gave added weight and legitimacy to male authority. With so many men having been called on to serve and sacrifice, the war had enhanced the prestige of male voters, irrespective of social class, and few politicians wished to denigrate their accomplishments. Republicans, in particular, welcomed the chance to appeal to their male constituents as a unified body of manly combatants, thereby countering the Democratic tendency to divide their own working-class supporters from the Republican "aristocrats." In this context, extending the right of suffrage to those who had not, and could not, be soldiers seemed to question the power and authority demonstrated so recently by men in their fight to preserve the Union.[21]

The suffrage debates repeatedly cast women in the part of dependent and protected wards of the state. Sons, argued Senator Williams, "defend and protect the reputation and rights of their mothers; husbands defend and protect the reputation and rights of wives; brothers defend and protect the reputation and rights of their sisters; and to honor, cherish, and love the women of this country is the pride and the glory of its sons." Debating the question two years later, John Broomall, a Republican representative from Pennsylvania, concurred. "Adult males," he argued, "are supposed to represent the family, and the government is not bound to look further than this common consent or submission." When the question of female enfranchisement was raised in the debate over the Fifteenth Amendment to the Constitution in the winter of 1869, Senator Dixon expressed his general support for the proposal, although he thought it inexpedient at that time. To underscore his argument in favor of women's suffrage, the senator recalled the familiar wartime image of the sacrificing soldier's wife. Imagine, he explained, a woman coming into the Senate chamber and telling of her husband and two sons who "'lie in yonder national cemetery—their graves marked, cared for, cherished gratefully and tenderly by the nation . . . I have no husband, no son, no brother, no father, no man left to represent me. I pay taxes; every law you pass affects me and mine, and I demand a voice in this Government.'" In stating the case for women's right to vote, Dixon focused not on women's individual civic roles but on their ties to male family members who had made the ultimate sacrifice for the nation.[22]

Neither the Fourteenth nor the Fifteenth Amendment gave women the right to vote. The Fourteenth Amendment did, however, establish a new platform of federal power, reflecting the expansion of federal authority in the wartime era. By making all native and naturalized persons citizens of the United States, the amendment made the nation-state the protector, and the grantor, of civic rights, overriding the power of the state governments in this capacity. It thus codified the new civic ideology that brought Americans—black and white, male and female, Northern and Southern—into a new relationship with the federal government. But the amendment also established a formal distinction between citizen and voter, specifying that the right to vote should be extended only to citizens of a certain age (twenty-one and older) and gender (male). The Fifteenth Amendment extended the provisions of the preceding amendment by guaranteeing the right to vote to all, irrespective of "race, color, or previous condition of servitude," but with no reference to gender. In this way, the two amendments confirmed a new civic identity for American women: they were citizens of the nation, not to be denied "life, liberty, or property, without due process of law," but they were not, like men, politically engaged citizens who could participate in the central political activities of the nation.[23]

Female activists, of course, spent years disputing this interpretation of the new civic order. Many saw the Civil War as accelerating a new level of political engagement for American women, evident in the wartime petitioning and organizing spearheaded by groups like the Woman's National Loyal League on behalf of full emancipation. Inspired by the struggle for justice and equality, they continued to demand universal suffrage, linking the calls for female and African American enfranchisement. They also struck out on their own independent political path and severed their ties with former abolitionists, most of whom remained loyal to the Reconstruction principles of the Republican Party. Some feminists, Stanton and Anthony in particular, briefly attempted a political alliance with the Democratic Party, seeking allies wherever they might be. In 1867 they worked with Democratic Party organizers in their attempt to sway Kansas voters to endorse universal suffrage. The Kansas campaign failed, but feminists persisted in pushing their suffrage, and civic, agenda. During the 1870s a number of suffragists tried to erase the Constitution's new, formalized distinction between citizen and voter by urging women to assume they had the right to vote because the Fourteenth Amendment had defined them as citizens. Women activists simply went to the polls to vote and then filed lawsuits against those who prevented them.[24]

This legal strategy proved unsuccessful. In fact, during the 1870s the U.S. Supreme Court backed away from the Fourteenth Amendment's guarantee of national citizenship by allowing states to pass measures that infringed on civil rights—a decision that would pave the way for the disenfranchisement and segregation legislation of the Jim Crow era. Suffragists, in the meantime, also retreated from the civic vision that the Civil War had inspired, and argued that women should have the vote not because they were citizens just like men, but because they could bring a different, and uplifting, moral force to national politics. They emphasized the civilizing influence that white women could bring to the polls as a counterweight to the demoralizing influence of black and immigrant male voters. In abandoning their equal rights arguments in favor of sex-specific ones, suffragists again accepted the view that women's civic capacities were defined not by their own independent political judgments but by their family relations.[25]

Most women who had experienced the upheavals and transformations of the Civil War era did not become involved with the suffrage movement. They returned to tending to their own households and domestic lives, after the disruption and devastation of the war. Tens of thousands of widows had to make do without their husbands, who had died as a result of Civil War injuries or illnesses. As new federal dependents, these women became pensioners and received monthly stipends from the government. Tens of thousands of women moved west, many perhaps compelled to emigrate by male family members who, feeling restless in the postwar period, sought to recapture something of the adventure that they had known as soldiers. And to the extent that they remained actively involved in public activities, many affiliated with new postwar groups like the Woman's Christian Temperance Union (WCTU), which strongly condemned male intemperance for its debilitating effects on women and children.

The WCTU's popularity certainly had something to do with the message of domestic empowerment it offered to women. With the war nearly over, Mary Milner, sister of soldier Taylor

Peirce, worried about her brother's possible lapse into intemperance as a result of his wartime separation from his family. "Oh my dear brother," she wrote in January 1865, shortly before Taylor's return, "for the sake of thy wife and little ones never touch the hateful thing again." Soon after moving to Ohio, in the spring of 1862, Elizabeth Cooper became an active temperance worker. Anxious that antiliquor meetings were poorly attended since so many men had left for war, Cooper felt more committed than ever to the cause. Then, as the war intensified, Cooper sensed that the drinking problem was becoming more severe. Temperance workers must, she maintained in the winter of 1863, "pull all together to remove these demons of degradation and vice that are infesting this town and the morality of the community." With soldiers returning in the spring of 1865, and with many no doubt suffering from alcoholism, women like Elizabeth Cooper and Mary Milner may have felt the need to redouble their crusade against the demon of drink.[26]

Aside from temperance societies, among the most popular post–Civil War women's organizations were the various ladies' auxiliary groups that attached themselves to Union veteran societies. By the late 1860s, women in a number of Northern states had begun to gather in clubs and fund-raising societies, lending support and encouragement to the men who had begun to meet regularly in veterans' alliances. Foremost among the veterans' organizations was the Grand Army of the Republic (GAR), founded in 1866 as a group in which former soldiers could come together to share memories and concerns from their war experiences, and to strategize on specific political issues, pensions in particular, that affected them. In 1882, with assistance and support from the GAR high command, a group of Massachusetts women led the way in consolidating a number of women's clubs and societies around the country into the GAR's official female auxiliary, the Woman's Relief Corps (WRC). Their ranks, or so the leadership contended, included many women who "were never before associated with any organization outside of church work." Relief Corps posts appeared throughout the country, including the South, gathering both black and white participants. By 1900 the WRC had about 3,000 local chapters and counted nearly 120,000 members.[27]

In its early years, the Woman's Relief Corps concentrated its efforts on supporting Union veterans and their activities. Foremost on the WRC agenda was the group's presence at Memorial Day celebrations throughout the North. Begun as an informal day of mourning after the war, Memorial Day gradually took its place as a widely observed holiday for remembering the Union dead. From the outset, GAR posts and WRC auxiliaries played central roles in Memorial Day ceremonies. Indeed the women frequently took the lead in this work, lending a sentimental cast to postwar memorialization and offering members of the community, including men, the opportunity to mourn and reflect on the human costs of the war. Relief Corps women gathered flowers for the graves, summoned local schoolchildren to pageants and parades, and placed flags on burial sites. To some extent the day offered women an opportunity for public expression, and WRC members often spoke or read poems at the ceremonies. Even the smallest and most remote chapters of the WRC joined in the Memorial Day work, including a tiny group of black women who reported they were "few in numbers and poor, but not a grave was forgotten."[28]

Over time the WRC expanded its mission to include a broader range of "patriotic" activities, especially the promotion of patriotism in the public schools. Along with the GAR, the WRC distributed American flags and encouraged the "proper" teaching of Civil War history, being particularly mindful to counteract

Confederate influences in the curriculum. As was true for many other women's patriotic organizations of the era, the WRC saw national loyalty as something uncritical and automatic. Anxious to combat "foreign" and immigrant influences, women—like those in the WRC—believed children, especially urban children of immigrant parents, should be inculcated with relatively simplistic notions of civic obedience and allegiance. Hence they devoted considerable effort to promoting patriotic rituals in American schools, like reciting the Pledge of Allegiance and singing the national anthem, traditions that continue to the present day.[29]

When it came to its own membership, however, the Woman's Relief Corps adopted a more nuanced perspective on the question of loyalty. From the time of its inception the WRC faced criticism and competition from rival organizations that admitted only the female relatives of Union soldiers into their ranks. Although some WRC affiliates likewise included only soldiers' kin, the organization officially condemned this approach and urged that "all loyal women" be admitted into the society. As a result of taking this stand, the WRC won the support of the GAR leadership and also managed to gather a far larger following than the competing organizations. The WRC's position on the "loyalty question," however, represented far more than a strategy for winning more members. Ideologically, its position bore the imprint of the civic transformations of the Civil War era, when American women learned to embrace the higher claims of country over home and when they were increasingly judged on their individual expressions of patriotism. Toward this end, WRC leaders repeatedly berated those who believed that only relatives of Union men should find a place in their society. "The relatives of the Union veteran," intoned the WRC president at the organization's fifth convention, "have no right to trade on an excess of loyalty and to arrogate to themselves all the patriotism of the women of our land." The true American spirit, she claimed, did not honor ties of blood but judged women on an individual basis, especially on their individual expressions of patriotism. At the eleventh convention of the Massachusetts WRC, President Emma Lowd made a similar point when she condemned "that false sentimentality which makes the claim of kinship to the veteran more sacred than that Divine impulse of loyalty, which prompted the woman during the war to offer up her heart's dearest treasure, or her own life for her country and humanity." The point was not a woman's familial associations but her own "impulse" and initiative. Leaders frequently argued that kinship was "accidental" or that "woman is loyal by birth, not marriage." Just as wartime loyalty oaths had made it impossible for Southern women to hide behind their family attachments, making them politically accountable to the Union military on an individual basis, so the WRC's loyalty criteria celebrated Unionist women for their own personal expressions of patriotism. The WRC was even prepared to admit Southern women who had been married to rebel soldiers, so long as that "lady had always remained loyal, notwithstanding the influence of her husband." In 1891 the Missouri WRC affirmed the right of a "loyal" wife of a Confederate soldier to join its ranks. "It would," they asserted, "be an act of gross injustice to exclude her."[30]

With its mission of including all "loyal women," the Woman's Relief Corps honored a wide array of women who, as individuals, had made their own contributions to the Union war effort. Most WRC leaders, at least initially, supported the full and equal participation of black women in the organization and were in theory committed to the notion that patriotism could not be racialized. Even when white Southern members attempted to keep black chapters segregated outside the parameters of their state organizations, the WRC national leadership came to African American women's defense. The black chapters, maintained one Relief Corps president, "are about all that is down there [in the South] that is patriotic." Nonetheless, the WRC was hardly a biracial sisterhood. The organization offered little assistance to bolster black women's chapters, many of which were impoverished and poorly organized. And eventually the national WRC acquiesced to a de facto segregation in a number of Southern states, fearful of alienating its Southern white membership.[31]

While it vacillated on the question of race, the Relief Corps remained steadfast in its commitment to loyal women who had no familial ties to Union soldiers. They paid homage to the army nurses who "had no tie of blood in husband, son, father or brother" but acted only out of "divine instinct of humanity and their undying loyalty to principle and country." In fact, the "loyal woman" criterion allowed the WRC to focus on women's wartime deeds in ways that groups who admitted only soldiers' relatives did not. "Let us remember," urged the WRC president at the second national gathering, "that from the soldier alone came not all the sacrifice; many a brave woman's duty in the hospital— yes, in the march and in the field—would compare in deeds of valor with that of the soldier." Relief Corps women were advised to honor not only fallen soldiers but also "the graves of the patriotic women." And even women who had made no tangible contribution to the war effort could join the WRC, so long as they subscribed to the principles of loyalty. In these ways the WRC upheld the civic outlook of the war years by placing a premium on women's individual accountability to the nation.[32]

That civic view, over time, propelled the WRC into the vibrant world of postbellum reform. In 1893 the WRC affiliated itself with the National Council of Women, a wide-ranging coalition of women's groups—including women from the WCTU and the national women's club movement—that focused on the progressive reforms of the day. Many WRC members went so far as to endorse women's suffrage, arguing that women's work in patriotic education would be better served if they had the power of the franchise. In its overall mission and objectives, though, the Woman's Relief Corps reflected the ambivalent legacy that the Civil War bequeathed to American women. The organization was defined by, and remained dedicated to, a conservative agenda of paying tribute to the military might and authority of Northern Union men. While members of the WRC may have begun to embrace a few of the progressive causes of the day, the organization's raison d'être kept them tied to an ideology of female submissiveness. WRC rules, for example, demanded that each corps of the WRC be attached to a specific GAR post, and required each corps to take the name of the GAR post with which it was affiliated. Corps members were forbidden to adopt a female name for their organization. When it came to spending money, GAR demands again assumed priority over WRC needs. Women from the Tennessee WRC agreed to forgo a monument they had hoped to build in tribute to the women of the Union, because their main work, they believed, had to focus on "the needy veteran and his family." A Pennsylvania member opposed using special flags on Memorial Day to pay tribute to WRC members who had died. This, she argued, would "detract from Memorial Day, which is the Soldiers' Day." In its most important activities, then, the WRC reaffirmed the exceptional contributions made by the male warriors of the wartime era. As a result, the organization could take only limited steps in challenging fundamental gender inequalities.[33]

Perhaps the most unfortunate, albeit unintended, consequence of the WRC's priorities was that they contributed to the diminishing place of Union women in American memory. With money generally being spent for the veterans and the GAR, few bothered to build monuments to women of the North, and little attention was directed toward public tributes or memorials to Yankee ladies. Through the 1880s and 1890s the WRC often called attention to the work of Union army nurses, but efforts were concentrated not so much on memorializing those women as on the problem of obtaining federal pensions for female hospital personnel, a goal that was finally achieved in 1892. In an era when countless statues appeared to commemorate the work of Civil War participants, few—including those sponsored by the WRC—made any mention of Northern women's sacrifices. For the most part, the WRC spent its money, and its time, paying tribute to men.[34]

If even the Woman's Relief Corps failed to memorialize Northern women, there were few outside that body who could be counted on to undertake such a task. A few celebratory words were spoken on Northern women's behalf soon after the war ended, mainly accounts compiled by men to honor some of the women who had contributed to the sanitary and medical needs of the soldiers. These speeches and writings generally lauded women for their self-sacrifice and modesty, singling out, for example, female nurses who had exhibited "thoroughness and punctuality" in their work and were always "obedient to the surgeons." Even more worthy of emulation were those women who, when the war ended, "slipped back into the happy routine of domestic usefulness." In these descriptions, the authors suggested that women would best be served by downplaying their wartime contributions, by remaining anonymous in the celebratory memorials of the postwar era. "There is a character 'of no reputation,'" explained former Sanitary Commission leader Henry Bellows in one account of Northern women's war work, "which formed in strictest retirement, and in the patient exercise of unobserved sacrifices, is dearer and holier in the eye of Heaven, than the most illustrious name won by the most splendid services." Women's wartime contributions were certainly praiseworthy, Bellows suggested, but it would be better to remember them quietly, with little public discussion.[35]

Female authors struck a more boisterous and celebratory tone, especially women like Mary Livermore, who published her wartime memoirs in the 1880s. But Northern women's memoirs were few and far between, even in a literary culture that was clogged with Civil War remembrances. Livermore explained her urge to write by noting the lack of Civil War literature that told of the people on the home front. She hoped, in particular, to call attention to the great "uprising" among women to sustain the war effort. "Who," she wondered, "has fully narrated the consecrated and organized work of women, who strengthened the sinews of the nation with their unflagging enthusiasm?" No one, Livermore believed, had yet accomplished this task.[36]

Other than Livermore, few would persist in this endeavor. As Livermore observed, by the late nineteenth century, American culture stood awash in Civil War memories, but they were mainly the memories of men's accomplishments and sacrifices, of the great "Battles and Leaders"—as one magazine series was titled—of the 1860s. Men took center stage in the postwar culture of reunion that focused on the common military heroism of Northern and Southern soldiers, applauding both sides for their proud demonstrations of martial valor. When women did make an appearance in Civil War literature, they were usually Confederate women, and they generally appeared, as they had during the war, as vociferous defenders of the Southern cause. Indeed, the hottempered Dixie female became a staple of postwar fiction, essential to the reconciliation drama in which she, in the end, renounces her Confederate sympathies and takes a Northern lover. Well into the twentieth century, authors would create some of the most enduring literary portraits in American fiction by re-shaping that image of the fiery and tempestuous rebel girl. They would, as a result, give Southern Civil War women a lasting, if not always accurate, place in American memory.[37]

As much as the Civil War captivated the American imagination in the nineteenth and twentieth centuries, little was said of the women of the North in either fiction or nonfiction. Certainly their experiences often lacked the drama and excitement that pervaded the lives of many Confederate women, making them less appealing as literary subjects. In one of the few post-war novels to deal with the subject of Yankee women, Louisa May Alcott's *Little Women* (1868), the tensions of the book focus largely on the inner, emotional conflicts that plague the March girls, while the war stands as a distant point of turmoil. Ultimately, the Civil War teaches Jo March not to trumpet her accomplishments but to control her emotions and curb her desires. Real-life Northern women seemed to have learned a similar lesson, and they chose not to call attention to their wartime heroics. As many had said repeatedly during the war, their own contributions paled in comparison to the work of men. And even the Northern women who made it their business to memorialize Union triumphs—specifically the ladies in the Woman's Relief Corps—agreed that the main tributes and laurels should go to men. Perhaps Alcott meant to imply only youthfulness when she described the March women of her most well-known and beloved novel as "little." Still, plenty of Northern women, whether old or young, might have given a different meaning to that word when they contemplated their own Civil War experiences.

Epilogue: An Ambiguous Legacy

❦ ❦ ❦

Soon after the end of the Civil War, the editors of the *New York Herald,* a newspaper that generally stood at odds with the Republican administration, posed some telling questions about the war's legacy for Northern women. In September 1865 the *Herald* directed its attention to the newly created Bureau of Refugees, Freedmen, and Abandoned Lands, also known as the Freedmen's Bureau. Created by Congress in March 1865 and charged with managing the former slaves' transition to freedom, especially by creating new contractual labor relations between ex-slaves and white landowners, the bureau represented one of the most significant extensions of federal responsibility into the private lives of American citizens. It signaled the growing entanglement of the American people in the workings of the nation-state. It signaled, too, the government's relatively brief moment of racial inclusiveness in extending its mantle of protection to black citizens.[1]

The New York newspaper, like many Americans, questioned the idea of extending a significant government commitment, not to mention a considerable budgetary outlay, to a class of people whom many despised. The *Herald* recognized and embraced the notion of expanded federal authority, but challenged the idea that freed slaves were the appropriate recipients of government assistance. "The war has left a great many niggers unprovided for," the *Herald*'s editors opined, ". . . .It is feared that they will not be happy. Somebody is afraid that somebody else will oppress them; that they will be made to exert their immense muscle in a little labor." Distressed at the protections being offered this particular group of individuals, the *Herald* implied the utter wastefulness and futility of an organization like the Freedmen's Bureau that was designed to secure "the interests of the niggers" who, apparently, had little need to have their interests secured.[2]

But there was a class of genuinely "helpless persons" who did deserve government protection, the newspaper maintained. Why, the editors asked, did federal authorities not extend their protective posture toward white women "and young girls who are poor and depend upon their own efforts for a living" and who were the victims of cheating employers and ruthless husbands? Where was the government bureau for these women? "And if the government" would not construct such an agency, the *Herald's* writers insisted, "how absurd is its act in making its immense provision for the protection and assistance of the gigantic nigger and his brood!"[3]

Embedded in the *Herald's* racist cant was one of the most significant developments of the Civil War era: the expansion of the nation-state into the lives of ordinary American citizens. The war had demonstrated that private mechanisms and support systems could not, by themselves, mobilize and prepare Americans to wage a monumental conflict. The government had to assume greater responsibility for the economic and social welfare of the American people, in both positive and negative ways. Throughout the conflict, this had taken a variety of forms, including new federal income taxes that were levied to help defray the costs of war, federal conscription laws that compelled able-bodied Northern men to serve in the army, federal pension benefits directed to soldiers and their kin, and labor contracts negotiated between landowners and former slaves who grew cotton (and sometimes between private employers and employees who produced military supplies) that required federal oversight. The wartime expansion of national power, as this book has demonstrated, represented a critical point of change in the lives of American women. As the state expanded its influence and power, Northern women, as well as Southern ones, found themselves drawn into a new relationship with civic and political authorities and occupying a new position in the public arena.

This civic relationship unfolded gradually over the course of the war, becoming more pronounced after the summer of 1862, when the Union military effort was faltering. By that point Union officials, as well as writers and commentators in the Northern states, had begun to recognize the need to keep home-front forces mobilized through propaganda efforts and financial incentives. Just as Gail Hamilton began to pen her laments over Northern women's insufficient patriotism, federal programs, most noticeably the new pension system, offered a stronger economic foundation to bolster women's apparently waning support for the war. This process proceeded apace through the rest of the conflict, as the federal government began to hire more female employees, especially in the Treasury Department, and as federal officials became more responsive to the needs and demands of subcontracted women workers. By 1863 the Republican Party had begun to pay keener attention to its female constituency, targeting women in its political activities and showcasing female lecturers, like Anna Dickinson, as its spokeswomen. Although at odds with the Republican wartime agenda, the *New York Herald*'s call for a government bureau to protect the interests of white working-class women is in many ways a logical result of the enhanced civic ties that the Civil War initiated between women and the state. It suggests, too, another theme highlighted in this book: that the new relationship forged between the government and the former slaves resonated in certain ideas about women's new ties with government. The Civil War nation-state increasingly broke down the somewhat imperfect barrier that separated the private from the public sphere, casting a more intense public spotlight on women's previously unrecognized domestic, economic, and emotional experiences.

But the stronger civic relationship was not simply the result of a new attitude on the part of federal officials or the Republican leadership. In various ways, Northern women asserted themselves more forcefully in the civic arena. Some of this change was apparent from the outset of the conflict. As men and women recognized that the Union struggle meant elevating national obligations over domestic ones, women learned to embrace new national priorities. By the latter half of the war, tens of thousands of women had responded to this sense of obligation by organizing thousands of soldiers' aid societies and spearheading dozens of successful fund-raising fairs on behalf of the United States Sanitary Commission. In Republican ranks especially, many Northern women became noticeably more engaged in the nation's political life, as observers and commentators and also as speakers and political organizers. When they became teachers and missionaries to the freedpeople, hundreds of Northern women helped advance the unfolding relationship between the former slaves and the U.S. government, and thereby gained a new appreciation for the expanded power of the Civil War nation-state. And thousands of women tied their fate even more directly to the work of the Union administration when they became nurses in army hospitals and in military camps throughout the South.

Northern women's passage into the civic arena led to a sense of both empowerment and subordination. Countless women spoke with more forceful and articulate political voices as a result of their Civil War experiences: they recognized the importance of their political influence, especially when male relatives were absent from the home-front scene, and they felt more confident about pressing certain kinds of political and economic demands. They worked to further their professional training, particularly as teachers and nurses, and they acquired numerous skills as organizers and fund-raisers that many would carry with them into postwar activities. But whereas previous scholars have read—and many continue to read—these experiences as evidence of women's wartime emancipation, I have tried to suggest a more complex story by demonstrating how the march into civic life also brought a redefinition of women's subordination. Women during the Civil War years learned new lessons about submission to male power. As pension recipients, many shifted their sense of dependency from male breadwinners at home to the nation-state and in the process submitted to public officials' scrutiny of their private lives. Through their participation in wartime politics, and relief work, women learned much about patriotic expression, but the emphasis was often placed on uncomplaining loyalty and obedience, as opposed to critical engagement and thoughtful interaction. Female nurses, perhaps more than others, gained a new appreciation for obeying the commands of male superiors in the difficult and demanding climate of wartime hospital work. Finally, the lessons of civic subordination were extended to Southern women, especially as Union control spread through the Confederacy in the later stages of the war. Women in the occupied South felt the enhanced power of the nation-state in the form of an intensified loyalty campaign that required them, often under the threat of punishment or exile, to express their commitment and devotion to federal officialdom.

The Civil War shaped a new civic identity for all American women, Northern as well as Southern, and it forced women to reorient their own struggle for change and equality. In the aftermath of the Civil War, women increasingly recognized the need to direct their demands and their political energies toward the nation-state, and to press forward their claims in the civic arena. This impulse became evident in the work of late nineteenth-century suffragists, many of whom sought to advance the purview of the Fourteenth Amendment by demanding action, at the federal level, that would give women the right to vote. But women's civic vision could be found in more than just the suffrage movement. The thousands who joined forces in the General Federation of Women's Clubs, unified in 1890, embraced a shift away from female self-improvement and toward national initiatives to study and influence federal policy with respect to working conditions and health care. Temperance activists also pushed women's claims in the civic sphere. By the 1880s the president of the Woman's Christian Temperance Union, Frances Willard, was urging supporters to advocate a "Home Protection Ballot" that would give women limited suffrage rights with respect to a variety of domestic concerns. Recognizing that the most effective means for social change lay in the ever-expanding nation-state, female activists became more explicit about presenting themselves as politically accountable citizens of the nation, furthering a process that had taken root in the Civil War era. As a number of historians have noted, women's reform activities—including protective labor legislation, public health efforts for women and children, and consumer advocacy—became increasingly essential components in the emerging welfare state of the Progressive Era. In fact, these developments eventually led to the creation of the very bureau that the *New York Herald* had called for in 1865: a Women's Bureau was formed in 1920 as part of the Department of Labor, to study and advocate for legislation on behalf of working-class women. With fifty years of women's civic activism behind it, the Women's Bureau was not simply a paternalist gesture toward women on the part of federal officials; rather, it flowed for the most part from the initiative of female professionals and reformers.[4]

The Civil War, because it set in motion a new relationship between women and the nation-state, must be seen as an important launching pad for many civic-minded initiatives, as well as for the turn-of-the-century welfare state that increasingly directed its attention to women's needs. But as this book has suggested, there was hardly a straight path from Civil War activism to the politically energized work of Progressive Era women. Many women emerged from the Civil War not with a sense of empowerment and opportunity but with a profound sense of civic estrangement, political weakness, and even economic victimization. In witnessing the awesome power of the Union military machine and political hierarchy, women learned, in new ways, how subordinate they were. Few voiced this sentiment as precisely as Cornelia Hancock, the Union army nurse who devoted herself to the Army of the Potomac in the aftermath of the Battle of Gettysburg. Seeing soldiers "faithfully plodding through the dust protecting me" had made her "feel more insignificant than words can express," she said. Hancock, it seems, accepted her insignificance as a necessary by-product of war. Others, though, may have been more disturbed by their lack of power. A sense of resentment suffused Elizabeth Livermore's evaluation of male voting strength when she observed in November 1864 that the men "must think themselves . . . almost kings in their powers & prerogatives." Nor can we be sure that Laura Beatty felt content about her own observation of women's ineffectiveness. "All that a woman could say," she had written to her soldier husband in the fall of 1864, "would not make a particle of difference in the fate of our country." Trying to respond to her husband's desire that she discard such feelings of political uselessness, Beatty no doubt felt herself caught between the impulse toward political engagement and the reality of persistent male supremacy.[5]

Perhaps the conflict and frustration Union women felt in the Civil War years were necessary preconditions for their political actions in the Gilded Age and the Progressive Era. Perhaps before they could advance their struggle for civic and political equality, women had to become more keenly aware of their subordinated status outside the domestic realm. The war did not emancipate women so much as teach them about their second-class status, in new and previously unimagined roles—as nurses, as pension recipients, as government employees, and as politically engaged actors in a wartime nation. Women glimpsed new possibilities but were quickly reminded of the limitations and restrictions that came with them. The Civil War did set the stage for later initiatives won by American women, although not so much by directly inspiring and energizing a new women's movement as by pushing the struggle for women's advancement beyond the home and into the nation.

Notes

ABBREVIATIONS

AAS	*American Antiquarian Society, Worcester, MA*
CHS	*Connecticut Historical Society, Hartford*
HL	*The Huntington Library, Art Collections, and Botanical Gardens, San Marino, CA*
HU	*Harvard University, Cambridge, MA*
LC	*Library of Congress, Washington, DC*
MHS	*Massachusetts Historical Society, Boston*
MnHS	*Minnesota Historical Society, St. Paul*
MSU	*Michigan State University, East Lansing*
NA	*National Archives, Washington, DC*
NHHS	*New Hampshire Historical Society, Concord*
NYPL	*New York Public Library*
PSA	*Pennsylvania State Archives, Harrisburg*
SL	*Schlesinger Library, Harvard University*
SSC	*Sophia Smith Collection, Smith College, Northampton, MA*
USAMHI	*U.S. Army Military History Institute, Carlisle Barracks, Carlisle, PA*

PROLOGUE

1. Among the historical accounts that have examined Confederate women's patriotism, or lack thereof, are George Rable, *Civil Wars: Women and the Crisis of Southern Nationalism* (Urbana, IL, 1991); Drew Faust, *Mothers of Invention: Women of the Slaveholding South in the American Civil War* (Chapel Hill, NC, 1996); and Elizabeth Varon, *We Mean to Be Counted* (Chapel Hill, NC, 1998), 169–177. On wartime images of Confederate women, see Reid Mitchell, *The Vacant*

Chair: The Northern Soldier Leaves Home (New York, 1993), 89–113, and Nina Silber, "The Northern Myth of the Rebel Girl," in Christie Farnham, ed., *Women of the American South* (New York, 1997), 120–132.

2. *New York Herald,* September 3, 1864; quote on "courage and energy" of Southern women in "A Few Words in Behalf of the Loyal Women of the United States by One of Themselves" (New York, 1863), in Frank Freidel, ed., *Union Pamphlets of the Civil War, 1861–1865,* vol. 2 (Cambridge, MA, 1967), 766; *New York Herald,* May 12, 1863.

3. Gail Hamilton [Mary Abigail Dodge], "Courage! A Tract for the Times," (New York, 1862), in Frank Freidel, ed., *Union Pamphlets of the Civil War,* vol. 1 (Cambridge, MA, 1967), 322; Gail Hamilton, "A Call to My Countrywomen," *Atlantic Monthly* 6 (March 1863): 345–349.

4. Linda Kerber, *Women of the Republic: Intellect and Ideology in Revolutionary America* (New York, 1980), 35–67.

5. Ibid., 189–231.

6. Varon, *We Mean to Be Counted,* 71–102.

7. Ibid., 137–168.

8. On the domestic manifestations of the sectional crisis, see Leeann Whites, "The Civil War as a Crisis in Gender," in Catherine Clinton and Nina Silber, eds., *Divided Houses: Gender and the Civil War* (New York, 1992), 3–21.

9. Caroline Cowles Richards Clarke, *Village Life in America, 1852–1872* (New York, 1913), 130; letters of Elizabeth D. Cabot to Ellen Twisleton, November 6 and December 16, 1860, in Hugh Cabot Family Papers, Box 2, Folder 19, SL; Caroline Dunstan, diary entry for December 4, 1860, NYPL.

10. Letter of Elizabeth D. Cabot, November 26, 1860, in Hugh Cabot Family Papers, Box 2, Folder 19, SL; Diary of Annie G. Dudley Davis (transcript copy of original), HM 58019, HL.

11. Elizabeth Cady Stanton, Susan B. Anthony, and Matilda Gage, eds., *History of Woman Suffrage,* vol. 2 (New York, 1882), 23; Jeanie Attie, *Patriotic Toil: Northern Women and the American Civil War* (Ithaca, NY, 1998), 275; Mary Massey, *Bonnet Brigades: American Women and the Civil War* (New York, 1966), 24; Gail Collins, *America's Women*

(New York, 2003), xv. A different type of analysis that both confirms and challenges this "conventional wisdom" can be found in Jean Bethke Elshtain, *Women and War* (New York, 1987).

12. *New York Herald,* April 30, 1861.

1. LOYALTIES IN CONFLICT

1. Letters of Ann Cotton, October 7, 1862, and January 1, 1863, in Papers of Josiah Dexter Cotton, LC.

2. Letters of Ann Cotton, June 25, 1863, October 14, 1863, and October 23, 1863, ibid.

3. Letter of Ann Cotton, October 2, 1864, ibid.

4. Information on the ages and marital and economic status of Union soldiers can be found in James McPherson, *For Cause and Comrades: Why Men Fought in the Civil War* (New York, 1997), viii, 182, and W. J. Rorabaugh, "Who Fought for the North in the Civil War? Concord, Massachusetts, Enlistments," *Journal of American History* 73, no. 3 (1986): 695–701.

5. *Arthur's Home Magazine,* quoted in Alice Fahs, *The Imagined Civil War: Popular Literature of the North and South, 1861–1865* (Chapel Hill, NC, 2000), 42–43; "The Volunteer's Wife to Her Husband" and *Harper's Weekly* cartoon in Charles Judah and George W. Smith, eds., *Life in the North during the Civil War: A Source History* (Albuquerque, NM, 1966), 42–43; Diary of Annie G. Dudley Davis, HL.

6. Caroline B. White Papers, octavo vol. 9, AAS; Diary of Caroline Dunstan, April 22, 1861, NYPL; *The Valley Spirit* (Chambersburg, PA), May 15, 1861; Haverhill and Bradford Soldiers Relief Society Records, AAS; Richmond Ladies' Soldiers Aid Society, Minute Book, PSA.

7. Diary of Caroline Dunstan, April 19 and May 10, 1861, NYPL; letter of Susan Hale, March 19, 1862, in Hale Family Papers, SSC; Harold E. Hammond, ed., *Diary of a Union Lady, 1861–1865* (New York, 1962), 15; Ethel Alice Hurn, ed., *Wisconsin Women in the War between the States* (Madison, WI, 1911), 11; excerpt from William H. Russell in Judah and Smith, eds., *Life in the North,* 46; letter of A. C. Hinckley, May 21, 1861, in Henry Rose Hinckley Papers, Historic Northampton, Northampton, MA.

8. Ann Gorman Condon, ed., *Architects of Our Fortune* (San Marino, CA, 2000), 108; Marjorie Ann Rogers, "An Iowa Woman in Wartime," part 1, *Annals of Iowa* 35 (Winter 1961): 543; Hammond, *Diary of a Union Lady*, 19; James C. Mohr, ed., *The Cormany Diaries: A Northern Family in the Civil War* (Pittsburgh, 1982), 253.

9. Letter of Sophia Buchanan, August 3, 1862, in George M. Blackburn, ed., "Letters to the Front: A Distaff View of the Civil War," *Michigan History* 49 (1965): 54; Charles Larimer, ed., *Love and Valor: Intimate Civil War Letters between Captain Jacob and Emeline Ritner* (Western Springs, IL, 2000), 19; letter of Augusta Kidder, May 18, 1862, quoted in Steven E. Woodworth, *Cultures in Conflict: The American Civil War* (Westport, CT, 2000), 127; letter of Harriet Jane Thompson to Major William G. Thompson, in Glenda Riley, ed., "Civil War Life: The Letters of Harriet Jane Thompson," part 2, *Annals of Iowa* 44 (1978): 306–307. Mrs. Thompson went by her middle name, Jane.

10. Letter of Harriet Jane Thompson to Major William G. Thompson, in Riley, ed., "Civil War Life," part 1, *Annals of Iowa* 44 (1978): 225.

11. McPherson, *For Cause and Comrades*, 98–99, 135; Stephanie McCurry, "'The Soldier's Wife': White Women, the State, and the Politics of Protection in the Confederacy," in Alison Parker and Stephanie Cole, eds., *Women and the Unstable State in Nineteenth-Century America* (College Station, TX, 2000), 15–36. On the conflicted loyalties of the Union soldier, see also Reid Mitchell, *The Vacant Chair: The Northern Soldier Leaves Home* (New York, 1993), 29–30.

12. On motivations of Northern soldiers, see McPherson, *For Cause and Comrades*, 98–100; on constructions of nationalism among civilians in the Civil War North, see Melinda Lawson, *Patriot Fires: Forging a New American Nationalism in the Civil War North* (Lawrence, KS, 2002).

13. Samuel Cormany, diary entry for September 1862, in Mohr, ed., *The Cormany Diaries*, 229; Skelton quoted in Glenn C. Altschuler and Stuart M. Blumin, *Rude Republic: Americans and Their Politics in the Nineteenth Century* (Princeton, NJ, 2000), 159; all others quoted in McPherson, *For Cause and Comrades*, 23, 99.

14. Letter of James Madison Bowler, September 27, 1862, to Elizabeth Sarah Caleff, Bowler Family Papers, MnHS; letter of Taylor Peirce,

August 20, 1862, in Richard L. Kiper, ed., *Dear Catharine, Dear Taylor: The Civil War Letters of a Union Soldier and His Wife* (Lawrence, KS, 2002), 24.

15. Rogers, "An Iowa Woman in Wartime," 543; Condon, ed., *Architects of Our Fortune*, 118.

16. McPherson, *For Cause and Comrades,* 133; letter of Sara Billings, September 21, 1864, in Billings Family Papers, State Historical Society of Wisconsin, Madison; for an example of a wife asking her husband not to go into battle, see letter of Marshall Phillips, June 2, 1863, in Letters of Marshall and Diana Phillips, S-166mb 6/3–6/8, Maine Historical Society, Portland; letter of James Madison Bowler, April 4, 1862, to Elizabeth Sarah Caleff, Bowler Family Papers, MnHS.

17. Correspondence of James Madison Bowler and Elizabeth Sarah Caleff, especially letters of February 26 and March 7, 1863, Bowler Family Papers, MnHS.

18. Linda Kerber, *No Constitutional Right to Be Ladies* (New York, 1998), xxii.

19. Letter of Josiah Corban, June 24, 1863, in Letters of Josiah B. Corban, MS 69465, CHS; Ohio soldier quoted in McPherson, *For Cause and Comrades*, 139; letter of Taylor Peirce, April 18, 1864, in Kiper, ed., *Dear Catharine, Dear Taylor,* 189–190.

20. Letter of Catharine Peirce, September 24, 1863, in Kiper, ed., *Dear Catharine, Dear Taylor,* 140; letters of Fanny Pierce, August 6, October 13, and August 29, 1861, in Thayer Family Papers, MHS.

21. Letters of Grace Weston, November 26, 1863, and January 7, 1864, in Weston-Allen Papers, SSC.

22. Condon, ed., *Architects of Our Fortune,* 119–127; Hurn, ed., *Wisconsin Women in the War,* 40.

23. Eric Foner, *Reconstruction: America's Unfinished Revolution* (New York, 1988), 24; letter of Catherine Buckingham, May 16, 1864, quoted in McPherson, *For Cause and Comrades,* 139; letter of Sophia Buchanan, January 1, 1863, in Blackburn, ed., "Letters to the Front," 55–56; letter of Emeline Ritner, August 17, 1864, in Larimer, ed., *Love and Valor,* 336; letter to Abraham Lincoln from Miss Mollie E., in Harold Holzer, ed., *Dear Mr. Lincoln: Letters to the President* (Reading, MA, 1993), 270–271.

24. Diary of Helen Grinnell, NYPL; letter of A. C. Hinckley, May 1, 1861, Henry Rose Hinckley Papers, Historic Northampton.

25. Quote from the *United States Service Magazine* appears in William Blair, "We Are Coming, Father Abraham—Eventually: The Problem of Northern Nationalism in the Pennsylvania Recruiting Drives of 1862," in Joan Cashin, ed., *The War Was You and Me: Civilians in the American Civil War* (Princeton, NJ, 2002), 191.

26. Examples of literary rebukes of "shoddy" womanhood can be found in "The Fortunes of War," *Harper's Monthly*, July 1864, and "The Russian Ball," *Harper's Weekly*, November 21, 1863.

27. Gail Hamilton, "A Call to My Countrywomen," *Atlantic Monthly* 6 (March 1863): 346.

28. Fanny Fern, "Soldiers' Wives," *New York Ledger*, November 8, 1862, 4.

29. Mrs. O. S. Baker, "The Ladies' Loyal League," *Continental Monthly* 4 (July 1863): 51–56.

30. *A Few Words in Behalf of the Loyal Women of the United States by One of Themselves* (New York, 1863), in Frank Freidel, ed., *Union Pamphlets of the Civil War*, vol. 2 (Cambridge, MA, 1967), 766–786, 780.

31. Ibid., 780.

2. THE ECONOMIC BATTLEFRONT

1. Mary Austin Wallace's account can be found in her wartime diary, which is reprinted in Julia McCune, ed., "Mary Austin Wallace: Her Diary," in Michigan Civil War Centennial Observance Commission, *Michigan Women in the Civil War* (Lansing, MI, 1963), 133–146; upbeat interpretations of Wallace's and other Northern women's experiences, can be found in Mary Livermore, *My Story of the War* (New York, 1995), 146–149.

2. Jeanne Boydston, *Home and Work: Housework, Wages, and the Ideology of Labor in the Early Republic* (New York, 1990), 56–74.

3. Emerson David Fite, *Social and Industrial Conditions in the North during the Civil War* (New York, 1910), 187–188; Boydston, *Home and Work*, 75–98; John Mack Faragher, *Sugar Creek: Life on the Illinois Prairie* (New Haven, 1986), 209.

4. Norma Basch, *In the Eyes of the Law: Women, Marriage and Property in Nineteenth-Century New York* (Ithaca, 1982), 15–29.
5. Boydston, *Home and Work*, 142–163.
6. Michael Grossberg, *Governing the Hearth: Law and the Family in Nineteenth-Century America* (Chapel Hill, NC, 1985), 27; Basch, *In the Eyes of the Law*, 224–232.
7. Fite, *Social and Industrial Conditions*, 85, 184.
8. Letter of Frank Lincoln, December 29, 1862, in Lincoln Family Letters, Hitchcock Free Academy, Brimfield, MA, transcribed and made available to author by Larry Lowenthal; letter of Anne Saylor, April 17, 1865, in Letters of Anne Saylor, Shelby County Historical and Genealogical Society, Shelbyville, IL; letter of Benjamin Morse, October 22, 1862, in Collection of Carole A. Fontana; letter of Louisa Phifer, in Carol B. Pye, ed., "Letters from an Illinois Farm, 1864–65," *Journal of the Illinois State Historical Society* 66 (1973): 400.
9. Fite, *Social and Industrial Conditions*, 288–289. Fite suggests that "undoubtedly over half" of all bounty money was "turned over by the soldiers to their needy relatives" (288). Ethel Alice Hurn, ed., *Wisconsin Women in the War between the States* (Madison, WI, 1911), 61; J. Matthew Gallman, *Mastering Wartime: A Social History of Philadelphia during the Civil War* (Cambridge, UK, 1990), 123.
10. For discussions of women moving to live with others during the war, see, for example, Nancy Grey Osterud, "Rural Women during the Civil War: New York's Nanticoke Valley, 1861–1865," *New York History* 62 (1990): 357–385; case of James and Abby Hood in Bristol County Supreme Judicial Court Records, April 1866, Bristol County, Massachusetts State Archives, Boston; Richard L. Kiper, ed., *Dear Catharine, Dear Taylor: The Civil War Letters of a Union Soldier and His Wife* (Lawrence, KS, 2002), 4; George M. Blackburn, ed., "Letters to the Front: A Distaff View of the Civil War," *Michigan History* 49 (1965); letter of John Pardington, March 23, 1863, in Coralou Peel Lassen, ed., *Dear Sarah: Letters Home from a Soldier of the Iron Brigade* (Bloomington, IN, 1999), 87; letter of Harriet Jane Thompson, in Glenda Riley, ed., "Civil War Life: The Letters of Harriet Jane Thompson," part 2, *Annals of Iowa* 44 (1978): 301.
11. Letter of Rhoda Southworth, September 28, 1862, in Southworth

Family Papers, MnHS; letter of Emeline Ritner, August 15, 1862, in Charles Larimer, ed., *Love and Valor: Intimate Civil War Letters between Captain Jacob and Emeline Ritner* (Western Springs, IL, 2000), 60; letter of Levi Perry, July 26, 1862, Letters of Levi Perry, S-1954mb 93/15 ms178, Maine Historical Society, Portland.

12. Letter of Julia Underhill, January 31, 1864, in Papers of Julia Underhill, MnHS; letter of George Shepherd, January 6, 1864, in Letters of George Shepherd, State Historical Society of Wisconsin, Madison; pension files of O'Donnell, Batson, and Matthew Bates, in Civil War pension records, NA.

13. Lyman Gray and John Benton are both discussed in Osterud, "Rural Women during the Civil War"; letter of Samuel Potter, April 9, 1864, in *Valley of the Shadow: Two Communities in the American Civil War,* Virginia Center for Digital History, University of Virginia (http://valley.vcdh.virginia.edu/lettersp2.html), hereafter cited as *Valley of Shadow;* letter of John Beatty, September 10, 1864, in Papers of John Beatty, MnHS; letter of Taylor Peirce, September 12, 1862, in Kiper, ed., *Dear Catharine, Dear Taylor,* 25.

14. Letter of Taylor Peirce, September 21, 1862, in Kiper, ed., *Dear Catharine, Dear Taylor,* 31.

15. Osterud, "Rural Women during the Civil War," 371; letter of Anne Saylor, April 25, 1865, Shelby County Historical and Genealogical Society, Shelbyville, IL; letter of Rebecca Lincoln, undated (1863?) in Lincoln Family Letters; letter of Ann Cotton, February 16, 1863, in Papers of Josiah Dexter Cotton, LC.

16. Letter of Fanny Pierce, December 15, 1861, in Thayer Family Papers, MHS; Osterud, "Rural Women during the Civil War," 374–375.

17. Letter of George Shepherd, January 17, 1864, in Letters of George Shepherd, State Historical Society of Wisconsin, Madison; letter of Richard Henry Tebout, September 26, 1865, in Ira Berlin, ed., *The Black Military Experience* (Cambridge, UK, 1982), 669; letter of Louisa Phifer, March 15, 1865, in Pye, ed., "Letters From an Illinois Farm," 400; letter of Emeline Ritner, November 27, 1862, in Larimer, ed., *Love and Valor,* 68–69; Rosella Benton quoted in Osterud, "Rural Women during the Civil War," 376.

18. Letters of Emeline Ritner, May 6, 1863, and September 19, 1863, in Larimer, ed., *Love and Valor,* 164, 207; Marjorie Ann Rogers, "An

Iowa Woman in Wartime," part 2, in *Annals of Iowa* 35 (Spring 1961): 598–599.

19. Fite, *Social and Industrial Conditions*, 8–9; Phillip Paludan, *"A People's Contest": The Union and the Civil War 1861–1865* (New York, 1988), 157–160; Mary Livermore, *My Story of the War* (New York, 1995), 146; Susan Rugh, "'Awful Calamaties Now Upon Us': The Civil War in Fountain Green, Illinois," *Journal of Illinois State Historical Society* 93 (Spring 2000): 21–22.

20. Lee Craig and Thomas Weiss, "Agricultural Productivity Growth during the Decade of the Civil War," *Journal of Economic History* 53 (1993): 527–548; letter of Emeline Ritner, August 7, 1863, in Larimer, ed., *Love and Valor*, 204; letter of Lydia Watkins, August 14, 1864, in *Michigan Women in the Civil War*, 55; diary entry of Rachel Cormany in James C. Mohr, ed., *The Cormany Diaries: A Northern Family in the Civil War* (Pittsburgh, 1982), 449. Emerson David Fite, in *Social and Industrial Conditions in the North during the Civil War*, attributes much of the increase in agricultural productivity to westward immigration from both the East Coast and Europe. See, in particular, pages 9–11.

21. Letter of Catharine Peirce, January 31, 1864, in Kiper, ed., *Dear Catharine, Dear Taylor*, 175–176; letter of Susan Eaton, September 11, 1864, in Southworth Family Letters, MnHS.

22. Letter of Samary Sherman, November 25, 1862, in Lucretia Sibley Papers, AAS; Nancy Osterud, "Rural Women during the Civil War," 377; letter of Anne Saylor, June 21, 1865, Shelby County Historical and Genealogical Society; diary entry for Rachel Cormany, in Mohr, ed., *The Cormany Diaries*, 442.

23. Letter of Catharine Peirce, January 31, 1864, in Kiper, ed., *Dear Catharine, Dear Taylor*, 175–176; diary entry of Emily Elliot, in Steven E. Woodworth, *Cultures in Conflict: The American Civil War* (Westport, CT, 2000), 179; Fite, *Social and Industrial Conditions*, 246; letter of Lydia Watkins, May 26, 1863, in *Michigan Women in the Civil War*, 38; letter of Frances Ingersoll, June 2, 1863, in Walter Rundell, ed., "'Despotism of Traitors': The Rebellious South through New York Eyes," in *New York History* 45 (October 1964): 353; letter of Julia Underhill, January 31, 1864, in Papers of Julia Underhill, MnHS.

24. Mary Massey, *Bonnet Brigades: American Women and the Civil War*

(New York, 1966), 142–143; diary entry of March 13, 1863, for H. A. Severance, SL (microfilm); letter of Susan Eaton, September 11, 1864, in Southworth Family Letters, MnHS.

25. Mark Wilson, "The Extensive Side of Nineteenth-Century Military Economy: The Tent Industry in the Northern United States during the Civil War," *Enterprise and Society* 2 (2001): 329; Paludan, *"A People's Contest,"* 182–183; Fite, *Social and Industrial Conditions*, 186–188; reprint from *Fincher's Trades' Review*, March 18, 1865, in John R. Commons, ed., *A Documentary History of American Industrial Society*, vol. 9 (New York, 1958), 72–73.

26. *U.S. House Reports 140*, 38th Congress, 1st sess., Select Committee to Investigate Charges against the Treasury Department (Washington, DC, 1864), 220–221; letters of David and Mary Demus in *Valley of the Shadow;* letter of Mrs. John Wilson, May 27, 1865, in Berlin, *Black Military Experience*, 682; letter of Rosanna Henson, July 11, 1864, in Berlin, *Black Military Experience*, 680; pension file of Lavinia Brown in Pension Records, NA.

27. Osterud, "Rural Women during the Civil War," 376; letter of Emeline Ritner, October 11, 1863, in Larimer, ed., *Love and Valor*, 220.

28. Finding aid and letters of Julia Underhill, October 11, 1863, December 4, 1863, January 31, 1864, and April 8, 1864, in Papers of Julia Underhill, MnHS.

29. Letter of Julia Underhill, July 28, 1864, in ibid.

30. Letter of Leemon Underhill, September 4, 1864, and newspaper clipping, in ibid.

31. "Special Report on Prisons and Prison Discipline by Massachusetts Board of State Charities," quoted in Edith Abbott, "The Civil War and the Crime Wave of 1865–1870," *Social Service Review* 1 (June 1927): 220.

32. Sheila Cumberworth and Daniel Biles, *An Enduring Love: The Civil War Diaries of Benjamin Franklin Pierce and His Wife Harriett Jane Goodwin Pierce* (Gettysburg, PA, 1995), 154; Lassen, ed., *Dear Sarah*, 87.

33. Letters of Ann Cotton, February 16 and February 25, 1863, in Papers of Josiah Dexter Cotton, LC; letter of Emeline Ritner, June 3, 1864, in Larimer, ed., *Love and Valor*, 283.

34. Letter of Benjamin Morse, May 29, 1862, in Letters of Benjamin F.

Morse, Collection of Carole A. Fontana; letter of Sylvester McElheney, November 29, 1864, in *Valley of the Shadow;* letter of John Pardington, October 23, 1862, in Lassen, ed., *Dear Sarah*, 26; letter of George Shepherd, March 1864, in Letters of George Shepherd, University of Wisconsin at Eau Claire; letter of Taylor Peirce, July 4, 1864, in Kiper, ed., *Dear Catharine, Dear Taylor*, 220.

35. *Harper's Weekly*, October 24, 1863, 677.
36. Letter of Emeline Ritner, October 14, 1864, and letter of Jacob Ritner, November 7, 1864, in Larimer, ed., *Love and Valor*, 375, 383; letter of Harriet Jane Thompson, November 11, 1862, in Riley, ed., "Civil War Life," part 2, 309.
37. Letter of Emeline Ritner, October 4, 1863, in Larimer, ed., *Love and Valor*, 214; diary entry of Emily Elliot, in Woodworth, *Cultures in Conflict*, 182; diary entry of Rachel Cormany, April 20, 1864, in Mohr, ed., *The Cormany Diaries*, 442.
38. Various entries for 1861, 1862, and 1863, in Diaries of Caroline Dunstan, NYPL.
39. Elizabeth Rogers Cabot, diary entries for April 18, 1863, and January 6, 1864, in Papers of Elizabeth Rogers Cabot, SL; Massey, *Bonnet Brigades*, 143, 145; information on labor organizing among sewing women can be found in Rachel Seidman, "Beyond Sacrifice: Women and Politics on the Pennsylvania Home Front during the Civil War," PhD diss., Yale University, 1996, 146–154.
40. Massey, *Bonnet Brigades*, 144–147; "The Sewing Women," in Commons, *Documentary History of American Industrial Society*, vol. 9, 72–73; letter from J. Andrew Harris, January 23, 1865, to Abraham Lincoln, transcribed and annotated by the Lincoln Studies Center, Knox College, Galesburg, IL, available at Abraham Lincoln Papers at the Library of Congress, Manuscript Division (Washington, DC, 2000–2002), http://memory.loc.gov/ammem/alhtml/alhome.html, accessed March 10, 2004, hereafter cited as Lincoln Papers at LC; letter from "workingwomen of the City of New York" to Stanton, *New York Times*, September 4, 1864.
41. Massey, *Bonnet Brigades*, 131–135; Cindy Aron, *Ladies and Gentlemen of the Civil Service: Middle-Class Workers in Victorian America* (New York, 1987), 70.
42. Aron, *Ladies and Gentlemen of the Civil Service*, 70–71; Massey, *Bon-*

net Brigades, 144, 133; letters in Treasury Department files, RG 56, NA; Ulysses Grant letter on behalf of Mrs. Lionel Booth reprinted in Roy Basler, "And For His Widow and His Orphan," *Quarterly Journal of the Library of Congress* 27 (October 1970): 294; *U.S. House Reports 140,* 38th Congress, 1st sess., Select Committee to Investigate Charges against the Treasury Department (Washington, 1864), 17.

43. Seavey and Clark letters in Treasury Department files, RG 56, NA; letter of Jennie Gaughran, July 14, 1864, to Abraham Lincoln, transcribed and annotated by the Lincoln Studies Center, Knox College, Galesburg, IL, in Lincoln Papers at LC.

44. Megan McClintock, "Civil War Pensions and the Reconstruction of Union Families," *Journal of American History* 83 (September 1996): 456–480; Rebecca Edwards, *Angels in the Machinery: Gender in American Party Politics from the Civil War to the Progressive Era* (New York, 1997), 12–38.

45. McClintock, "Civil War Pensions," 461–471; Nancy Cott, *Public Vows: A History of Marriage and the Nation* (Cambridge, MA, 2000), 103–104.

46. *Congressional Globe,* 37 Cong., 2nd sess., May 13, 1862, 2100–2105.

47. Letter of Catherine Spielman, June 17, 1864, in Harold Holzer, ed., *Dear Mr. Lincoln: Letters to the President* (Reading, MA, 1993), 107.

3. DOMESTICITY UNDER SIEGE

1. Books that address the antebellum ideal of female domesticity include: Jeanne Boydston, *Home and Work: Housework, Wages, and the Ideology of Labor in the Early Republic* (New York, 1990); Nancy Cott, *The Bonds of Womanhood: "Woman's Sphere" in New England, 1780–1835* (New Haven, CT, 1977); Kathryn Kish Sklar, *Catharine Beecher: A Study in American Domesticity* (New York, 1976); Harriet Beecher Stowe, *Uncle Tom's Cabin: Or, Life among the Lowly* (New York: Penguin, 1986), quotations from 214–217.

2. Jeanie Attie, *Patriotic Toil: Northern Women and the American Civil War* (Ithaca, NY, 1998), 9–13.

3. Vermont soldier quoted in James McPherson, *For Cause and Comrades: Why Men Fought in the Civil War* (New York, 1997), 134.

4. On the distinct domestic ideal of the antebellum South, see Elizabeth

Fox-Genovese, *Within the Plantation Household: Black and White Women in the Old South* (Chapel Hill, NC, 1988), 100–145.

5. "The Volunteer's Wife to her Husband" in Charles Judah and George W. Smith, eds., *Life in the North during the Civil War: A Source History* (Albuquerque, NM, 1966), 42.

6. Letter of Ann Cotton, June 25, 1863, in Papers of Josiah Dexter Cotton, LC; letter of Elizabeth Caleff, December 23, 1861, in Bowler Family Papers, MnHS; diary of Mary E. Baker (Pierce) in Thayer Family Papers, MHS.

7. Nancy Grey Osterud, "Rural Women during the Civil War," 360–363; letters of Sophia Buchanan, August 17 and August 5, 1862, in George M. Blackburn, ed., "Letters to the Front: A Distaff View of the Civil War," *Michigan History* 49 (1965): 58, 60; letter of Clara Wood, 1862(?), in Wood Family Letters, unpublished manuscripts from the South Hadley Historical Society, available at the Web site The American Civil War: Letters and Diaries (accessed March 9, 2004; hereafter cited as Civil War in Letters and Diaries); letter of Harriet Jane Thompson, September 19, 1862, in Glenda Riley, ed., "Civil War Life: The Letters of Harriet Jane Thompson," part 1, *Annals of Iowa* 44 (1978): 231; letter of Elizabeth Bowler, January 21, 1863, in Bowler Family Papers, MnHS.

8. On camp visits by soldiers' female relatives, see Mary Massey, *Bonnet Brigades: American Women and the Civil War* (New York, 1966), 65–72; on Julia Grant's presence in camp, see John Y. Simon, "A Marriage Tested by War: Ulysses and Julia Grant," in Carol Bleser and Lesley Gordon, eds., *Intimate Strategies of the Civil War: Military Commanders and Their Wives* (New York, 2001), 123–137.

9. Massey, *Bonnet Brigades,* 65–66; Emily Elliot, diary entries for January 16 and January 19, 1864, in Steven E. Woodworth, *Cultures in Conflict: The American Civil War* (Westport, CT, 2000), 172–173; letter of Elizabeth Bowler, November 17, 1864, in Bowler Family Papers, MnHS; letter of Sarah Butler, May 2, 1862, in *The Private and Official Correspondence of Gen. Benjamin F. Butler, during the Period of the Civil War* (Norwood, MA, 1917), 439.

10. Union soldier's letter quoted in Bell Irvin Wiley, *The Life of Billy Yank: The Common Soldier of the Union* (Baton Rouge, 1952), 256–257;

Eunice Tripler quoted in Michigan Civil War Centennial Observance Commission, *Michigan Women in the Civil War* (Lansing, 1963), 14.

11. Letters of Lucinda Ingersoll, August 26, 1861, and October 2, 1861, in Walter Rundell, Jr., ed., "'Despotism of Traitors': The Rebellious South through New York Eyes," *New York History* 45 (October 1964): 332, 334; letter of Rhoda Southworth, July 1862, in Southworth Family Papers, MnHS; letters of Elizabeth Caleff, December 23, 1861, and James Bowler, January 23, 1861, in Bowler Family Papers, MnHS.

12. Letter of Harriet Jane Thompson, September 7, 1862, in Riley, ed., "Civil War Life," part 1, 222; letter of Catharine Peirce, October 25, 1863, in Richard L. Kiper, ed., *Dear Catharine, Dear Taylor: The Civil War Letters of a Union Soldier and His Wife* (Lawrence, KS, 2002), 146; letter of Mattie Blanchard, March 26, 1863, in Letters of Mattie and Caleb Blanchard, CHS; letter of Emeline Ritner, October 19, 1863, in Charles Larimer, ed., *Love and Valor: Intimate Civil War Letters between Captain Jacob and Emeline Ritner* (Western Springs, IL, 2000), 228. Rachel Seidman, in "Beyond Sacrifice: Women and Politics on the Pennsylvania Home Front during the Civil War," PhD diss., Yale University, 1996, makes a similar point about the difficulty women in Pennsylvania had in dispensing moral advice to men at war.

13. Letter of George Shepherd, March (?) 1864, in Letters of George Shepherd, University of Wisconsin at Eau Claire; letter of Mary Pierce, March 9, 1864, in Thayer Family Papers, MHS.

14. Letter of Clara Wood, January 25, 1863, in Wood Family Papers, unpublished manuscripts from the South Hadley Historical Society available online at Civil War in Letters and Diaries; letter of Melissa Wells, January 20, 1864, in Albert Castel, ed., "Dearest Ben: Letters from a Soldier's Wife," *Michigan History* 71 (May/June 1987): 20; James C. Mohr, ed., *The Cormany Diaries: A Northern Family in the Civil War* (Pittsburgh, PA, 1982), 287.

15. Letter of Melissa Wells, December 20, 1863, in Castel, "Dearest Ben," 19; letter of Clara Wood, February 9, 1863, in Wood Family Papers, unpublished manuscripts from the South Hadley Historical Society available online at Civil War in Letters and Diaries; letter of John Pardington, December 21, 1862, in Coralou Peel Lassen, ed., *Dear Sarah: Letters Home from a Soldier of the Iron Brigade* (Bloomington, IN, 1999), 49.

16. Letter of James Bowler, November 14, 1863, and letter of Elizabeth Bowler, January 8, 1864, in Bowler Family Papers, MnHS; case of James Hood in Bristol County Supreme Judicial Court Records, Bristol County, Massachusetts (microfilm reel #1), Massachusetts State Archives, Boston.

17. Letter of Laura Beatty, September 3, 1864, in Beatty Papers, MnHS; Mohr, ed., *The Cormany Diaries*, 440; diary of Emily Elliot, entry for January 13, 1864, in Woodworth, *Cultures in Conflict*, 171.

18. Letter from Fairchild Papers in Wisconsin State Historical Society, reprinted in Judah and Smith, eds., *Life in the North*, 316–317; letter of Lucinda Ingersoll, October 2, 1861, in Rundell, "Despotism of Traitors," 334; letter of Elizabeth Bowler, March 7, 1863, in Bowler Family Papers, MnHS.

19. On Union soldiers' religious attitudes, see Wiley, *Life of Billy Yank*, 262–274; letter of Ann Cotton, October 19, 1862, in Papers of Josiah Dexter Cotton, LC.

20. Letter of Lucius Mox, undated, available at *Valley of the Shadow: Two Communities in the American Civil War*, Virginia Center for Digital History, University of Virginia (http://valley.vcdh.virginia.edu/lettersp2.html); letters of James Bowler, May 24, 1863, and July 5, 1863, in Bowler Family Papers, MnHS; letters of James Beatty, April 26, 1864, and September 15, 1864, in Beatty Papers, MnHS.

21. James Boyd Jones, "A Tale of Two Cities: The Hidden Battle against Venereal Disease in Civil War Nashville and Memphis," *Civil War History* 31 (September 1985): 270–276; Amy Stanley, *From Bondage to Contract* (Cambridge, UK, 1998), 249–250.

22. Diary of Harrison Otis, entry for September 15, 1862, in Ann Gorman Condon, ed., *Architects of Our Fortune* (San Marino, CA, 2000), 244; letter of Elizabeth Bowler, March 7, 1863, and letter of James Madison Bowler, November 1, 1864, in Bowler Family Papers, MnHS; letter of John Pardington, October 25, 1862, in Lassen, ed., *Dear Sarah*, 27.

23. Letter of Edwin Horton, January 14, 1865, in Letters of Edwin and Ellen Horton, MSS 21, no. 16, Vermont Historical Society, Montpelier; letter of Emeline Ritner, November 20, 1864, in Larimer, ed., *Love and Valor*, 387.

24. Diary of Rachel Cormany, entry for August 24, 1863, in Mohr, ed., *The*

Cormany Diaries, 379; letter of Julia Underhill, April 8, 1864, in Papers of Julia Underhill, MnHS.

25. Letters of James Beatty, April 26 and April 30, 1864, in Beatty Papers, MnHS; Edith Abbott, "The Civil War and the Crime Wave of 1865–1870," *Social Service Review* 1 (June 1927); J. Matthew Gallman, *The North Fights the Civil War: The Home Front* (Chicago, 1994), 17–18.

26. Norma Basch, *Framing American Divorce: From the Revolutionary Generation to the Victorians* (Berkeley, CA, 1999); Glenda Riley, *Divorce: An American Tradition* (New York, 1991), 78. Case of Thomas Rodman, November 1865; case of Allen Howland, April 1866; case of Alexander Duckworth, November 1865, all cited in Bristol County Supreme Judicial Court Divorce Records, Bristol County, MA (microfilm reel #1), Massachusetts State Archives, Boston.

27. Massey, *Bonnet Brigades,* 46–47; Elizabeth Leonard, *Yankee Women: Gender Battles in the Civil War* (New York, 1994), 14–17; Judith Ann Giesberg, *Civil War Sisterhood: The U.S. Sanitary Commission and Women's Politics in Transition* (Boston, 2000), 43–47.

28. Letter of Cornelia Hancock, August 8, 1863, in Harriet S. Jaquette, ed., *South after Gettysburg: Letters of Cornelia Hancock from the Army of the Potomac, 1863–1865* (Philadelphia, 1937), 21; Harold E. Hammond, ed., *Diary of a Union Lady, 1861–1865* (New York, 1962), 173; John R. Brumgardt, ed., *Civil War Nurse: The Diary and Letters of Hannah Ropes* (Knoxville, TN, 1980), 61.

29. Reid Mitchell, *The Vacant Chair: The Northern Soldier Leaves Home* (New York, 1993), 75–76.

30. Letter from Mrs. James Harlan, March 31, 1862, in National Freedmen's Relief Association, By-Laws and Minutes, 1862–1868, Boston Public Library; *Continental Monthly* 1 (June 1862): 728.

31. Letter of Cornelia Hancock, August 8, 1863, in Jaquette, ed., *South after Gettysburg,* 21; Kristie Ross, "'Women Are Needed Here': Northern Protestant Women as Nurses during the Civil War, 1861–1865," PhD diss., Columbia University, 1994, 158–164; diary entry of Esther Hill Hawks, October 21, 1865, in Gerald Schwartz, ed., *A Woman Doctor's Civil War: Esther Hill Hawks' Diary* (Columbia, SC, 1984), 201; Stephen B. Oates, *A Woman of Valor: Clara Barton and the Civil War* (New York, 1994), 148–151; Brenda Stevenson, ed., *The Journals of Charlotte Forten Grimke* (New York, 1988), 45–47; diary entry

of Eliza Otis, June 25, 1863, in Condon, ed., *Architects of Our Fortune*, 195.

32. Massey, *Bonnet Brigades*, 137–138; *U.S. House Reports 140*, 38th Congress, 1st sess., Select Committee to Investigate Charges against the Treasury Department (Washington, DC, 1864), 8–21.

33. Letter of Sallie Bridges, September 28, 1865, in Records of the Division of Appointments, Applications and Recommendations for Positions in the Washington, DC, Offices of the Treasury Department, 1830–1910, Box 217, RG 56, NA; Bernice M. Deutrich, "Propriety and Pay," *Prologue* (Fall 1971): 73–74.

34. *Allegheny Arsenal Investigation Report*, in Letters Received by the Office of the Adjutant General, 1861–1871, M619, Roll 72, RG 94, NA; Megan McClintock, "Civil War Pensions and the Reconstruction of Union Families," *Journal of American History* 83 (September 1996): 471–479; Nancy Cott, *Public Vows: A History of Marriage and the Nation* (Cambridge, MA, 2000), 103–104.

35. Cott, *Public Vows*, 92–94.

4. FROM PATRIOTS TO PARTISANS AND BACK AGAIN

1. Arthur J. Larsen, ed., *Crusader and Feminist: Letters of Jane Grey Swisshelm, 1858–1865* (Westport, CT, 1976), 176.

2. Larsen, ed., *Crusader and Feminist*, 1–27; Melanie Gustafson, *Women and the Republican Party, 1854–1924* (Urbana, IL, 2001), 15–17; Robert J. Dinkin, *Before Equal Suffrage: Women in Partisan Politics from Colonial Times to 1920* (Westport, CT, 1995), 50.

3. Janet Coryell, "Superseding Gender: The Role of the Woman Politico in Antebellum Partisan Politics," in Alison Parker and Stephanie Cole, eds., *Women and the Unstable State in Nineteenth-Century America* (College Station, TX, 2000), 84–112. Coryell notes the emergence of a group of women in the Civil War era whom she identifies as "female politicos," women who focused less on gender and more on partisan politics.

4. There is a growing literature on women and politics in antebellum America, including Elizabeth Varon, *We Mean to Be Counted* (Chapel Hill, NC, 1998); Parker and Cole, eds., *Women and the Unstable State*; Dinkin, *Before Equal Suffrage*.

5. Rebecca Edwards, *Angels in the Machinery: Gender in American*

Party Politics from the Civil War to the Progressive Era (New York, 1997), 3–35; Dinkin, *Before Equal Suffrage*, 55–59; letter of Lillie Chace, June 17, 1861, in Anna Dickinson Papers (microfilm), HU.

6. On the Republicans' wartime vision of national loyalty, see Melinda Lawson, *Patriot Fires: Forging a New American Nationalism in the Civil War North* (Lawrence, KS, 2002), 65–97.

7. Susan Rugh, "Awful Calamities Now upon Us: The Civil War in Fountain Green, Illinois," *Journal of the Illinois State Historical Society* 93 (Spring 2000): 16; Thomas Rodgers, "Hoosier Women and the Civil War Home Front," *Indiana Magazine of History* 97 (June 2001): 115.

8. The political battle between Republicans and Democrats is nicely summarized in Lawson, *Patriot Fires*, 65–97.

9. Letters of Eleanor Bereman, August 10, 1862, and March 15, 1863, in Charles F. Larimer, ed., *Love and Valor: Intimate Civil War Letters between Captain Jacob and Emeline Ritner* (Western Springs, IL, 2000), 56, 136; letter of Maria Patec, February 16, 1863, in Lucretia Sibley Papers, AAS; Martha Jane Smith quoted in Rodgers, "Hoosier Women and the Civil War Home Front," 121.

10. Letter of Elizabeth Caleff, February 9, 1862, in James Madison Bowler Papers, MnHS; letter of Sophia Buchanan, September 12, 1862, in George M. Blackburn, ed., "Letters to the Front: A Distaff View of the Civil War," *Michigan History* 49 (1965): 56.

11. Letter of Harriet Jane Thompson, November 2, 1862, in Glenda Riley, ed., "Civil War Life: The Letters of Harriet Jane Thompson," part 2, *Annals of Iowa* 44 (1978): 306; letter of Elizabeth Bowler, September 28, 1864, in James Madison Bowler Papers, MnHS; letter of Laura Beatty, August 19, 1864, in Beatty Papers, MnHS.

12. Letter of Robert Hubbard, February 25, 1863, in Letters of Robert Hubbard, Civil War Manuscripts Collection, Yale University Library; letter of Taylor Peirce, July 16, 1864, in Richard L. Kiper, ed., *Dear Catharine, Dear Taylor: The Civil War Letters of a Union Soldier and His Wife* (Lawrence, KS, 2002), 230.

13. Letters of Ann Cotton, January 1, June 14, and October 23, 1863, in Josiah Dexter Cotton Papers, LC.

14. Rachel Seidman, in her dissertation "Beyond Sacrifice: Women and Politics on the Pennsylvania Home Front during the Civil War," PhD

Diss., Yale University, 1996, estimates that about 30,000 letters were written by women to the federal government during the Civil War. An extensive collection of Lincoln correspondence, including numerous letters from women, can be found at *Abraham Lincoln Papers at the Library of Congress,* Manuscript Division (Washington, DC: American Memory Project, [2000–02]), http://memory.loc.gov/ammem/alhtml/alhome.html (Web site hereafter cited as Lincoln Papers at LC). Mary Herrick quoted in Seidman, "Beyond Sacrifice," 207; letter of Mrs. L. C. Howard, September 17, 1861, and letter of Mrs. A. A. Moor, January 13, 1865, in Lincoln Papers at LC; letter of Hannah Johnson quoted in Ella Forbes, *African American Women during the Civil War* (New York, 1998), 206–207; letter of Mattie Blanchard, March 26, 1863, in Letters of Mattie and Caleb Blanchard, CHS.

15. Letter of Sara Billings, September 24, 1864, in Billings Family Letters, Wisconsin Historical Society, Madison; letter of Catharine Peirce, May 17, 1863, in Kiper, ed., *Dear Catharine, Dear Taylor,* 111; letter of Sophia Buchanan, November 5, 1863, in Blackburn, ed., "Letters to the Front," 56; letter of Lydia Watkins, September 20, 1864, in "Letters from Home," in Michigan Civil War Centennial Observance Commission, *Michigan Women in the Civil War* (Lansing, 1963), 57; Lizzie Corning, Diary of Lizzie Corning, NHHS; letters of Mattie Blanchard, November 9, 1862, and March 26, 1863, in Letters of Mattie and Caleb Blanchard, CHS.

16. Letter of Harriet Jane Thompson in Riley, ed., "Civil War Life," part 2, 302; letter of Mary Parmelee, July 26, 1863, Letters of Mary Parmelee, Civil War Manuscripts Collection, Yale University Library; letters of Ruth A. Whittemore in Walter Rundell, Jr., ed., "'Despotism of Traitors': The Rebellious South through New York Eyes," *New York History* 45 (October 1964): 347, 349.

17. Rundell, ed., "'Despotism of Traitors,'" 356, 355.

18. Letter of Adelaide Fowler, July 1863, in Fowler Family Manuscripts, Peabody Essex Museum, Salem, MA; letter of Emeline Ritner, July 31, 1864, in Larimer, ed., *Love and Valor,* 322; letter of Catharine Peirce, February 7, 1864, in Kiper, ed., *Dear Catharine, Dear Taylor,* 183.

19. Octavia Roberts Corneau, ed., "A Girl in the Sixties," *Journal of the Illinois Historical Society* 22 (October 1929): 437; "The Draft," *Harper's*

Weekly, July 25, 1863, 466; Adrian Cook, *Armies of the Streets: The New York City Draft Riots of 1863* (Lexington, KY, 1974), 193–194, 310n.

20. Iver Bernstein, *The New York City Draft Riots* (New York, 1990), 36–39; William Hanna, "The Boston Draft Riot," *Civil War History* 36, no. 3 (1990): 262–273.

21. Marjorie Ann Rogers, "An Iowa Woman in Wartime," part 2, *Annals of Iowa* 35 (Spring 1961): 605; Thomas Rodgers, in his study of several Indiana counties, some of which were strongly Democratic, finds that smaller numbers of married and single Democratic men enlisted in the war. See Rodgers, "Hoosier Women and the Civil War Home Front"; letter of Ann Cotton, October 2, 1864, in Josiah Dexter Cotton Papers, LC.

22. Persis Black quoted in Ronald J. Zboray and Mary Saracina Zboray, "Cannonballs and Books: Reading and the Disruption of Social Ties on the New England Home Front," in Joan Cashin, ed., *The War Was You and Me* (Princeton, NJ, 2002), 244.

23. Dubuque newspaper quoted in Glenn Altschuler and Stuart Blumin, *Rude Republic: Americans and Their Politics in the Nineteenth Century* (Princeton, NJ, 2000), 172.

24. Forbes, *African American Women during the Civil War*, 43–45; Dorothy Sterling, *We Are Your Sisters: Black Women in the Nineteenth Century* (New York, 1984), 251–253, 296; letter of Frances Ellen Watkins Harper, 1862, in William Still, *From the Underground Rail Road: A Record of Facts, Authentic Narratives, Letters, &c: Narrating the Hardships, Hair-breadth Escapes and Death Struggles of the Slaves in Their Efforts for Freedom* (Philadelphia, 1872), available at Civil War in Letters and Diaries Web site.

25. On the politics of the nineteenth-century post office see Elizabeth Varon, "Patriotism, Partisanship and Prejudice: Elizabeth Van Lew of Richmond and Debates over Female Civic Duty in Post–Civil War America," in Parker and Cole, eds., *Women and the Unstable State*, 106.

26. Various letters to Lincoln available at Lincoln Papers at LC; Massey, *Bonnet Brigades*, 133; Marshall Henry Cushing, *The Story of Our Post Office: The Greatest Government Department in All Its Phases* (Boston, 1893), 453; Henry Ward Beecher quoted in Gustafson,

Women and the Republican Party, 36. According to Cushing, there were, as of 1893, 6,335 postmistresses in the United States.

27. Gustafson, *Women and the Republican Party,* 25–33; Dinkin, *Before Equal Suffrage,* 57–59; J. Matthew Gallman, "Anna Dickinson: Abolitionist Orator," in Steven E. Woodworth, *The Human Tradition in the Civil War and Reconstruction* (Wilmington, DE, 2000), 93–110.

28. Letters of Benjamin F. Prescott, February 12, February 21, March 25, April 2, and May 11, 1863, in Papers of Anna Dickinson (microfilm), HU; Gallman, "Anna Dickinson," 93–110.

29. J. Matthew Gallman, "An Inspiration to Work: Anna Elizabeth Dickinson, Public Orator," in Cashin, ed., *The War Was You and Me,* 171; diary of Annie G. Dudley Davis, HM 58019 (transcription), 9, HL; diary of Lizzie Corning, NHHS; letter of Lillie Chace, March 30, 1863, in Papers of Anna Dickinson (microfilm), HU.

30. Letter to B. F. Prescott, February 27, 1863, and letter from Everett Clapp, October 27, 1863, in Papers of Anna Dickinson (microfilm), HU; Gustafson, *Women and the Republican Party,* 25–33.

31. Gustafson, *Women and the Republican Party,* 25–33; Gallman, "Anna Dickinson," 93–110.

32. Letter from Mrs. J. Olmsted to B. F. Prescott, March 23, 1863, and letter of B. F. Prescott, April 2, 1863, in Papers of Anna Dickinson (microfilm), HU.

33. Letters of Joseph P. Allyn, May 31, 1863; Henry Homes, November 23, 1863; and Theodore Tilton, July 13, 1864, in Papers of Anna Dickinson (microfilm), HU.

34. Letter of Catharine Peirce, in Kiper, ed., *Dear Catharine, Dear Taylor,* 285–286; letter of Lillie Chace, August 21, 1864, in Papers of Anna Dickinson (microfilm), HU; letter of Rhoda Southworth, September 16, 1862, in Southworth Family Papers, MnHS.

35. Letters of Mrs. John Hodges, April 17, 1863; Mrs. W. H. Planck, February 1, 1864; and Ellie Reno, May 11, 1863, available at Lincoln Papers at LC Web site.

36. Letter of C. I. H. Nichols in Elizabeth Cady Stanton, Susan B. Anthony, and Matilda Gage, eds., *History of Woman Suffrage,* vol. 2 (New York, 1882), 887–888; letter of Ann Cotton, October 16, 1864, in Josiah Dexter Cotton Papers, LC.

37. Diary entry for November 8, 1864, Papers of Elizabeth Livermore,

NHHS; letter of James Beatty, September 17, 1864, in Beatty Family Papers, MnHS. On the growing power of the nation-state in the Civil War era, see Richard Bensel, *Yankee Leviathan: The Origins of Central State Authority in America, 1859–1877* (Cambridge, UK, 1990).

38. Letters of Cornelia Hancock, June 20, 1864, and July 14, 1864, in Harriet S. Jaquette, ed., *South after Gettysburg: Letters of Cornelia Hancock from the Army of the Potomac, 1863–65* (Philadelphia, 1937), 119, 134–135; Katharine Prescott Wormeley, *The Other Side of the War with the Army of the Potomac* (Boston, 1889), 29–30. Similar sentiments were expressed by Clara Barton in her letter of June 24, 1863, in Clara Barton Papers, AAS.

39. Information on the Woman's Loyal National League can be found in Wendy Venet, *Women Abolitionists in the Civil War* (Charlottesville, VA, 1991), 94–122; Faye Dudden, "The New York Strategy: the New York Woman's Movement and the Civil War," in Jean Baker, ed., *Votes for Women: The Struggle for Suffrage Revisited* (New York, 2002), 56–76; and Stanton, Anthony, and Gage, eds., *History of Woman Suffrage*, vol. 2, 51–86. Stanton's appeal appears on 53.

40. Mrs. Hoyt's remarks appear in Stanton, Anthony, and Gage, eds., *History of Woman Suffrage*, vol. 2, 63–64; the views of Mrs. Hoyt and other Wisconsin women can also be found in Ethel Alice Hurn, ed., *Wisconsin Women in the War between the States* (Madison, WI, 1911), 90–91.

41. Stanton, Anthony, and Gage, eds., *History of Woman Suffrage*, vol. 2, 898.

42. Call for Woman's Loyal National League meeting in *The Liberator,* May 6, 1864.

43. Caroline Dall, "To the Women of the Loyal League," letter in *The Liberator,* May 6, 1864; Dudden, "The New York Strategy," 69–71.

44. Dall, "To the Women of the Loyal League"; Dudden, "The New York Strategy," 69–71.

45. Harold E. Hammond, ed., *Diary of a Union Lady, 1861–1865* (New York, 1962), 219, 297; Massey, *Bonnet Brigades,* 246–247; letter of Elizabeth Dwight Cabot, May 8, 1864, in Hugh Cabot Family Papers, SL.

46. *New York Times,* May 5, 1864; editorial, *New York Times,* May 6, 1864; Clara Barton, Diary, in Clara Barton Papers, AAS.

47. Massey, *Bonnet Brigades*, 246–247.
48. *New York Herald*, July 14, 1863; *Harper's Weekly*, July 25 and August
    1, 1863; Hammond, ed., *Diary of a Union Lady*, 249; letter of Eliza-
    beth Gay to Abigail Hopper Gibbons, August 13, 1863, in Sarah Hop-
    per Emerson, ed., *Life of Abby Hopper Gibbons: Told Chiefly through
    her Correspondence* (New York, 1896), 58.
49. Letter of Sarah Chamberlain, 1866, in Chamberlain-Adams Papers,
    SL.
50. Ibid.
51. "Work and Incidents of Army Life," 1865 war lecture, in Clara Barton
    Papers, AAS.

5. AIDING THE CAUSE, SERVING THE STATE

1. Bardwell diary, SL.
2. Mary Livermore writes of "the loyal women of the North, who organized over ten thousand 'aid societies' during the war." *My Story of the
   War* (New York, 1995), 133.
3. Scholarly works that have appraised Northern women's wartime relief
   work include Jeanie Attie, *Patriotic Toil: Northern Women and the
   American Civil War* (Ithaca, NY, 1998); Judith Ann Giesberg, *Civil
   War Sisterhood: The U.S. Sanitary Commission and Women's Politics
   in Transition* (Boston, 2000); and Lori Ginzberg, *Women and the Work
   of Benevolence: Morality, Politics, and Class in the Nineteenth-Century United States* (New Haven, CT, 1990).
4. Haverhill and Bradford Soldiers' Relief Society Records, AAS; Attie,
   Patriotic Toil, 34, 90–91; Bardwell diary, SL; Minute Book of Richmond Soldiers Aid Society, PSA.
5. Minute Book of Richmond Soldiers Aid Society, PSA; Diary of Mary
   E. Baker, in Thayer Family Papers, MHS; letter of Caroline Woolsey
   Mitchell, January 13, 1862, in Georgeanna W. Bacon and Eliza W.
   Howland, eds., *Letters of a Family during the War for the Union
   1861–1865*, vol. 1 (New Haven, CT, 1899); Caroline Cowles Richards
   Clarke, *Village Life in America, 1852–1875* (New York, 1913), 131.
6. Attie, *Patriotic Toil*, 34–35.
7. Ella Forbes, *African American Women during the Civil War* (New
   York, 1998), 77–105, 79; Dorothy Sterling, *We Are Your Sisters: Black
   Women in the Nineteenth Century* (New York, 1984), 245–254.

8. Letter of Harriet Jane Thompson, December 8, 1862, in Glenda Riley, ed., "Civil War Life: The Letters of Harriet Jane Thompson," part 2, *Annals of Iowa* 44 (1978): 311–312; diary, vol. 7, Elizabeth Rogers Cabot Papers, SL; letter of Ann Cotton, September 23, 1863, in Papers of Josiah Dexter Cotton, LC; diary of Caroline Dunstan, in Papers of Caroline Dunstan, NYPL.

9. Diary of Elizabeth Livermore, vol. 1, NHHS; diary of Caroline White, vol. 9, Caroline B. White Papers, AAS.

10. Octavia Roberts Corneau, ed., "A Girl in the Sixties," *Journal of the Illinois Historical Society* 22 (October 1929): 423; Clarke, *Village Life in America,* 132.

11. Letters of Fanny Pierce, August 29 and December 15, 1861, in Thayer Family Papers, MHS; Annual Report of Worcester Soldiers' Relief Society, octavo vol. 1, Worcester Soldiers' Relief Society Records, AAS.

12. Rochester Soldiers' Aid Society quoted in Nancy Hewitt, *Women's Activism and Social Change: Rochester, New York, 1822–1872* (Ithaca, NY, 1984), 197; Haverhill and Bradford Soldiers' Relief Society Records, AAS; Ethel Alice Hurn, ed., *Wisconsin Women in the War between the States* (Madison, WI, 1911), 42; Richmond Soldiers Aid Society, Minute Book, PSA; Worcester Soldiers' Relief Society, Octavo vols. 3, 1, Worcester Soldiers' Relief Society Records, AAS.

13. Diary of Emily Elliot quoted in Steven E. Woodworth, *Cultures in Conflict: The American Civil War* (Westport, CT, 2000), 186; letter of Caroline Woolsey Mitchell, January 13, 1862, in G. W. Bacon and E. W. Howland, eds., *Letters of a Family during the War for the Union, 1861–1865,* vol. 1 (New Haven, CT, 1899), 248; diary of Elizabeth Livermore, vol. 1, NHHS. For a discussion of the new premium placed on loyalty during the Civil War, see George Fredrickson, *The Inner Civil War: Northern Intellectuals and the Crisis of the Union* (New York, 1965), 130–150.

14. Letter of Ellen Matilda Orbison Harris, February 10, 1862, Folder 18 and Report for Philadelphia Ladies' Aid Society, Folder B-1, Papers of Ellen Matilda Orbison Harris (microfilm, MG #98), PSA; letter to Captain Miner in Haverhill and Bradford Soldiers' Relief Society Records, AAS.

15. Letter of Elizabeth Cabot, May 5, 1861, in Box 2, Folder 19, Hugh

Cabot Family Papers, SL; Caroline White diary, vol. 10, Caroline B. White Papers, AAS; Livermore, *My Story of the War,* 111.

16. *The Spirit of the Fair,* April 5, 1864, 6; Quote from Soldiers' Aid Society of Detroit in "For Loved Ones Far Away," in Michigan Civil War Centennial Observance Commission, *Michigan Women in the Civil War* (Lansing, 1963), 128; Livermore, *My Story of the War,* 109; Clarke, *Village Life in America,* 149–150; letter of Mary Chapin, February 18, 1862, in Papers of Ellen Matilda Orbison Harris (MG #98), PSA.

17. Livermore, *My Story of the War,* 110, 128–134; Henrietta Colt quoted in Hurn, ed., *Wisconsin Women in the War,* 53.

18. Melinda Lawson, *Patriot Fires: Forging a New American Nationalism in the Civil War North* (Lawrence, KS, 2002), 18–20, Bellows quoted on 19; Fredrickson, *Inner Civil War,* 136–137.

19. Attie, *Patriotic Toil,* 40, 50–86, and *passim.*

20. Letter of Abigail May, November 2?, 1862, and *First Annual Report of New England Women's Auxiliary Association of the United States Sanitary Commission,* January 7, 1863, both in New England Women's Auxiliary Association Records, 1861–1887, MHS.

21. Letter of Rebecca Lincoln, March 1, 1863, in Lincoln Family Letters, Hitchcock Free Academy, Brimfield, MA, transcribed and made available to author by Larry Lowenthal; letter of Emeline Ritner, March 12, 1863, in Charles F. Larimer, ed., *Love and Valor: Intimate Civil War Letters between Captain Jacob and Emeline Ritner* (Western Springs, IL, 2000), 131; letter of Fanny Pierce, October 13, 1861, in Thayer Family Papers, MHS.

22. Wisconsin appeal quoted in Hurn, ed., *Wisconsin Women in the War,* 34; Detroit appeal quoted in "For Loved Ones Far Away," in *Michigan Women in the War,* 128; Worcester Soldiers' Relief Society, vols. 1 and 2, in Worcester Soldiers' Relief Society Records, AAS.

23. Hannah Lamb, Soldiers' Charity accounts, vol. 2 (1861–1867), Lamb Family Papers, MHS; Elizabeth Livermore Diary, Elizabeth Livermore Papers, NHHS; letter of November 16, 1863, in Papers of Ellen Matilda Orbison Harris (MG #98), PSA.

24. *First Annual Report of New England Women's Auxiliary Association of U.S. Sanitary Commission,* January 7, 1863, 8–9, in New England

Women's Auxiliary Association Records, 1861–1887, MHS; letter of James Lesley, August 13, 1861, Folder 13, and "Appeal to the Ladies of Pennsylvania, New Jersey, and Delaware," Folder B-1, in Papers of Ellen Matilda Orbison Harris, 1816–1902, PSA; letter of Clara Barton, December 16, 1861, in Clara Barton Papers, Box 2, AAS.

25. Clara Barton, diary entry for December 5, 1863, in Clara Barton Papers, AAS; diary entry of Elizabeth Cooper, May 25, 1861, in Elizabeth Cooper (Mattheson) Diary, MSU; diary entry of Elizabeth Livermore, February 11, 1862, in Papers of Elizabeth Livermore, NHHS.

26. Attie, *Patriotic Toil,* 122–146, 130; letter of Mary Davenport, March 16, 1864, in New England Women's Auxiliary Association Records, 1861–1887, MHS; Livermore, *My Story of the War,* 139; letter of Miss Melville, August 10, 1861, in Folder B-1, Papers of Ellen Matilda Orbison Harris (MG#98), PSA; Attie, *Patriotic Toil,* 142.

27. Attie, *Patriotic Toil,* 135–137, 138.

28. Ibid., 198–219; Gail Hamilton, "A Call to My Countrywomen," *Atlantic Monthly* 6 (March 1863): 346; Frank Moore, *Women of the War: Their Heroism and Self-Sacrifice* (Hartford, CT, 1866), 575.

29. Letter of Louisa Schuyler, April 1, 1864, in Wead Family Papers, SSC; letter of Abigail May, November 28, 1863, New England Women's Auxiliary Association Records, 1861–1887, MHS.

30. Letter of Abigail May, November 28, 1863, and letter of Alfred Bloor, November 31, 1863, in New England Women's Auxiliary Association Records, 1861–1887, MHS.

31. Livermore, *My Story of the War,* 411; Lawson, *Patriot Fires,* 14–39.

32. *Spirit of the Fair,* April 5, 1864, 4; Lawson, *Patriot Fires,* 24–26; Attie, *Patriotic Toil,* 217–218; *Spirit of the Fair,* April 5, 1864, 4.

33. Hurn, ed., *Wisconsin Women in the War,* 157; *Spirit of the Fair,* April 5, 1864, 5.

34. Harold E. Hammond, ed., *Diary of a Union Lady, 1861–1865* (New York, 1962), 280; Livermore, *My Story of the War,* 433.

35. Beverly Gordon, *Bazaars and Fair Ladies* (Knoxville, TN, 1998), 58–93; *Spirit of the Fair,* April 5, 1864, 5, and April 13, 1864, 88.

36. Diary of Elizabeth Livermore, October 12, 1862, NHHS; Marjorie Ann Rogers, "An Iowa Woman in Wartime," part 3, in *Annals of Iowa* 36 (Summer 1961): 39.

6. SAVING THE SICK, HEALING THE NATION

1. Louisa May Alcott, *Hospital Sketches* (Boston, 1986), 28, 5.
2. Harold E. Hammond, ed., *Diary of a Union Lady, 1861–1865* (New York, 1962), 77.
3. *New York Herald,* April 30, 1861; letter of Mrs. Hummel, October 15, 1861, in Folder 24, Papers of Ellen Matilda Orbison Harris, 1816–1902 (MG #98), PSA; *New York Herald,* April 30, 1861.
4. Jane E. Schultz, "Seldom Thanked, Never Praised, and Scarcely Recognized: Gender and Racism in Civil War Hospitals," *Civil War History* 48 (2002): 220–236; Kristie Ross, "Women Are Needed Here: Northern Protestant Women as Nurses during the Civil War, 1861–1865," PhD diss., Columbia University, 1993.
5. Elizabeth Leonard, *Yankee Women: Gender Battles in the Civil War* (New York, 1994), 7–16; Schultz, "Seldom Thanked," 222.
6. Leonard, *Yankee Women,* 8–11; Kristie Ross, "Arranging a Doll's House: Refined Women as Union Nurses," in Catherine Clinton and Nina Silber, eds., *Divided Houses: Gender and the Civil War* (New York, 1992), 97–113.
7. Leonard, *Yankee Women,* 23–30; quotation on 29.
8. Bradley quoted in Schultz, "Seldom Thanked," 227–228; letter of Clara Barton, March 1862, in Clara Barton Papers, AAS; John R. Brumgardt, ed., *Civil War Nurse: The Diary and Letters of Hannah Ropes* (Knoxville, TN, 1980), 116.
9. Bucklin quoted in Leonard, *Yankee Women,* 3–4; Jane Woolsey, *Hospital Days* (New York, 1870), 63; letter of Sally Gibbons, November 12, 1864, in Sarah Hopper Emerson, ed., *Life of Abby Hopper Gibbons: Told Chiefly through Her Correspondence* (New York, 1896), 119.
10. Alcott, *Hospital Sketches,* 5; letter of May 31, 1865, Clara Barton Papers, AAS; Emily Parsons quoted in Ross, "Women Are Needed Here," 222; Harriet S. Jaquette, ed., *South after Gettysburg: Letters of Cornelia Hancock from the Army of the Potomac, 1863–1865* (Philadelphia, 1937), 28.
11. Julia Susan Freeman, *The Boys in White: The Experience of a Hospital Agent in and around Washington* (New York, 1870), 27; Brumgardt, ed., *Civil War Nurse,* 89.

12. For more on Northern nurses' maternal image, see Reid Mitchell, *The Vacant Chair: The Northern Soldier Leaves Home* (New York, 1993), 75–80; Livermore, *My Story of the War,* 345; Swisshelm quoted in Mitchell, *The Vacant Chair,* 80.

13. "How I Came to Be a Nurse—No. V," in *The Spirit of the Fair,* April 18, 1864, 137; Freeman, *The Boys in White,* 35; Katharine Prescott Wormeley, *The Other Side of the War with the Army of the Potomac* (Boston, 1889), 34.

14. 1865 War Lecture, in Clara Barton Papers, AAS.

15. Brumgardt, ed., *Civil War Nurse,* 86, 74–89; Livermore, *My Story of the War,* 289, 312–315.

16. Scholarly assessments that stress the empowering effects of wartime nursing include Judith Ann Giesberg, *Civil War Sisterhood: The U.S. Sanitary Commission and Women's Politics in Transition* (Boston, 2000), and Ross, "Women Are Needed Here"; Jaquette, ed., *South after Gettysburg,* 16; Brumgardt, ed., *Civil War Nurse,* 74–93.

17. Woolsey, *Hospital Days,* 155; diary entry of December 5, 1863 in Clara Barton Papers, AAS; "How I Came to be a Nurse—No. IV" in *The Spirit of the Fair,* April 16, 1864, 125.

18. "How I Came to be a Nurse—No. IV," in *The Spirit of the Fair,* April 16, 1864, 125; Arthur J. Larsen, ed., *Crusader and Feminist: Letters of Jane Grey Swisshelm, 1858–1865* (Westport, CT, 1976), 234; Wormeley, *Other Side of the War,* 59, 62, 113, 114.

19. Jaquette, ed., *South after Gettysburg,* 12, 13, 27, 28.

20. Ibid., 27, 156.

21. Ibid., 70, 134, 119.

22. Livermore, *My Story of the War,* 480, 509, 486–487.

23. WCRA quoted in "A Cool Hand for the Fever'd Brow," in Michigan Civil War Centennial Observance Commission, *Michigan Women in the Civil War* (Lansing, 1963), 90; Livermore, *My Story of the War,* 224; Ross, "Women Are Needed Here," 165–185.

24. Ross, "Women Are Needed Here," 110; Leonard, *Yankee Women,* 20–23; Jaquette, ed., *South after Gettysburg,* 36; Hancock also quoted in Leonard, *Yankee Women,* 20.

25. Sanitary Commission bulletin quoted in "A Cool Hand for the Fever'd Brow," in *Michigan Women in the Civil War,* 91; Woolsey, *Hospital Days,* 156.

26. Wormeley, *Other Side of the War,* 84; Jaquette, ed., *South after Gettysburg,* 36.

27. Olnhausen and Bradley quoted in Schultz, "Seldom Thanked," 229. See Schultz's article in its entirety for an incisive discussion of the nature of gender and racial power relationships in Civil War hospitals.

28. Susie King Taylor, *Reminiscences of My Life in Camp* (1902; repr., New York, 1968), 21.

29. Diary entries, June 3 and June 16, 1863, Clara Barton Papers, AAS; letter of Bell Robison, May 12, 1864, in Pardee-Robison Collection, USAMHI.

30. Alcott, *Hospital Sketches,* 27–28; Larsen, ed., *Crusader and Feminist,* 233; Jaquette, ed., *South after Gettysburg,* 119.

31. Jaquette, ed., *South after Gettysburg,* 21; Wormeley, *Other Side of the War,* 29–30, 137.

32. Letter of Clara Barton, June 24, 1863, in Clara Barton Papers, AAS; Nurse Hadley quoted in Ethel Alice Hurn, ed., *Wisconsin Women in the War between the States* (Madison, WI, 1911), 112.

7. WARTIME EMANCIPATION

1. Letter of Laura Hildreth, June 6, 1861, in *Private and Official Correspondence of General Benjamin F. Butler, During the Period of the Civil War,* vol. 1 (Norwood, MA, 1917), 128.

2. Letter of Maria Patec, January 1, 1861, in Lucretia Sibley Papers, AAS.

3. Wendy Hammond Venet, *Neither Ballots nor Bullets: Women Abolitionists and the Civil War* (Charlottesville, VA, 1991), 33; letter of Lillie Chace, June 17, 1861, in Papers of Anna Dickinson (microfilm ed.), HU; Mary Livermore, *My Story of the War* (New York, 1995), 91–92.

4. Letter of Fanny Pierce, November 6, 1861, in Thayer Family Papers, MHS. Letters of Mrs. L. C. Howard, September 17, 1861, and Mrs. E. A. Spaulding, September 23, 1861, available at Lincoln Papers at LC Web site.

5. Rose quoted in Elizabeth Cady Stanton, Susan B. Anthony, and Matilda Jocelyn Gage, eds., *History of Woman Suffrage,* vol. 2 (New York, 1881), 74–75.

6. Letter of Rhoda Southworth, September 28, 1862, in Southworth Family Papers, MnHS; letter of Sophia Buchanan, January 1, 1863, in

George M. Blackburn, ed., "Letters to the Front: A Distaff View of the Civil War," *Michigan History* 49 (1965): 55–56; Boynton quoted in Alice Fahs, *The Imagined Civil War: Popular Literature of the North and South, 1861–1865* (Chapel Hill, NC, 2001), 193; diary entry for May 2, 1863, in Diary of Elizabeth Livermore, NHHS.

7. Ann Gorman Condon, ed., *Architects of Our Fortune* (San Marino, CA, 2000), 138–139; letter of Mattie Blanchard, November 9, 1862, in Letters of Mattie and Caleb Blanchard, CHS; letter of Catharine Peirce, December 13, 1863, in Richard L. Kiper, ed., *Dear Catharine, Dear Taylor: The Civil War Letters of a Union Soldier and His Wife* (Lawrence, KS, 2002), 162–163.

8. Letter of Rebecca Lincoln, undated (probably February 1863), in Lincoln Family Letters, Hitchcock Free Academy, Brimfield, MA, transcribed and made available to author by Larry Lowenthal; letter of Ann Cotton, March 1, 1863, in Papers of Josiah Dexter Cotton, LC; letter of Clara Pierce Wood, March 1862, in Wood Family Letters, unpublished manuscripts from the South Hadley Historical Society, available at Civil War in Diaries and Letters Web site.

9. Jane Schultz, "Seldom Thanked, Never Praised, and Scarcely Recognized: Gender and Racism in Civil War Hospitals," *Civil War History* 48 (2002): 229–230; letter of Elizabeth Bowler, April 28, 1865, in Bowler Family Papers, MnHS; letter of Mrs. Bartlett in Steven E. Woodworth, *Cultures in Conflict: The American Civil War* (Westport, CT, 2000), 161; responses to Pennsylvania Abolition Society quoted in Dorothy Sterling, *We Are Your Sisters: Black Women in the Nineteenth Century* (New York, 1984), 255.

10. Ella Forbes, *African American Women during the Civil War* (New York, 1998), 70–80; Sterling, *We Are Your Sisters*, 250; Julie Roy Jeffrey, *The Great Silent Army of Abolitionists: Ordinary Women in the Antislavery Movement* (Chapel Hill, NC, 1998), 217–218.

11. Bardwell Diary, SL; letter of Elizabeth Dwight Cabot, undated fragment from 1862, in Hugh Cabot Family Papers, SL; Worcester Soldiers' Relief Society, octavo vol. 1, Worcester Soldiers' Relief Society Records, AAS; letter of Edward Atkinson, February 26, 1864, in New England Women's Auxiliary Association Records, 1861–1887, MHS.

12. Letter of J. Foster Jenkins, February 29, 1864, in New England

Women's Auxiliary Association Records, 1861–1887, MHS; letter of Ellen Collins, September 18, 1865, in Letters of Mary Wead, Wead Family Papers, SSC; Nancy Hewitt, *Women's Activism and Social Change: Rochester, New York, 1822–1872* (Ithaca, NY, 1984), 196–197; letter of Elizabeth Dwight Cabot, undated fragment from 1862, in Hugh Cabot Family Papers, SL.

13. Charles F. Larimer, ed., *Love and Valor: Intimate Civil War Letters between Captain Jacob and Emeline Ritner* (Western Springs, IL, 2000), 255.

14. Forbes, *African American Women during the Civil War*, 73–96; Sterling, *We Are Your Sisters*, 263–264.

15. Diary of Ellen Mills, Low-Mills Papers, Container 15, LC; Henry Swint, ed., *Dear Ones at Home: Letters from Contraband Camps* (Nashville, TN, 1966), 24; Elizabeth Ware Pearson, ed., *Letters from Port Royal, 1862–1868* (New York, 1969), 126.

16. The literature on Northern teaching in the wartime and postwar periods includes Willie Lee Rose, *Rehearsal for Reconstruction: The Port Royal Experiment* (New York, 1964); James McPherson, *The Struggle for Equality: Abolitionists and the Negro in the Civil War and Reconstruction* (Princeton, NJ, 1964); Jeffrey, *Great Silent Army*, 222–229; Jacqueline Jones, *Soldiers of Light and Love: Northern Teachers and Georgia Blacks, 1865–1873* (Chapel Hill, NC, 1980); Ronald Butchart, *Northern Schools, Southern Blacks, and Reconstruction: Freedmen's Education, 1862–1875* (Westport, CT, 1980); Henry Swint, *The Northern Teacher in the South, 1862–1870* (New York, 1967). At one point Union General O. O. Howard estimated that more than 200,000 freedpeople had received some amount of instruction during the war.

17. McPherson, *Struggle for Equality*.

18. James McPherson, *The Abolitionist Legacy: From Reconstruction to the NAACP* (Princeton, NJ, 1975), 165; Jeffrey, *Great Silent Army*, 226–228.

19. Brenda Stevenson, ed., *The Journals of Charlotte Forten Grimke* (New York, 1988), 397–398; Swint, ed., *Dear Ones at Home*, 24, 119.

20. James McPherson, *Battle Cry of Freedom: The Civil War Era* (New York, 1988), 355–356; Chase quoted in Henry Noble Sherwood, ed., "Journal of Miss Susan Walker," *Quarterly Publication of the Historical and Philosophical Society of Ohio* 7 (1912): 9; Mrs. A. M. French,

Slavery in South Carolina and the Ex-Slaves; or, The Port Royal Mission (1862; repr., New York, 1969), 19.

21. Rupert S. Holland, ed., *Letters and Diary of Laura M. Towne* (New York, 1969), 16, 14; Henrietta S. Jaquette, ed., *South after Gettysburg: Letters of Cornelia Hancock from the Army of the Potomac, 1863–1865* (Philadelphia, 1937), 207.

22. Sherwood, ed., "Journal of Miss Susan Walker," 36–38, 39; Holland, *Letters and Diary of Laura Towne*, 86, 84.

23. Stevenson, ed., *Journals of Charlotte Forten Grimke*, 405–406; letter of Anna Gardner, January 1, 1865, *Freedmen's Record* 1 (February 1865): 21.

24. Edward Pierce, "The Negroes at Port Royal. Report of E. L. Pierce, Government Agent, to the Hon. Salmon P. Chase, Secretary of the Treasury" (Boston, 1862), 12; letter of H. R. Smith, November 5, 1864, in *Freedmen's Journal* 1 (January 1865): 5; *American Missionary*, October 1863, 235.

25. Elizabeth Hyde Botume, *First Days amongst the Contrabands* (1893; repr., New York, 1968), 30; New England Freedmen's Aid Society, Record Book, 1862–1874, Box 1, MHS; Sherwood, ed., "Journal of Miss Susan Walker," 35.

26. Kelley and Saxton quoted in Amy Stanley, *From Bondage to Contract* (Cambridge, UK, 1998), 140, 142; Gregory quoted in Linda Kerber, *No Constitutional Right to be Ladies: Women and the Obligations of Citizenship* (New York, 1998), 64; Swint, ed., *Dear Ones at Home*, 118.

27. Edward Pierce, "Freedmen at Port Royal," *Atlantic Monthly* 12 (September 1863): 307; Nina Silber, "'A Compound of Wonderful Potency': Northern Female Teachers in the Occupied Confederacy," in Joan Cashin, ed., *The War Was You and Me: Civilians in the American Civil War* (Princeton, NJ, 2003), 35–59.

8. AMERICAN WOMEN AND THE ENDURING POWER OF THE STATE

1. An excellent discussion of the case against Surrat and the imposition of the death penalty can be found in Elizabeth Leonard, "Mary Surratt and the Plot to Assassinate Abraham Lincoln," in Joan Cashin, ed., *The War Was You and Me: Civilians in the American Civil War* (Princeton, NJ, 2002), 286–309.

2. Diary of Helen (Lansing) Grinnell, Papers of Helen Grinnell, 1859–1867, NYPL; diary of Elizabeth Livermore, Papers of Elizabeth Livermore, NHHS; Walter Rundell, Jr., ed., "'Despotism of Traitors': The Rebellious South through New York Eyes," *New York History* 45 (October 1964): 364.
3. Diary of Caroline White, vol. 11, Caroline B. White Papers, AAS; Caroline Cowles Richards Clarke, *Village Life in America, 1852–1872* (New York, 1913), 183.
4. Richard L. Kiper, ed., *Dear Catharine, Dear Taylor: The Civil War Letters of a Union Soldier and His Wife* (Lawrence, KS, 2002), 402; Sheila Cumberworth and Daniel Biles, *An Enduring Love: The Civil War Diaries of Benjamin Franklin Pierce and His Wife Harriett Jane Goodwin Pierce* (Gettysburg, PA, 1995), 156; James C. Mohr, ed., *The Cormany Diaries: A Northern Family in the Civil War* (Pittsburgh, 1982), 582.
5. Gen. Benjamin F. Butler, "Woman Order," in *Private and Official Correspondence of General Benjamin F. Butler*, vol. 1, 486.
6. Letter of General Benjamin F. Butler, June 10, 1862, and letter of Simon Cameron, June 23, 1862, in *Private and Official Correspondence of General Benjamin F. Butler*, vol. 1, 581–583, 631.
7. Harold Hyman, *To Try Men's Souls: Loyalty Tests in American History* (Berkeley, CA, 1959), 139–153; the new intellectual premium placed on loyalty in the Civil War period is discussed in George Fredrickson, *The Inner Civil War: Northern Intellectuals and the Crisis of the Union* (New York, 1965), 132–135.
8. Hyman, *To Try Men's Souls*, 168–183; memo from Department of the South, June 20, 1862, in *The War of the Rebellion: A Compilation of the Official Records of the Union and Confederate Armies* (CD-ROM, Carmel, IN, 1997), hereafter cited as *OR*, series 2, vol. 4, 47; memo of Brig. Gen. Stoughton, March 1, 1863, *OR*, series 1, vol. 25, part 2, 114; letter of Joseph Darr, September 2, 1862, *OR*, series 2, vol. 4, 486.
9. Hyman, *To Try Men's Souls*, 177–183.
10. Letter of Gen. William Sherman, August 6, 1862, in Brooks D. Simpson and Jean V. Berlin, eds., *Sherman's Civil War: Selected Correspondence of William T. Sherman, 1860–1865* (Chapel Hill, NC, 1999), 276–277. I am grateful to James McPherson for his insights into Sherman's letter.

11. Linda Kerber, *No Constitutional Right to Be Ladies* (New York, 1998), 17, 18, 25.

12. Virginia woman quoted in Hyman, *To Try Men's Souls*, 178; Mary Lee quoted in Drew Faust, *Mothers of Invention: Women of the Slaveholding South in the American Civil War* (Chapel Hill, NC, 1996), 214.

13. For examples of orders linking oath taking to suffrage (and specifying "male citizens" in the directive), see General Orders No. 24 from the Department of the Gulf, February 13, 1864, and Orders No. 9 from Vicksburg, MI, March 11, 1864, in *OR*, series 3, vol. 4, 96–97, 478–479; memo from Department of Arkansas, January 18, 1865, in *OR*, series 1, vol. 48, part 1, 575.

14. On teachers taking oaths in postwar Missouri, see http://civilwarstlouis.com/History/Oathofloyalty.html. Jonathan Dorris, *Pardon and Amnesty under Lincoln and Johnson: The Restoration of the Confederates to Their Rights and Privileges* (Westport, CT, 1977), 137.

15. Letter of Sarah Butler, May 15, 1862, in *Private and Official Correspondence of General Benjamin F. Butler*, vol. 1, 490; Evelyn Leasher, ed., *Letter from Washington, 1863–1865* (Detroit, 1999), 262; Annie Wittenmyer, *Under the Guns: A Woman's Reminiscences of the Civil War* (Boston, 1895), 137.

16. Leasher, ed., *Letter from Washington*, 37–38; Arthur J. Larsen, ed., *Crusader and Feminist: Letters of Jane Grey Swisshelm, 1858–1865* (Westport, CT, 1976), 270; Gerald Schwartz, ed., *A Woman Doctor's Civil War: Esther Hill Hawks' Diary* (Columbia, SC, 1984), 243.

17. An excellent analysis of gender and the Surrat case can be found in Elizabeth Leonard, "Mary Surrat and the Plot to Assassinate Abraham Lincoln," in Cashin, ed., *The War Was You and Me*, 286–309.

18. Leonard, "Mary Surrat," 300–305; Diary of Annie G. Dudley Davis (transcript of original), 23, HL; Leasher, ed., *Letter from Washington*, 280–281.

19. Martha Wright and *New York Herald* quoted in Mary Massey, *Bonnet Brigades: American Women and the Civil War* (New York, 1966), 164; Ellen DuBois, *Feminism and Suffrage: The Emergence of an Independent Women's Movement in America, 1848–1869* (Ithaca, NY, 1978), 53–62.

20. Ellen DuBois, "Outgrowing the Compact of the Fathers: Equal

Rights, Woman Suffrage, and the United States Constitution, 1820–1878," *Journal of American History* 74 (1987): 836–862; Eric Foner, *The Story of American Freedom* (New York, 1998), 108.

21. Kerber, *No Constitutional Right*, 243; Senator Frelinghuysen, December 11, 1866 (39th Cong., 2nd sess.), in *Congressional Globe*, 66; Senator Morrill, July 25, 1866 (39th Cong., 1st sess.), ibid., 40; Senator Williams, December 11, 1866 (39th Cong., 2nd sess.), ibid., 56.

22. Senator Williams, December 11, 1866 (39th Cong., 2nd sess.), in *Congressional Globe*, 56; Representative Broomall, February 25, 1868 (40th Cong., 2nd sess.), ibid., 1956; Senator Dixon, February 4, 1869 (40th Cong., 3rd sess.), ibid., 862.

23. DuBois, "Outgrowing the Compact."

24. DuBois, *Feminism and Suffrage,* 53–202; DuBois, "Outgrowing the Compact," 851–854.

25. DuBois, "Outgrowing the Compact," 857–860.

26. Kiper, ed., *Dear Catharine, Dear Taylor,* 339; Diary of Elizabeth Cooper (Mattheson), MSU.

27. Information on the GAR and the WRC can be found in the following: Stuart McConnell, *Glorious Contentment: The Grand Army of the Republic, 1865–1900* (Chapel Hill, NC, 1992); Wallace E. Davies, "The Problem of Race Segregation in the Grand Army of the Republic," *Journal of Southern History* 13 (August 1947): 354–372; Cecilia O'Leary, *To Die For: The Paradox of American Patriotism* (Princeton, NJ, 1999), 70–90; Mary R. Dearing, *Veterans in Politics: The Story of the GAR* (Baton Rouge, LA, 1952).

28. David Blight, *Race and Reunion: The Civil War in American Memory* (Cambridge, MA, 2001), 64–77; O'Leary, *To Die For,* 100–109; black WRC chapter quoted in ibid., 103.

29. O'Leary, *To Die For,* 97–98.

30. Ibid., 75–81; Woman's Relief Corps, *Journal of the Fifth National Convention of the Woman's Relief Corps, auxiliary to the Grand Old Army of the Republic* (Boston, 1887), 39; Massachusetts Woman's Relief Corps, *Eleventh Annual Convention of the Department of Mass. WRC* (Boston, 1890), 18; Woman's Relief Corps, *Report of the National Organization, 1883, and Proceedings of the Second National Convention, 1884* (1884; repr., Boston, 1903), 15; Woman's Relief Corps, Department of Missouri, *Proceedings of the Seventh Annual Convention of*

the Woman's Relief Corps: auxiliary to the Grand Army of the Republic, Department of Missouri, Moberly, Missouri, April 2nd and 3rd, 1891 (Moberly, MO, 1891), 31–32.

31. O'Leary, *To Die For,* 82–90.

32. Woman's Relief Corps, Department of Massachusetts, letter of May 5, 1888, in Papers of Massachusetts Woman's Relief Corps, SL; Woman's Relief Corps, *Report of the National Organization, 1883, and Proceedings of Second National Convention, 1884,* 13; Woman's Relief Corps, *Journal of the Third National Convention of the Woman's Relief Corps* (Boston, 1885), 206.

33. Woman's Relief Corps, *Journal of the Sixth National Convention of the Woman's Relief Corps, auxiliary to the Grand Old Army of the Republic* (Boston, 1888), 103; Woman's Relief Corps, *Journal of the Fourteenth National Convention of the Woman's Relief Corps* (Boston, 1896), 207–209; Woman's Relief Corps, Department of Pennsylvania, *Journal of the Eighth Annual Convention, Department of Pennsylvania, Woman's Relief Corps: auxiliary to the Grand Army of the Republic, Altoona, PA, February 24, 1891* (Erie, PA, 1891), 89.

34. *Patriotic Review* (November 1901), 56. I am grateful to Professor Thomas Brown for his research and insights on Civil War memorials, and his observations concerning the dearth of statuary for Northern women.

35. Frank Moore, *Women of the War: Their Heroism and Self-Sacrifice* (Hartford, CT, 1866), 156–169; Henry Bellows, "Introduction," in L. P. Brockett and Mary C. Vaughan, *Woman's Work in the Civil War: A Record of Heroism, Patriotism, and Patience* (Philadelphia, 1867), 55.

36. Mary Livermore, *My Story of the War* (New York, 1995), 9.

37. Alice Fahs, *The Imagined Civil War: Popular Literature of the North and South, 1861–1865* (Chapel Hill, NC, 2001), 311–318; Nina Silber, *The Romance of Reunion: Northerners and the South, 1865–1900* (Chapel Hill, NC, 1993).

EPILOGUE

1. Eric Foner, *Reconstruction: America's Unfinished Revolution* (New York, 1988), 31–32.

2. *New York Herald,* September 13, 1865.

3. Ibid.

4. Works examining female reformers' national focus in the Gilded Age and the Progressive era include Paula Baker, "The Domestication of Politics: Women and American Political Society, 1780–1920," *American Historical Review* 89 (June 1984): 620–648; Ruth Bordin, *Woman and Temperance: The Quest for Power and Liberty, 1873–1900* (Philadelphia, 1980); Kathryn Kish Sklar, *Florence Kelley and the Nation's Work: The Rise of Women's Political Culture, 1830–1900* (New Haven, CT, 1995). Some of these works, along with Theda Skocpol's *Protecting Soldiers and Mothers: The Political Origins of Social Policy in the United States* (Cambridge, MA, 1992), also consider how the turn-of-the-century welfare state was shaped in response to women's demands and domestic needs. Skocpol specifically focuses on the Civil War pension system as a central element of state welfare policy.

5. Henrietta S. Jaquette, ed., *South after Gettysburg: Letters of Cornelia Hancock from the Army of the Potomac, 1863–1865* (Philadelphia, 1937), 119; diary entry for November 8, 1864, Papers of Elizabeth Livermore, NHHS; letter of James Beatty, September 17, 1864, in Beatty Family Papers, MnHS.

Acknowledgments

Standing now at the end of this long, multiyear project, I feel somewhat daunted by the task of acknowledging all those who offered various forms of support and assistance that helped me see this work through to completion. I hope my words here can convey at least some of my gratitude.

I first gave serious attention to this work in the fall of 1996, when I began a year as a fellow at the Charles Warren Center in American History at Harvard University. The project then was more about Northern women and Civil War memory, but a number of ideas that finally worked their way into this book began to see the light of day during that fellowship year. For their warm support and encouragement during my days at the Warren Center, I am grateful to Bruce Schulman, Jill Lepore, Kristin Hoganson, Kathleen Dalton, and David Blight. I was especially pleased, during that year, to have the opportunity to get to know the late William Gienapp, who took a special interest in the Warren Center's Civil War scholars.

I've learned over the years that the true workhorses of the history profession are the librarians and archivists who labor at historical societies, manuscript rooms, and special collections repositories. Many gave me tremendous aid in tracking down sources and identifying particularly rich collections. I am especially grateful to Hampton Smith, archivist at the Minnesota Historical Society, who pointed me in the direction of some extraordinary letters. Effusive thanks are also due to Dick Sommers at the U.S. Army Military History Institute in Carlisle, Pennsylvania, for his very careful consideration of my project during my all-too-brief visit to that library. Larry Lowenthal cannot be thanked enough for letting me see his transcription of the wonderful Lincoln family letters. And I will be forever indebted to the Civil War specialists at the National Archives, who have fine-tuned the art of finding needles in haystacks.

Over the years several scholars have given me valuable feedback on my written work, as well as the opportunity to articulate different pieces of this argument as it was taking shape. In this regard, I owe special thanks to Drew Faust, who both commented on some of the early written work and allowed me, twice, to lecture to interested high school teachers on my findings. I was pleased to have the chance to present some of my work to the Boston University History faculty at a History Department seminar, and I am grateful for the insightful commentary that was generated. James McPherson offered timely and useful advice about loyalty oaths. Doug Wilson clued me in to some terrific letters at the Abraham Lincoln letters Web site. And Eric Foner delivered some thoughtful comments on an early version of my chapter on Northern teachers.

For their wonderful and timely efforts in tracking down sources, I also extend thanks to two Boston University graduate students: Benjamin Varat, who, despite being a Europeanist, took a keen interest in searching Civil War–era newspapers; and Bill Leeman, who tracked down a number of leads on oath taking.

Thanks to Nanci Edwards and Bryan Sieling for their warm hospitality and (always excellent) food during my visits to Washington, D.C. Also to David Blight for giving me shelter in Amherst, and for his constant support and friendship. I have been cheered by Tony Rotundo's friendship and collegiality, and by the yeoman service he did in carefully reading and intelligently commenting on half this manuscript. Special thanks go to my good friend Liz Varon. Together we learned about the special trials of being the "girls" in the manly world of Civil War scholarship. And, like Tony, she was a fantastic supporter and reader of a significant portion of this work.

I owe a special debt to my editor at Harvard University Press, Joyce Seltzer. She was keenly enthusiastic about this project at the outset and has helped shaped the final outcome in countless ways. She has challenged me to be a better scholar and a better writer.

I will always be grateful for the encouragement I received from my parents, Irwin and Sylvia Silber, to pursue my work as a historian. I am greatly saddened that my mother—undoubtedly my single biggest fan—did not live to see this book completed. I know she would have been genuinely interested and profoundly pleased.

My children, Benjamin and Franny, were terrific sports through all of this and will, I hope, be glad to have the chance to see me again. I know I'll be glad to see them. About my husband, Louis Hutchins, enough cannot be said. Through his own work as a public historian, he has helped me to ask new questions about my research. As a friend, he has been supportive and encouraging. As a father, he devoted considerable time and energy to making sure I had the time to finish this book. And as my partner in life, he gives meaning to everything I do.

Index

Italics indicate pages that contain illustrations.